The Anatomy of Work

GEORGES FRIEDMANN

The
Anatomy
of Work

LABOR, LEISURE AND THE
IMPLICATIONS OF AUTOMATION

translated by WYATT RAWSON

THE FREE PRESS OF GLENCOE, INC.

A DIVISION OF THE CROWELL-COLLIER PUBLISHING COMPANY

For information, address:

THE FREE PRESS OF GLENCOE, INC.
A DIVISION OF THE CROWELL-COLLIER PUBLISHING COMPANY
60 Fifth Avenue, New York 11

Library of Congress Catalog Card No. 61-9165

Contents

CONTENTS

CONTENTS

Perhaps after all the division of labour is a necessary evil. Labour having been simplified to its extreme limit, the machine takes the place of man and man engages in other more complicated work, which he then proceeds to subdivide and simplify in order to give more business to the machine. And so it goes on. Thus, more and more, the handworker's domain is invaded by the machine, and, as the system is extended to its extreme limits, the worker's function becomes increasingly intellectual. This ideal attracts me greatly; but the transition period is a hard one, since, until the new machines are created, the worker is himself made into a machine by the simplification of his work, and suffers the unfortunate effects of a debasing necessity. . . . Let us then accept the division of labour where it is proved necessary, but with the hope that the machine will increasingly take over all simplified jobs; and let us insist with the same urgency as for the workers of other classes, that the workers of this class shall receive an education not only saving them from mental torpor, but also stimulating them to find a way of controlling the machine instead of being themselves the machine-controlled. — ANTHIME CORBON, *Worker, Vice-President of the Constituent Assembly of 1848*

Without work all life goes rotten. But when work is soulless life stifles and dies. — ALBERT CAMUS

Foreword

SOME years ago I accompanied an industrial psychologist on a visit to a factory engaged in the mass-production of watches and alarm-clocks. He was a specialist in the problems of the division of labour, and, wherever his advice was sought, tried as far as possible to eliminate physical and mental strain from the simplified motions into which the work had been broken down. The plant was equipped with the most modern machines, and from a technical standpoint was highly rationalized. Everywhere in the workshops we saw semi-skilled workers repeating several times a minute the same operation, which consisted in a few elementary and carefully studied movements. There were stampers, cutters, drillers, polishers, etc. among whom stood out here and there, like survivors from an age long extinct, a few professional watch-makers, 'finishers' or foremen, who knew all the mechanisms of a watch and could take one to pieces and put it together again singlehanded.

My companion stopped for a while in front of a young workman, who with a few stereotyped motions was punching holes in the plates of watches brought to him every ten seconds on a mechanical belt. 'You see,' he said after a moment's thought, 'here *the man is bigger than his job.*'

This remark could very well have served as the title of this short book. While not neglecting, as will be seen, any of the more general and complex kinds of work which our industrial society still demands, and even in certain sectors tends to increase, what follows is particularly concerned with those occupations, now highly sub-divided by the progress of technology, which are much too limited in scope to involve the worker's whole personality, however much his intellectual needs and personal ambitions may have been restricted by his upbringing and social environment. All those engaged in such work, and there are still tens of millions, indeed perhaps hundreds of millions of them in different parts of the world, are 'bigger than their jobs'; those repetitive and frag-mentary operations of all kinds, performed in factories, in mines, steelworks and shipyards, as well as in offices, shops and distribution centres; jobs which lack variety, initiative and responsibility, and all sense of belonging to a whole — which are in fact devoid of any real meaning at all. These occupations, unlike those in which the worker can find ever-renewed interest, as well as intrinsic satisfactions which in privileged cases may even amount to real enjoyment, consist in cycles of movements of short duration, lasting occasionally no more than a few seconds, which only call for short-term motivations.

What do those engaged, day in, day out, for weeks or for years, in this kind of job feel about it? How does it affect their attitude to their work? And, outside working hours, how does it affect their free-time interests, the way they spend their leisure? What place does it occupy in the whole phenomenon of specialization, and what is the reaction in the workshop to-day to the constantly increasing break-down of jobs into tiny units, a fragmentation which certain industrialists, and among them some of the most authoritative, already consider excessive? Have we now arrived, as some recent scientific inquiries suggest, at a new turning-point in the evolution of the division of labour — a division which began when *homo sapiens* first rose above the level of the animal, and which has been going on for thousands of years? What part, too, is being played by this state of affairs in the crisis which to-day faces both the individual and civilization itself? And what in consequence is the outlook for man's development in the near future?

These are some of the questions that I have been led to ask in the course of the following pages, as the result of my observations and reflections — questions to which I do not pretend to offer an answer, save in the form of certain hypotheses and further questions. Some of my interpretations may seem over-bold to those used to methods founded upon systematic inquiries and the statistical elaboration of results. In fact, there are still very few such studies dealing with the problems of which I am trying to present a general picture here. Many of them indeed have not been tackled at all. Are we then to wait until they have been explored by pioneer groups, theoretically well-prepared and technically fully equipped? Are we to close our eyes and ears, ignore our misgivings and stifle the hopes derived from certain salutary reactions? May we not insist upon the seriousness of the problem and try, tentatively at least, to discover ways of preventing human beings from being crushed beneath its weight?

I beg the indulgence and understanding of research workers in the social sciences. First of all, I have to deal with a vast subject without being able to examine all its aspects in the compass of this book. Thus, for example, no consideration has been given to the relations that exist between the jobs performed by semi-skilled workers and their absenteeism or unreliability. Secondly, a limited number of observations have occasionally been made the basis for suggesting general hypotheses which, in the present state of our means of investigation at least, cannot be tested upon samples of the population.

How large a proportion of the whole of industry is engaged upon these simplified operations is a highly controversial subject. Some people, dazzled by the progress (and the myth) of automation, talk as if they had already vanished from off the face of the globe! That is going a bit too fast. In fact it would need a large volume to discuss the statistical problem from this standpoint in detail, singling out data of like kind and comparable criteria,* and analysing into different types the occupational categories concerned with production, distribution and administration. No such attempt can be undertaken here. Nevertheless, since this book deals primarily with occupations classed as unskilled, or semi-skilled, it seems desirable that it should provide, at least in outline, an idea of the area they cover in highly industrialized countries. For this reason, a summary of the known facts, together with an explanation of the difficulties and obscurities that still remain, will be found in an appendix at the end of this volume.

I hope therefore that specialists in sociological research will not be too hard on me because of the gaps and over-bold generalizations to which I have referred. In fact, in writing this study, I was not thinking of specialists, but of a larger public (of which they form of course a part) that consists of all those decent people alive to-day who accept their responsibilities as human beings and long for clarity in a topsy-turvy world full of threats as well as of promises. For these pages are directly addressed to those, whatever their profession, who have not allowed specialization with its multi-

* M. Pierre Naville has recently published an important contribution concerning this problem in his *Essai sur la qualification du travail*, Marcel Rivière, Paris, 1956.

farious pressures and demands to stifle their desire to see things as a whole, to *understand*. By avoiding the use of terms that are too technical I hope to make this public aware of some of the major problems now facing our industrial civilization, and to show how the social sciences throw light upon some aspects of them. Perhaps some of my suggestions may later on serve as hypotheses for teams of investigating psychologists and psychiatrists, sociologists and demographers. That at least is my hope.

Others may object that most of the facts·and inquiries mentioned deal with labour in capitalist societies. That is true. I could have wished it otherwise. But reliable accounts of Soviet factories and their technical organization, and of the way in which semi-skilled workers there regard their highly simplified jobs, are rare; indeed, at the time when these pages are going to press, almost non-existent.* I am convinced myself that the human problems of specialization as they appear in the economic, social and cultural context of the Soviet Union assume quite a different form from the one they take here. It can be agreed, however, that it is impossible in matters of this kind to consider as objective the attitudes and values attributed to characters in Soviet novels, since these are mostly ideal types, which the author, carrying out thereby the function of Soviet literature as it exists to-day, sets before his fellow-citizens as models to be followed. The most informative reports are really those contained in industrial manuals (such as those of Maslova, Arakelian and Kamenizer), or else in certain letters of self-criticism published in the press. From these it appears that planned economies of the Soviet type, including those of the peoples' democracies of Eastern Europe, and more and more of communist China, contain large sectors in which technical progress has multiplied the number of simplified jobs — we shall give many examples later on — and has thus started, and is developing, that separation between planning and execution which seems to be in our day a common denominator linking all industrial societies together, however different their populations and structures.†

* The best book on the U.S.S.R. to appear in France since the recent war (*Visa pour Moscou*, Gallimard, Paris, 1951), the work of an intelligent and sensitive journalist who knows the Russian language well, tells us nothing about this subject — for a very good reason; its author, Michel Gordey, was not able to visit a single plant during his stay.

† A comment on this published in the *Komsomolskaya Pravda* is to be found in Chapter VI, p. 99.

Finally it is worth while to remind ourselves that the last work published by Stalin, a kind of ideological testament, lays stress upon the hours spent outside the factory, upon the leisure that will constantly increase during the advance towards communism, considering this leisure time as the real centre of human life in so far as it makes for a full flowering of the personality.* Such ideas are also to be found in a different form in the works of the most clear-sighted critics of capitalist industrialism.

This book is nearing completion at a moment when 'automation' is very much to the fore. The new techniques designated by this hybrid term, which nevertheless seems to have overcome all opposition and secured a place by assault in the international vocabulary, have caught the attention of a great number of intelligent business men and observers. Moreover, around these techniques a whole lurid journalistic literature has grown up, which has become fashionable and has spread in recent years throughout Europe and the United States, being fed by speculations derived from 'cybernetics', many of which are devoid of any scientific basis.

Without entering into details I should like to say a word about these matters at the outset of this book. If, as some popular writers would lead us to suppose, automation is really destined to spread with lightning speed throughout the factory and office world, if it were to come into general use tomorrow, these atomized jobs would almost wholly disappear in a very short time, and the problems we are considering here would be rendered completely out-of-date.

In fact, according to the majority of specialists in France and elsewhere, we are not at present faced by a 'new industrial revolution', but by a new stage, a very important one of course, in the development of 'automatism',† which, as is too often forgotten, has a long history behind it. This stage is characterized by three main features: (a) the integration into one continuous productive chain (through which the product passes without being touched by hand) of various manufacturing operations, previously performed separately. This is what is often called 'Detroit automation', because the most striking examples of it are to be found in the

* *Problèmes économiques du Socialisme en U.R.S.S.*, special number of *Études soviétiques*, November 1952, p. 43.

† As it appears from the *Journées d'Information sur l'Automatisme* organized by the Commissariat général à la Productivité, Paris, 8–10 February, 1956. Cf. *Documents*, June 1956.

automobile industry. In France the 'transfer machines' of the Renault works are a well-known instance of this; (b) feedbacks or automatic regulators with electronic amplifying circuits, allowing for a comparison of the actual outcome of an operation with its intended result, and making the necessary adjustments by means of a servo-mechanism; (c) electronic computers, capable of registering and accumulating information, on the basis of which they perform a variety of mathematical operations, from the simplest to those so complicated that they lie beyond the highest reaches of the human brain.

In short, the most important novelty in automation, the one that seems to be most fraught in the long run with consequences for the life of mankind in industrial civilizations, is the development of techniques of communication and control, as applied to the processes of production, distribution and even administration.

But will this development alter the character of our factories, offices and workshops, immediately or in the near future? I doubt it. While taking into account the possible future effects of automation upon our societies and upon the worker's freedom, we have to face the present situation, which seems likely to continue as it is for the rest of the century over a large part of our planet. Work in factory and office, in mine and field, is far from reaching the stage of automation. In an authoritative investigation made in the United States in 1952, the branches of industry said to be ripe for automation affected only 8 per cent of the working population. Furthermore this process, even in the most favourably situated sectors, can only take place quite slowly, because of technical and financial difficulties, as well as of the problem of training the new specialists required. The total of unskilled and semi-skilled operators in the U.S.A., which was 14·3 million in 1930, had risen to 15·5 million in 1950.* A considerable proportion of the working population throughout the globe remains absorbed in fragmentary and repetitive jobs. These are in fact increasing in the sectors in process of industrialization in the so-called 'under-developed' countries, where abundant and low-paid labour militates against the introduction of costly machinery, requiring highly qualified technicians to manage and supervise it.

The chief reasons, it seems to me, why automation cannot in the short run revolutionize industrial societies are three: (1) whatever

* *Statistical Abstract of the United States*, Washington, 1954.

people may say, or rather though people may forget to say so, since the beginning of the century automation has already made great strides in certain industries; (2) the number of industrial and administrative jobs actually ripe for automation is limited; (3) the general introduction of automation depends upon complex economic and social factors, which are not understood by the pure technician, and which are equivalent, as will be seen from what follows,* to a radical transformation in capitalist society.

The prophets, who are not worried about such small matters, already seek to dazzle the public with a picture of industry freed from all labour causing physical or mental strain, and involved in a vast upgrading movement which will multiply qualified and responsible jobs on higher levels. In the long run this may very well take place. But in fact, predictions of a general kind in this matter are highly speculative, particularly as there exists at present, even in the United States, no wide scientific inquiry dealing with the effects of the new automatic techniques upon the transformation and distribution of different types of occupation. Such investigations are being made in England† and have been adumbrated in France. In any case it is much too early to consider atomized jobs and their problems as out-of-date. Without denying the great potentialities inherent in automation — far be it from me to do so — my study is definitely concerned only with the present and the immediate future.

Moreover, when in due course automation has eliminated manual work and has greatly reduced the hours of labour, when it has deprived men of the essential element upon which their mental balance and the possibility of self-realization have been based (the role traditionally assigned to work), the need to find a new centre for human development in the hours thus freed, i.e. in the active use of leisure, will become all the more acute. Automatism does not eliminate the problems forming the core of this book. Its results *may* be as marvellous as its most enthusiastic supporters have imagined. But they may also contribute to man's downfall, should they occur in a world lacking just institutions, and deprived of liberty and wisdom.

* Chapter VII, p. 103.

† A first report has been published by the Department of Industrial and Scientific Research; *Automation, a Report on the technical trends and their impact on management and labour*, London, 1956.

Introduction

THE DIVISION of labour began tens of thousands of years ago, during man's first efforts to adapt himself to his natural surroundings and thereby to transform them. In this sense it may be said to have started at the same time as the ascendancy of man, and to explain the extraordinary expansion of mankind among the higher primates, in spite of a hostile world, from the time of the last glacial period. An examination of collections of objects produced by prehistoric industry shows us that all these flint and bone implements — scrapers, polishers, awls, planes, axes, saws, etc. — imply different aptitudes among those making and using them. These differences are still further accentuated in mesolithic times, when such implements and arms, skilfully fashioned and encased in new materials, such as reindeer hoofs or antlers, become finer and more exact and complicated, and when the first canoes appear on the shores of the Baltic and the North Sea. Moreover, how can we avoid the assumption that in the higher palaeolithic age the Aurignacian and Magdalenian artists, whose wonderful and astonishing drawings, sculptures and mural paintings — signs of the first human civilization — have only been discovered in our own day, already formed a special class several hundreds of centuries ago? A class of specialists quite separate from those concerned with food production, and living among the small group of human beings who found shelter in the caves of Altamira and of the Dordogne, or on the valley slopes of the Vézère and the Corrèze?[1]

Neolithic times saw the utilization of flint deposits, the shafts leading down to them being surrounded by villages for the specialized workmen, as at Spiennes in Belgium;[2] it saw also the birth of metallurgy and the use of the first alloys. All this increased the division of labour, which began to take its first historical form, already visible in outline in the products made by the artisans of the empires of the Near East and of predynastic Egypt, as well as in the objects discovered recently in the palaces of Crete — pottery, frescoes, statuettes and jewels — in which art and industry are to be found happily associated for the first time.[3]

In all the civilizations of the East, of Asia and of America, which have left traces of their activities, a specialization of functions is to be seen. Among the Persians, Xenophon tells us, the royal dishes were specially prepared, and the arts in general attained a higher perfection in the large towns.

For in small towns the same workman makes chairs and doors and plows and tables, and often this same artisan builds houses, and even so he is thankful if he can only find employment enough to support him. And it is, of course, impossible for a man of many trades to be proficient in all of them. In large cities, on the other hand, inasmuch as many people have demands to make upon each branch of industry, one trade alone, and very often even less than a whole trade is enough to support a man: one man, for instance, makes shoes for men, and another for women; and there are places even where one man earns a living by only stitching shoes, another by cutting them out, another by sewing the uppers together, while there is another who performs none of these operations but only assembles the parts. It follows, therefore, as a matter of course, that he who devotes himself to a very highly specialized line of work is bound to do it in the best possible manner.

Exactly the same thing holds true also in reference to the kitchen: in any establishment where one and the same man arranges the dining couches, lays the tables, bakes the bread, prepares now one sort of dish and now another, he must necessarily have things go as they may; but where it is all one man can do to stew meats and another to roast them, for one man to boil fish and another to bake them, for another to make bread and not every sort at that, but where it suffices if he makes one kind that has a high reputation — everything that is prepared in such a kitchen will, I think, necessarily be worked out with superior excellence.[4]

But by then specialization had not invaded only the economic sphere. According to Herodotus, 'the practice of medicine is so divided among the Egyptians that each physician is a healer of one disease and no more. All the country is full of physicians, some of the eye, some of the teeth, some of what pertains to the belly, and some of the hidden diseases'.[5]

In Western societies, which interest us particularly, the division of labour increases with the development of handicrafts and industries in the ancient civilizations of the Mediterranean, the most famous of which is that of Mycenae; while in the classical period of Athens and Rome it shows an extraordinary variety and complexity, already singularly like our own. Scarcely touched by the disintegration of the Roman Empire, it was definitely enshrined in the Middle Ages in the regulations governing the guilds and corporations. These guilds continued in various forms, meeting with different degrees of resistance according to the country and period as a result of new technical and economic developments, until the end of the eighteenth century and in certain parts of Europe until even later. Because craftsmen each worked in a particular trade to which they were apprenticed and in which they were protected, this system was the negation of competition and was in fact written into the very structure of society. But it was also based upon a rigid definition of the occupational unit, which was essentially manual and polyvalent and so opposed to the introduction of machines and the simplification of operations. The 'masterpiece' stood in the way of technical progress, which necessarily implied a rational redistribution of jobs as functions of the new tools. Thus in the eighteenth century the future master hat-maker, provided with a pound of wool and other raw materials, still had to make a complete felt hat, finished and dyed, for which he was responsible from the preparation of the cloth to the putting on of the feathers. By thus obstinately resisting new forms of the division of labour, and continuing to amalgamate skilled crafts at a time when the increase in demand and the complexity of the product required simple and rapid specialized processes, the guild system hardened into a routine and signed its own death warrant.[6]

The invention of the steam engine began the era of industrial revolutions and with it the division of labour entered upon a new phase and gained a new impulse. Until this turning-point, in spite of the appearance of a relatively limited number of large firms devoted to the subdivision of labour, of which Adam Smith has given a picture that is famous, the artisan or craftsman, incorporating his skill, experience and knowledge of materials in an object made from start to finish with *his own* tools, remained the typical workman of the Western world. From that time on, however, stimulated by mechanization, the division of labour continued at an accelerated pace. Machines were specialized, as can be seen in the success of Hargreaves's spinning-jenny, Arkwright's waterframe, Crompton's mule-jenny and Cartwright's combing machine.

Operations originally performed by a single professional weaver began to be divided up. This was the start of a phenomenon of dispersion, which continued on all sides and took innumerable forms. It was encouraged during the nineteenth century by a further specialization of machines and by the firm belief — one might almost call it a semi-mystical belief — which took possession of the engineering world and was strengthened by the development of Taylorism from 1880 on, that all 'scientific' rationalization of labour would imply a breaking down of jobs, increasing the output of the 'semi-skilled' worker and the volume of production with a lowering of the cost of such mass-produced goods.*

Apart from this conviction, another belief that was current at the end of the nineteenth century and the beginning of the twentieth inspired industrialists and often supported the first. Many people then, more or less consciously, conceived of the division of labour as part of a universal design, a development expressed throughout the world in the evolution in every sphere of life of the heterogeneous from the homogeneous, the concentrated from the diffuse. This was a principle to be found in the course of progress itself, the increasing division of labour and its functions being naturally completed by a happy harmonization of these specialities. So one can see how, for many engineers in Europe and America, specialization in the technical sphere formed part and parcel of the general myth of 'progress'.[7]

This evolution, in the intense form it has taken during the last half-century in Europe, the United States and Japan, is certainly linked with the history of industrial capitalism, which, owing to its intensive development of the forces of production and the opening up of vast outlets in colonial territories, was constantly compelled

---

* One can get an idea of the degree of specialization reached in the United States between the two wars by noting that the *Dictionary of Occupational Titles* (United States Department of Labor, Washington, 1939) devotes 1,040 pages to the listing in alphabetical order with short definitions of 17,452 distinct 'occupations', giving a complementary classification of 12,292 titles, making a total of 29,744 different types of employment, trades and professions. Even so the authors of this dictionary excuse themselves in the preface for publishing a work which 'is far from being complete', and that for administrative as well as financial reasons. See in this connection the comments of W. E. Moore, *Industrial Relations and the Social Order*, new ed., pp. 441–51, Macmillan, New York, 1951.

to discover ways of producing more at a minimum cost in order to meet the demands of invested capital and the growing requirements of an ever-expanding consumer market. This cycle of production and markets is admirably illustrated from 1913 onwards in the spirit (and the factories) of Henry Ford, in his theory of 'creative industry',[8] and in the boom of the assembly line, which spread from the workshops of Dearborn to the factories of all five continents.

But the development of specialization and the multiplication of hands whose work is restricted to repetitive and fragmentary operations, are not aspects of a specifically capitalist economy. Elsewhere we have drawn attention to the lucid articles published by Lenin in *Pravda* in 1918, while the civil war was still raging in Soviet territory, in which he stressed the need for adopting the progressive techniques to be found in Taylorism.[9] Forty years later an organization of labour based upon a strict specialization of jobs is more than ever the order of the day in the U.S.S.R. The party and the government have in recent years vigorously supported several movements derived from Stakhanovism, in particular the Agarkov movement, which stresses the subdivision of operations and the extension of the use of the assembly line.[10] Finally, the Soviet Union to-day, by equipping modern factories from Changchun to Yunnan, from Shanghai to Lanchow, and providing them with technicians, is drawing swiftly in her wake the China of Mao Tse-Tung.

CHAPTER I

Job Specialization in Industry: Some Recent Aspects

BEFORE considering the problems of specialization to-day and the possibilities it presents of humanizing labour, it is desirable, indeed indispensable, to refer here to certain aspects of it which we have recently observed on the spot. So let me run through the notebooks I have carried with me for some twenty years while visiting factories, workshops, mines, offices and centres of apprenticeship and of vocational training. Throughout these notes, scribbled on the corner of a table, or more often on a workshop bench, recurrent themes appear, having a certain general character in spite of the diversity of the plants visited, of their size, products, structure and geographic location. Let us note that the majority of the facts thus observed, the way in which jobs are being developed and individual and group reactions to this have never yet been studied systematically in sample groups. Indeed, in many cases it would be difficult, if not impossible, to make such investigations in view of the way in which enterprises are run. Therefore it seems to me that observations of an empirical and limited kind are by no means without value, and I shall continue to think them of interest in showing ways in which the facts can be interpreted and systematic studies be planned.

However, in order to give at least some idea of the general background against which these facts are to be viewed, I have added an Appendix to this book, in which I have examined a few statistical data concerning the more highly industrialized countries. These show the very considerable importance (in the present state of technical progress) of the sector still occupied in such countries by unskilled or semi-skilled labour, i.e. by those who have never had any systematic training for their job and perform very simple and fragmentary operations.

SPECIALIZATION AND THE DECAY OF APPRENTICESHIP

We ought not to be surprised then to observe every day at shop level many examples of the breaking down of jobs and of the decay of apprenticeship in the most diverse branches of production.* This is a definite policy, deliberately pursued by certain managers, though its effects may not be fully realized. One manager of a large British motorcar factory (1948) said to me, 'We try to reduce skill to a minimum.' Many others, who do not say this, think in the same way and act accordingly. Factories making toilet articles, brushes and combs, which often also manufacture various other plastic objects, such as knife-handles, fountain-pen holders, etc., are full of very simple specialized operations, performed at a rapid pace. In an English factory (Birmingham, 1933) the only work-people were young girls and women, who were given a fortnight's 'training' and worked at semi-automatic machines under the super-vision of a few 'forewomen' with the occasional help of a mechanic in charge of the machines. Operations such as the moulding, cutting out, sawing and drilling of combs were reduced to certain very restricted and repetitive motions, performed on individual, but interdependent, machines grouped in cycles. By 1933 many of these operations lasted less than a minute. At Lyons (textiles, 1936) the work of the weavers in certain firms was so subdivided and mechanized that it required only a fortnight's training and three months' experience in all to make 'a good worker'.

Let us stop a little longer in a remarkably well-run and highly organized clothing firm in Amsterdam, which I was able to study at close quarters in 1949. Clothing is one of the branches of industry in which job specialization has gone furthest. English industrial psychologists often quote the case of a firm in the Midlands, where the making of the waistcoat alone for a man's suit had been broken down into more than sixty-five different units of work. My Dutch factory had followed the same line, and at the time of my visit had increased the number of its coat units from forty in 1932 to fifty-four in 1949, thus reducing the total time required for manu-

* It is not usual for industrial sociologists to give the names of the firms they have had permission to study, and whose shops and reports, labora-tories and planning departments they have seen. In the course of this rapid sketch I have not had to refer to financial and technical data of a confidential nature, so that I have felt myself all the more free to com-ment on what I have observed on the spot.

facture. The division of operations in all clothing firms of any importance has taken the normal form of assembly-line work, needing careful planning. All the thought necessary for the work goes into this planning, which deals with the smallest details. 'To sew and stitch on our machines is not difficult,' a workshop manager said to me, 'the difficulty lies in planning the operations.' The designer's work is especially elaborate and minute. If a dress is required, for instance, he designs it in the material chosen, or rather to be experimented with, and two pattern-makers trace the design according to his instructions. Then the planning department examines this first project from three points of view: (1) the quality of the material in relation to the operations to be performed; (2) the difficulty of these operations, particularly of the cutting and sewing on the machines; (3) its commercial value, i.e. where, what and how large the market for such a dress is likely to be.

The next step is to simplify the dress, and this is one of the jobs of the pattern department, which for this purpose makes use of a 'catalogue' of all the parts and elements of dresses manufactured by the firm since it started. Thus it very often happens that the technicians discover that similar parts have already been created before. Then it is a question of profiting from these earlier experiments and the money invested in them by recombining the model and making a new synthesis, composed either of a smaller number of elements or of simpler ones. 'Real dressmaking chemistry,' one of the engineers said to me. The planning department, once the model has been definitely created and decided upon, works out a list of the operations to be performed on the conveyor belt, and makes detailed charts of these to one hundredth of a minute. Thus I noticed that each unit of dress no. 3389, the first issue of which would contain 20,000 samples, to be sold partly in Holland, but for the most part abroad, would be finished in forty-seven and a quarter minutes. The lay-out of the work, the position of the workers, and the pace of the belt, are then determined by the planning department. The responsibility of the 'belt-leader' (a former worker, possessing authority and experience) is reduced to deciding where particular workers are to be used. This is all the initiative left to her in the organizing of her section.

The machinists are classified into four categories: A, B, C, D — corresponding to the increasing difficulty of their jobs and to the amount of their pay. The 'D's are those capable of performing all the operations needed in making a whole 'ready-made' dress. But they would not be able to make this dress at home with the needle as a 'made-to-measure' garment.

Real tailors are rare in such a firm. There is no need of any trained cutters. The cutters on the machines are all former semi-skilled workers trained in the factory itself by former cutters. Some of them take external courses in cutting out. 'For us, strictly speaking,' Z, the technical director, told me, 'that is a luxury.' The belt forewomen themselves are old 'D's, able to make a whole 'ready-made' dress, but not necessarily qualified as dressmakers. Let us note, however, that Z considered it wise to add to his staff of semi-skilled workers a real tailor, to be consulted in certain circumstances in order to prevent mistakes in fitting and sewing together the parts. One such tailor, however, was quite enough!

It is hardly surprising that the amount of training necessary for such jobs is greatly reduced. The company has even introduced the conveyor-belt into the training shop — not a common innovation — so that trainees can be prepared for the actual conditions of production. A few days' training is enough for each unit of work, but these operations are so limited and so numerous that the beginner 'A', once admitted into the workshop itself, takes no less than a year and a half, if she gets so far, to become a multi-specialized worker and reach the 'D' level. After that a few hope to become 'belt-leaders' eventually — if they have not already left the factory in order to marry or to work in one of the many small shops of Amsterdam at a higher wage. The turnover is large and reaches 66 per cent; that is to say, in eighteen months the whole labour force is nearly replaced, save for a few workers who make the factory their career. Faced by a development which to him seemed the result of the inexorable logic of modern production, Z, an intelligent and clear-sighted engineer, was puzzled: 'We can't stop technical progress,' he said, 'but where is such specialization leading us?'

Let us visit other workshops employing only women workers. An abundant crop of specialized jobs awaits our study. They are to be found in factories producing special parts of watches, such as we have described in another book.[1] In a highly mechanized Swiss firm (Soleure, 1947 and 1950), planned, in part at least, according to the advice of an eminent industrial psychologist, the girls are trained to produce two at least of the 'parts' of a watch, each of which requires not more than four days' training. Many of the girls are conversant with six operations, and some with more: but the trade union, recognizing the attenuation of training caused by this so-called 'rationalization', refused to allow this process of multispecialization to spread, since it condemns to extinction the last skilled trades in watchmaking.

In the food industries, to which reference will frequently be made in this chapter, and in modern distilleries, we find a multitude of jobs which carry work simplification to its extreme limit; as, for instance, with those workers in France, whose time is spent on the assembly line filling bottles with a famous white liqueur. I have seen a girl there (1954) whose job it was, day in and day out, for a week or a year, to put on the bottle the brightly-coloured decorative ribbon which is the mark of the firm. But all she does is to place it on the neck: it is the job of one of her fellow-workers, the one 'below' her on the line, to do the sticking-on!

It is not only female labour that affords us examples of such minutely subdivided work. Many jobs done by men in very different industries, in the furniture, engineering, food, hide and leather trades, are the result of the same or a similar development. In my pre-war notebooks an account is to be found of a visit to an armament factory in the St Etienne district, where in 1937 a complete break-down of the skilled gunsmith's trade was taking place. The assembly line had not yet been introduced into these vast shops, but a far-reaching division of labour had left each workman in charge of an operation connected with only one element of a gun — the bolt, barrel, butt, or lever, etc. In a workshop mass-producing sports guns of a current model, the only fully trained person was the man in charge of twenty semi-automatic machines, which were being worked by semi-skilled operatives. Apprenticeship for the trade of a skilled gunsmith had already almost disappeared, and my attention was directed to a corner of the shop where there were a few old workmen maintained on supervisory jobs, the last representatives — certainly no longer there to-day — of the gunsmith 'who knew how to make a whole gun'.

In the chemical industry, although the division of labour does not as a rule take the form of the assembly line, the modernization of equipment has considerably lessened the time needed to train 'experienced' workers. In a factory for distilling coal-tar (Lyons, 1949), the training of a 'good distiller', which previously took about six months, to-day takes three weeks. This is due particularly to the process of continuous distillation, resulting from more numerous and more sensitive measuring devices.

One of the results of job specialization is the problem of promotion. The downgrading of many jobs, called the 'deskilling' process, makes it increasingly difficult for many workers, and in particular for those restricted to 'specialized' jobs, to gain access to more skilled posts when they have got as far as they can in the work they are doing. The company may offer them promotion courses within the firm as a means of advancement, or they themselves may make the painful effort of following theoretical and practical courses outside, once their week's work is finished. This actually happens in the case of those courageous workers who spend Saturdays or Sundays in the 'promotion' workshops, organized by the Department of Technical Education in Paris and a few big provincial centres. In this connection, however, we often find two distinct tendencies among the workers. On the one hand there is a reluctance to accept promotion with a view to becoming foremen, for reasons which are, I admit, diverse and complex. Thus in the textile industry of Manchester (Cotton Board, 1951) the recruitment of 'overlookers' from the bottom has become difficult on account of the considerable effort the semi-skilled worker is required to make for promotion, and of the greatly enlarged gulf that exists between him and the foreman. In other industries, however, such as the motorcar industry in the United States (Detroit, 1948), there is the desire and hope, expressed by many, of getting free of the assembly line, where the chance of promotion is nil, and being transferred (if possible) to supervisory or repair work, or of leaving the factory altogether. We shall mention later certain statistical data on this subject collected by C. R. Walker and R. H. Guest in their excellent book *The Man on the Assembly Line*.[2]

KNOWLEDGE OF MATERIALS

I shall not here discuss one aspect of job specialization, the importance of which I have stressed elsewhere, although I have encountered it often enough in my different studies, i.e. the decline in the knowledge of materials.[3] One may say, generally speaking, that rationalization has split up the inherited crafts of the artisan, in which the worker's experience consisted largely in the slowly acquired knowledge of his materials and of their properties when worked by hand or tool — knowledge, too, of the qualities of different samples, and of the effect upon them of seasonal alterations, changes of weather and of temperature (to-day we would speak of their hygrometric state). In so doing, sometimes slowly and sometimes at a rapid rate, rationalization has deprived the worker of one of the most precious contents of his working life — contact with, and knowledge of, his materials. In the book mentioned[3] I have given many examples of this, taken from the most varied industries — engineering, the timber trade, shoe, glove and paper manufacture, pottery and porcelain, textiles and food.

To-day, even in the case of workers termed skilled in the collective agreements of industry owing to the way in which it has developed, the knowledge of materials is declining, having lost the place it occupied in job evaluation in favour of other kinds of proficiency. Thus in a rubber factory (Lyons, 1949), where the trimmers are classed as 'highly skilled workers' and given more pay as such, they are really, according to the engineers, only poorly skilled in the rubber trade. The main object of their training is to enable them to read a plan and trace a model. 'Eight hours are enough for that in the case of any intelligent person,' said the manager. This opinion, in the highly disputable form in which we give it, represents the managers' point of view. But we find a similar attitude among the workers, though the causes, naturally, are quite different. In the course of the same inquiry, militant trade unionists told me that certain 'tensions' exist in rubber firms, particularly between the trimmers and the toolshop mechanics, whose training for their own job is much more complete, their qualifications being also greater, but who are nevertheless rated lower in the evaluation of their work and paid less.

In quite another trade, the milk industry, in Denmark (a cooperative milk plant at Enigheden, 1953) I had a similar experience. I was in a huge hall, painted all white and containing the magnificent separators of sparkling stainless steel belonging to the cooperative. Here the butter, some of which is exported, is separated from the skimmed milk, which is sold to the Danes who are very fond of it. The supervisor of these machines is classed as 'highly skilled' and gets 200 Kroner a week, which puts him at the top of the hierarchy of production workers in this firm. The girls who wash and look after the bottles get about 135 Kroner. The machines are excellent and breakdowns are rare. The supervisor had had a four years' apprenticeship in a small country dairy so as to learn all about the properties of milk and the different kinds of butter. He had thus acquired an extensive experience of the materials of production. D., a responsible member of the co-operative, who had been a dairyman in the past himself, declared that his expert knowledge was of value to the machine supervisor. He had to see to it if the butter was defective, and vary certain controls according to seasonal changes affecting the milk's composition and water content. On the other hand, a technician of the factory, to whom I spoke a few minutes later, told quite another story. 'The machine is perfect,' he said, 'nothing ever goes wrong. The occasional regulating required does not need any "dairy knowledge". In reality,' he added, 'D. keeps talking like that because he was once a skilled dairyman and wants to maintain the prestige of his old trade, to which he is still attached.' According to the technician, this dairy worker was 'definitely overskilled'.

The fact is that in the case of many considered 'overskilled', specialized or multispecialized workers, performing several fragmentary operations, knowledge of materials has practically disappeared owing to extreme mechanization and the very minute division of labour. Many technicians, however, do not seem to have realized that ability and experience are now required in other forms, particularly as manual skill, dexterity and speed, which does not exclude carefulness. This overvaluation has still another aspect, which is clear enough in the case of the Danish dairy supervisor. Workers are classed as 'skilled' whose job it is to take charge when the unexpected happens or when changes are made or something goes wrong with the machine. Even when these things rarely occur, such workers are still maintained as skilled hands. From this point of view they can be likened to former stokers on the old steam locomotives — although of course their case is not the same — who now act as deputies on the electrified lines, being empowered to step in, should the driver-mechanics of the electric engines suddenly be taken ill, but then *only* authorized to bring the train to a stop (S.N.C.F.,* 1954). In fact, according to my information,

* *Société Nationale des Chemins de Fer.*

there has never yet been a single occasion on which they have been called upon to intervene. Idle, and often embittered, they feel themselves reduced to the position of mere luggage in the engine cabin.

SPEED AND HABITUATION

Speed, precision and dexterity constitute a new set of skills in many specialized jobs, and claim increasing attention from industrial psychologists. In this connection, as we shall see, British investigators have made some interesting comments, coining the phrase 'speed as a skill'.[4] In textiles (weaving, Lille) since 1935, it has been a striking spectacle to watch the deftness of the motions made by the girls working on the continuous power-looms and looking after 'three sides', i.e. a machine and a half, as they run along the looms to tie broken threads or to regulate the speed of the machine. A job that most certainly demands precision, attention and dexterity, even though it is highly specialized, since the girls do not have to clean, or to replace the threads, or to arrange the removal of the bobbins.

A factory specializing in making tins (London suburb, 1948) has organized its entire production around semi-automatic machines, looked after mainly by girls. The sight of the factory rooms is unforgettable, fantastic! Tins move everywhere in a continuous and noisy flow, on rails forming a tracery skirting all round us and above our heads. Sparkling cascades, elsewhere, swing about in all directions, their accumulated shocks causing an unheard-of racket with a high-pitched noise, giving rise, so the personnel manager told me, to awkward problems of selection, since for certain people the sound is intolerable. The girls work in teams of four, and take turns in doing different jobs on the assembly line and in the packing shed. Some of them grumble to begin with, but most of them get used to it and settle down to the work. During my investigations I have often met with this phenomenon of getting used to the conditions of a disagreeable job, which we have called 'habituation'. Let me add in passing that it is one which should be systematically studied on the spot by teams of physiologists and psychologists.[5] It does not exclude a process of psychomotor adaptation to a rapid rhythm, nor certain forms of skill. Moreover, it points to the problem of 'routine', and to the dislike of changing habits of work which often accompanies it. Finally, I would suggest that psychologists wishing to make a systematic survey of the realities of industrial labour should ask themselves whether this kind of habituation — at least in the case of certain people of a type to be defined — does not lead to a serious impoverishment or alteration of the personality.

JOB ALTERNATION

'Speed as a skill' seems clearly to be a feature of certain specialized jobs considered in isolation. But another series of observations draws our attention to the alternation of jobs and to the new form of skill contained in the performance of several highly specialized operations one after another.

Let us take the case of a large French bacon and meat packing firm (Paris, 1953). Most of the men and women employed in this firm S., which possesses modern equipment and is highly rationalized, being thus comparable in character, although not in size, to the famous slaughter-houses of Chicago, are semi-skilled workers, performing highly subdivided tasks carefully worked out by the planning department. One job is solely concerned with the removal of the navel and ovary (or testicles), another with evisceration, while the removal of the pig's claw is a special operation entrusted to a particular worker using a special apparatus. The sausage-making is done by a team of three semi-skilled men, the filler, the linker and the packer, and is a good example of 'speed as a skill'. The linker, in particular, showed striking manual ability and precision. Timing him by a stop-watch, I calculated that his speed over a period of several minutes was such that he linked a sausage every three seconds. The average production, calculated over a week, was said by the factory technician to be a sausage every five seconds — no mean performance!

In the pig preparation room the management keeps professional workers who have been trained as pork-butchers, men who for various reasons — the expense of setting up on their own, or actual failure or the fear of it — have taken refuge in big industry. A refuge, however, which may not last for long, since the logical development of the division of labour is leading this company, like so many others, to train its own men by job rotation, thus procuring workers who, if not fully skilled and qualified in the traditional sense of the words, are at least 'multispecialists'. Thus the 'cutters' and 'bleeders' hold important posts but are not all professionals with a polyvalent training. There are semi-skilled workers among them, 'trained on the spot' for these jobs and so getting promoted to them. The firm retains the services of a relatively large number of fully trained pork-butchers, who know all aspects of the trade; but this is because of the need for flexibility and of the varying nature of the demand, particularly during the boom at the end of the year before Christmas, when they are taken off their ordinary work to prepare special pork dishes — *pâtés*, galantines and so on.

Many examples of work rotation are to be seen in these factories. Thus the three members of the sausage-making team go and work at certain times in the brine room, while the women in the scalding room and those dealing with the offal alternate their jobs. The girls who prepare the runners are encouraged to learn about linking and about trimming the paunch, so as to be able to work at any one of these operations.

I have stressed elsewhere[6] the importance for modern industry of what I have proposed to call the 'by-passing' of trained skill, and no doubt we meet here with one of its manifestations. The technicians, when breaking down jobs, quite naturally tend to use their semi-skilled workers to perform all the operations required by the planning department, and so to let them do all types of work as far as possible in a rationalized business. This is the principle of substitutes, of 'utility men' as they are called in the United States, who fill the 'gaps' in the assembly line and who will turn up again in the course of our discussions. Semi-skilled workers in the slaughter-house, who have no general knowledge of the pork-butcher's trade, may become quite expert in cutting out the veins, or as preparers, and will learn other jobs as well. Their wages and status in the firm will rise accordingly. They learn, that is, a number of particular skills, but not a trade as a whole, as a synthesis. The multispecialist will never become a polyvalent craftsman, unless he acquires another training elsewhere. The firm S. thus tends to form a replacement staff for its own internal use, and to decrease the sector in which it employs skilled workers, trained in vocational schools or as apprentices. In doing so, it provides for promotion within the business, though it is still only on a modest scale, and also offers its semi-skilled workers, who as a rule mark time without any hope of advance, some sort of further objective.

Such a policy is not possible in all branches of industry. The limits within which it can be carried out depend not only upon economic conditions and social structure, but also upon techniques of production, which in any systematic investigation should be studied from this point of view. However that may be, the tendency to substitute multispecialized workers for the polyvalent craftsman is new and important. The craftsman — apart from the classical occupations of tool-setting, repair and maintenance work — retains his place in all sectors where complexity of work and variations in demand require a peculiarly flexible type of skilled labourer, an 'all-round man'.

A similar development seems to be taking place in the trades connected with air transport (Air-France, 1954). The maintenance of machines in operation has been split up into a number of different jobs, performed more and more in the planes themselves by semi-skilled workers, who check the many elements, connections and measuring devices according to a check-list system. Their programme may include the inspection of parts of the aeroplane body as well as of the engine. In case of serious defect, the whole part is taken down and sent to the workshop to be overhauled by a highly skilled workman and, if time presses, a standard exchange part is fitted. Here, too, we see the emergence of a kind of multi-specialist as distinct from a real craftsman.

But the most remarkable symptom of this development is certainly the increasingly frequent appearance of utility men in firms using the assembly line. To-day they are normally employed in American factories, and I already saw some at work when I visited the United States in 1948. This is a new function, now formally recognized by industrialists, of which we shall have to take account, for some time at least, when studying labour problems.

The utility man was born of the needs of the assembly line, where, in order to provide stop-gaps in the case of unexpected illness or absence, the technicians were obliged to put into practice the principle of job alternation for the benefit of certain semi-skilled workers, selected and trained with this end in view. This alternation of jobs is an irregular one, not a systematic rotation, since by definition it takes place unsystematically and without any possible prevision. Let us note that the utility man's existence in no way contradicts the principle of specialization and does not imply that the technicians introducing it are abandoning their belief in the dogma of the division of labour or are recognizing the value of regrouping jobs — much less the need to do so. The experiment is taking place within the actual framework of specialization and as the result of its requirements. When a substitute performs half a dozen different jobs in the course of a day, the job programme, as analysed and laid out by the planning department, is not modified in any way. But the inner experience, personal value and status of this type of employee are very different from those of a specialized worker performing one single operation the whole time. The remarks made by utility men about their work are very significant.[7] They like the absence of monotony, the chance they have of getting an idea of 'the whole line' on one segment of the belt, and even show a certain pride in knowing all the operations. Thus variety is introduced, at any rate for a privileged group of workers, among the specialized tasks of mass-production, without its suffering in the smallest degree, either economically or financially. This flatly contradicts the views of the technicians, who have considered such experiments impossible without serious injury to the business.

The utility man, as we have said, is clearly not a skilled workman of the type ordinarily so named in industrial circles. Although, for instance, he may know how to fill a dozen places on the belt in the pig preparation room, he does not thereby become anything like a pork-butcher. On the assembly line of a motorcar factory a substitute knowing how to install correctly a number of different parts is not the equivalent of a fitter-mechanic in a repair shop capable of repairing a whole engine by himself. Nevertheless, is there not something more than a purely additive process in what he does? Has not this juxtaposition of jobs in time an integrating effect? That their work is lifted by this kind of synthesis or *Aufhebung* to a higher level seems to be shown by the new way these workers come to regard it. They begin, we are told,[8] to understand the whole job of production for the segment of the line on which they work, for instance the fitting of a wireless condenser or the installation of an engine, thus finding satisfaction in what they do and even taking a certain pride in the task when finished, in the total product. For my part, in the absence to date of fuller empirical data systematically collected, and without denying that the utility man, owing to the enlargement of his job, looks upon himself as different from what he was as a semi-skilled worker, I doubt whether he can really re-evaluate his work intellectually, or gain an authentic *understanding* of it, without his experience of a number of operations being completed by further technological knowledge and vocational training. Only after that can a multispecialist *realize* what a condenser or a motor really is, and a true integrative process take place. Without it his status in the company is bound to remain much lower than that of a skilled workman, and the satisfaction he gets out of his work will not take him very far. But if job alternation is given significance and at the same time filled out by sound technical knowledge we should really be in the presence of a revaluation of labour.

SATISFACTION AND COMPLEXITY

That the worker's satisfaction often increases with the complexity of the work performed is a fact commonly observed, not only in industry but also in office work, as a recent inquiry carried out by Nancy S. Morse among American office employees has shown.[9] Nevertheless, it is always interesting to find such facts confirmed by one's own observations on the spot. In a highly rationalized watchmaking factory (Switzerland, 1949) the work, which was minutely subdivided, was particularly tiring, an industrial psychologist told me, *because* it could not give any satisfaction. The jobs many of the workers were forced to perform were, he thought, definitely below those they were capable of doing, had they been given the opportunity. That was one of the chief reasons for their ageing prematurely, he added. 'Much of the work done in our factory,' he continued, 'could and should be done by half-wits; for instance, inserting a little spring in a drum.' This view of the kind of work suitable for mental defectives hardly agrees with the successful experiments recently carried out by occupational therapists in many different lands.[10] However that may be, this psychologist is gradually getting work alternation introduced, and is trying to make the management agree to certain jobs never being performed for more than one day at a time.

In a factory making electrical wireless material (Paris, 1954) I questioned some women employed on the conveyor-belt. We were

at the dead season. The manager had retained only the best workers, for whom the jobs on the assembly lines had been regrouped. Thus, at the time of my visit they had to make some thirty connections, whereas this number was reduced to five when the belt was working full out. 'It's much less tiring and more interesting,' they said. But the manager, speaking as a technician, was of quite a different opinion. 'The ideal,' he declared, 'would be for each of them to have only one connection to make. Many of our workers, when they first come, prefer simple work, consisting of a small number of elementary operations. When the work they have to do grows, when they have to weld, for instance, or to make connections, their output falls. Besides, even if well trained, they will have moments of hesitancy which makes it difficult to plan, and in particular to time, their operations.'

In a British firm manufacturing electric fans (Middlesex, 1951), where some jobs also involved the making of a number of connections, I made similar observations. Those to be employed in connecting have six weeks' training, followed by another six weeks in the workshop, before being able to do the work at the normal production pace. The job then seems tedious, but gives them satisfaction. 'One feels one has done something,' one of them said to me, 'something really useful. We are making the core of the machine.' Others from the same room made similar remarks, in which one could sense their difficulties, their feeling of achievement and a certain pride.

At the opposite pole we have the attitudes, so often (and correctly) observed by those using the Metro in Paris, of the members of its staff engaged in performing small fragmentary jobs. Their work and attitudes, when issuing or clipping tickets, closing gates, etc. have never, so far as I know, been made the object of systematic inquiries and psycho-sociological study. I shall not attempt to outline these tasks in a few words here. They are clearly not always, or uniquely, a matter of reflex action, and often give rise to little problems and unexpected situations (the giving of information, for instance), requiring from time to time various forms of attention, such that, in France at all events, the use of 'human nervous systems' is to-day more economical than that of servo-mechanisms. However, casual conversations across the lines from one platform to another in between the passage of trains, the constantly interrupted reading of a newspaper paragraph, and the doing of crossword puzzles, are hardly enough to make life interesting for those whose activity makes no demands on them, and whom automatic equipment will soon, we hope, deliver from their slavery.

DISLIKE OF CHANGE

Thus worker satisfaction seems often to depend upon a certain inner complexity in the job. Nevertheless, throughout my factory observations I have come across many instances of men, and more particularly of women, who are attached to their highly subdivided, routine tasks and do not wish to change.

In the rubber industry (Lyons, 1949), the trimming of parts coming from the mould is done by semi-skilled women workers, either by hand or with a chisel or with the help of small lathes and various machines. The management has to take into account the fact that they want to work as long as possible on the same part. They are timed for each of these by the planning department, and every change entails a slight readaptation and so a slowing up, which is translated into a loss of pay. A worker occupied in trimming a large batch of teats for calves told me she was satisfied. 'Doing this I don't lose any time, and I can think of other things.' Other workers engaged in trimming handles for bicycle bars, or rubber gloves, showed the same dislike of change. 'When there are changes, we have to think of our work,' was the way they put it. They were annoyed when sent 'ends' to do or batches for a small order. At the same time, they insisted that the objects they had to trim, for example the bicycle handles, were never exactly alike, each requiring a slightly different attack from the tool or the machine. Certain kinds of attention were therefore necessary. But the similarity between the objects, even when they differed slightly, seemed to them an element of security. 'One gets the hang of it.'

At Liverpool (a company making telephone apparatus, 1949), not infrequently the girls refuse to change their work even if the change will benefit them. 'Many people here don't want any interesting work,' a personnel officer said to me. The girls were quite content to settle down in a job. It was the same story in a Belgian clothing firm (Binche, 1952), where the girls make difficulties if they are transferred from one assembly line to another, and even occasionally leave the firm if they are forced to change. But it is clear that each case of 'routine' must be examined separately and in detail. At Binche, for example, I noted that this transfer was accompanied by a more advanced mechanization and a corresponding decrease in the number of operations performed by hand. The workers' attitude may partly have been due to fear of extra fatigue, a fatigue not compensated, they thought, by a fair increase in pay. Many observations point in the same direction and prove that under the economic, family and moral conditions in which many working-class women live in our societies, they tend to prefer routine jobs, not demanding constant attention but bringing in a regular wage, even if the pay is less than if they changed their job. In the case of male workers such observations are less common, although they are by no means exceptional. We find, particularly with certain men, that they become 'habituated' to work on the assembly line after a fluctuating period lasting for a shorter or a longer time, though seldom for more than six months. I have noticed this in large motorcar factories in England (Dagenham, 1948) and in France (Billancourt, 1948, 1950). Here again I have only impressions to go on for the moment, and not systematic studies of significant samples, which alone would enable us to discover the real causes, doubtless complex in character.

THE 'AWAKE' AND THE 'STEREOTYPED'

If many workmen and particularly workwomen find 'satisfaction' in simple jobs, what is the reaction to these jobs of the intellectually more mature? In actual fact industry tends to keep such people away from this type of work: the 'misgivings' felt by many personnel officers, and by some factory psychologists, in regard to the more alert minds take curious forms — forms that will only appear paradoxical to those who are unaware of the realities of industrial life. In a highly rationalized factory manufacturing meters in a Brussels suburb (1948), where a third of the workers are women, the unskilled jobs are divided into five categories: 'elementary, simple, medium, difficult, and particularly difficult'. When hands are taken on, a first selection is made (with the help of the psychologist) of those suited for 'moderately skilled' jobs, which absorb 65 per cent of the employees. This is a preliminary screening. 'But,' said the psychologist R., with whom I had a long talk before making my visit, 'it can happen later that the foremen or team-leaders may point out certain employees who are "not adapted" to "fine work", as the tiny, fragmentary operations belonging to the "simple" and "elementary" categories are called here. These women must then be moved to jobs with more scope, "medium" or even "difficult" ones.'

R., who had worked for a long time in the firm and acquired its spirit, his horizon being largely limited to it, seemed to me one of those technicians who are themselves victims of a certain kind of specialization. . . . At any rate, I have seldom heard a factory psychologist express so crudely his mistrust of workers with minds too open and alert. R. established a pragmatic distinction between the 'awake' and the 'stereotyped'. 'The "awake" never get accustomed to elementary jobs. On the other hand, when we have to make changes in the work, a large percentage of the "stereotyped" leave.' The personnel department, which he directs, gives a series of tests to all those seeking employment in 'fine work'. Their object is to test for good sight, precision, manual skill, speed of movement, comprehension and judgement. Apart from the testing of motor abilities, the aim is to keep the 'stereotyped' and eliminate the 'awake'. A good way of doing this, according to R., is to note the women who grasp the test procedure and orders at once. They will probably be the 'awake' ones. They must not be given 'elementary' jobs, but must be moved to more complicated ones, such as the microscopic inspection of parts, in which ten different instructions have to be carried out, or the delicate adjustment of a time switch.

'The women in the suburb from which we mainly recruit our staff are "little developed",' said R., a fact which explains why the firm finds it comparatively easy to obtain workers who are 'not awake'. Nevertheless, I was unable to get an exact idea of the turnover and of the attitude taken towards their job by those whom he called the 'stereotyped'.

Make no mistake, R. is not the only factory psychologist to encounter difficulties of this kind in the selection of workers for very simple jobs. Moreover, one finds similar worries among factory doctors. In a huge Dutch firm, making electric lamps and apparatus (Holland, 1949), one of the medical staff told me that his attention had been drawn to the psycho-somatic troubles that arise when a job is definitely 'above' or 'below' the capacity of the worker. 'Everything then depends,' he said, 'not only on the physical constitution but also on the psychical level of the worker, on how developed and mature he is. With "simple folk" there are few problems: they are seldom above the level of their work, and in any case they settle down and declare themselves "satisfied". On the other hand, with the "more intellectual" workers we meet with difficulties, with problems of adaptation and transfer, which are sometimes extremely awkward in spite of the size of our factories and the great variety of jobs we are able to offer.'

In a large English company making telephonic apparatus (Liverpool, 1949), to which I have already referred more than once, selection is organized with the help of the National Institute of Industrial Psychology of London; but it still admits into the factory girls who cannot adapt themselves to very simplified operations. In the bank wiring shop, the psychologist told me, the girls are aware of signs of discouragement and 'frustration' among some of them, and there is always a heavy turnover. These girls are then offered other jobs of greater complication and variety, this being possible since the factory is very large and is still expanding. They have then to accept these jobs — or leave.

CHAPTER II

Decline of an Orthodoxy

THE CONSTANTLY increasing specialization of industrial jobs is thus a widespread phenomenon of our time. Nevertheless, a whole group of symptoms presenting disturbing likenesses is noticeable to-day in factories, workshops and offices, and corresponds to what we can note of life as lived during working and leisure hours. It leads us to ask a vital question. In this mid-twentieth century, have we not reached a new moment in the evolution of the division of labour — have we not come to a turning point — which, if the present trend continues, will be of cardinal importance for the future of all human societies?

A DISQUIETING SITUATION

In fact, in a more detailed study we should here have to point first of all to the correspondence existing between the practical reactions and worries felt by managers and technicians during the course of their work and noticeable among many of their staff, and the results of the scientific studies made by teams of psychologists belonging to institutions specializing in the study of the human aspects of industry. This convergence of views is not a chance matter, since in England, for instance, the investigations carried out by the National Institute of Industrial Psychology, to which reference will be made later, have been supported by a Panel on Human Factors, set up by the government because of its concern over a problem which is now officially recognized as of great practical importance.* We might make similar remarks concerning

---

* This Panel was itself formed by the Committee on Industrial Production which was dissolved in 1950 to make way for two new organs created in 1953: the Committee on Individual Efficiency in Industry and the Committee on Human Relations in Industry, both of which now work under the combined direction of the Department of Industrial and Scientific Research and of the Medical Research Council.

the experiments in job enlargement carried out during and after the Second World War in large American firms. Let us first stress the fact that these are not the sentimental reactions of journalists and writers; the effect of their criticisms of industrial life, however intrinsically justified, would have been very slight. Nor is it a purely theoretical and scientific movement, due to groups of industrial psychologists and sociologists, whose views would not have carried the weight they have, had they not voiced the anxieties increasingly felt by more and more industrialists, technicians and workshop personnel.

These new facts are part of a growing disquiet aroused by the effects, judged harmful in certain circumstances, of assembly line work and the breakdown of jobs. The studies made by specialists in the fields of industrial psychology and sociology during the last twenty-five years have increasingly drawn attention to the be- haviour of workers performing this kind of job, to the forms, degrees and prerequisites of their satisfaction in it, and to the many aspects of the delicate problem of monotony. The publications of Morris S. Viteles, devoted to experimental studies on attitudes to work, have also underlined the complication and interrelation of the factors upon which these attitudes depend.[1] Systematic investigations have been made and alterations introduced into the workshop, where, in order to lessen the physical and mental dangers connected with highly simplified jobs, various methods have been tried out, such as the introduction of rest periods, physical training, competition between groups, the diffusion by loudspeakers of 'music while you work', and even the distribution of headphones, allowing workers to listen to talks and reports and thus enabling them to use their minds while their psychomotor automatisms continue to work.

TRANSFER AND WORK ROTATION

Frequent transfer from one job to another, and work rotation, both come much closer to a real grasp of the problem, and I shall here give a few examples of both of these, taken from different branches of industry. In a highly mechanized Parisian biscuit factory, which I studied not long ago, the management had followed the advice of one of the best French planning specialists and had introduced regular rotation of jobs.[2] The girls, grouped in teams, changed their work each week, going from the baking department to 'detoasting', and then to weighing and to packing. They liked this variation in their work, although each job by itself when performed for a long time was 'monotonous'. In spite of the fact that many French engineers, not understanding the psychological and social aspects of production about which they have heard nothing either before or after their training, persist in considering all such measures as disturbing and costly *a priori*, these reforms are gradually spreading under the pressure of daily workshop experience. I have already described some striking examples in a large meat and bacon factory near Paris.[3]

In the United States these methods are now widespread, and certain American companies have introduced some bold innovations of this kind. Thus the firm R., which makes car battery boxes and controls various factories in Illinois, Indiana and Texas, has set up a regular system of job alternation within teams, the members of which are allowed a certain freedom in apportioning between themselves the work required by the general plan, such as that on castings and on presses.[4] The semi-skilled workers have at the same time had restored to them a large part of the supervision of the quality of the product.

Examples of this procedure known to me are so numerous, not only in workshops but also in offices, that it is difficult to make a choice. In a big American public utility corporation, distributing gas and electricity, the book-keeping requires seven specialized operations. At first, one group of employees only entered the meter readings, while another listed the customers' payments, and so on. Now the office is divided into sections, each composed of four employees working as a team. These share the jobs between them, often making exchanges, the team being supervised by one member who takes responsibility for it. The Bristol-Myer Company, in its Hillside factory (New Jersey), trains its semi-skilled workers to perform jobs in 'blocks' of twelve, between which they alternate. Their pay rises each time they successfully master a new 'block'. Job rotation organized in this way has led to a higher output than the classical method of individual job assignments.[5] In a shop belonging to a large motorcar factory engaged on assembly-line work, a foreman had taken the initiative and introduced a system of job rotation. The workmen showed an unusual amount of satisfaction over their work, and they were well aware that this was due to the innovation. Moreover, the speed and quality of the work of these 'rotating' men was just as great as those of their 'stationary' comrades. Even when, as happened in certain cases, there was a smaller output after a change, the improvement in quality and the decrease in labour turnover and in absenteeism may largely have counterbalanced it. Walker and Guest note in this connection that if one asks workers to give up routine work and to make the effort to learn new operations, they must be offered substantial compensation in exchange. For many, the attractions of variety and of learning a repertory of skills will suffice. Others will need more if their dislike of change is to be overcome. This accounts for the interest shown by firms in pilot experiments introduced with the guarantee that workers or employees 'rotating' can, if they wish, return to the 'stationary' assignments they had before.[6]

In the clothing factories of Binche (Belgium, 1952) we also noticed the place given to the alternation of jobs and to the establishment of 'flying squads', made up of fifteen or so multi-specialized workers, who can step in when someone is ill or absent and a gap occurs in the assembly line, and who are used when not so needed in repair and supervision. In the Hoover factory at Greenford, Middlesex, near London, the assembly line for vacuum-cleaner motors was organized by the engineers (1951) in such a way that the members of each team of sixteen men and women were partly free to apportion jobs among themselves and could also help one another, thus forming a sub-assembly group when the conveyor-belt in the segment on which they were employed became over-full.

This interchangeability of workers within a group, together with the margin of freedom allowed in the apportioning of jobs, seems to me also one of the characteristic features of the new rolling sheet foundries. Thanks to the doubling of the 'cage', one now holds two roughing cylinders and the other two finishing ones. Alongside each cage there is a comparatively comfortable, air-conditioned cabin, in which the work done in the old foundries by six men is now performed by two. In both cabins one mechanic, using buttons, pedals and levers that are much more accurate, now executes work formerly carried out by three semi-skilled men.

The sheet worker on the ground near each train retains his essential function of calibrating the steel plating, as well as a certain general authority. But, and this is what interests me most, the four mechanics are themselves sheet-workers and all six men are interchangeable. They form a single team, which to function properly must be homogeneous, each man being able to do the work performed by the other five. As an engineer said to inquirers, 'We leave them free to organize themselves, to find the job that suits them best and to take one another's place when they want to, or when it is necessary.' Even when there is in fact specialization in the interests of output, the principle of interchangeability remains, and has in addition a further sanction in the fact that all six men have equal status and equal pay.[7]

It is worth while noting what is being done in France by an organization of a strictly technical kind, the *Centre d'Études pratiques des Techniques de Production* (C.É.P.T.P.), which is concerned with the introduction of up-to-date methods in the many metal-using firms engaged in medium or small scale mass-production. It would be out of place here to describe the methods advocated by its inspirers, who have achieved remarkable results. It is enough to say that they recommend an ultra-rapid changeover from one tool or machine to another, the creation of partial assembly lines — i.e. of separate segments of the line replacing the old grouping by type of machines — and the reorganization by 'families' of parts requiring to be manufactured or worked on during quite long periods of time. The rapid change of tools allows of many operations being performed on the same spot and of reducing the time taken by the manufacturing cycle — what industrial psychologists in England call the 'total cycle of the unit of work'.* Here too we see that the purely technical development of organization tends to create teams and heighten their importance, thereby increasing the worker's interest in a reduced manufacturing cycle, which he is now more able to grasp and understand as a whole. That is the point made by M. Louis Longchambon, the chairman of the *Conseil de Perfectionnement* of the C.É.P.T.P., when he says: 'The methods of our Centre, in so far as they tend to decrease the work cycle and regroup certain processes by entrusting different jobs to the same person on the same working day, and also to develop teamwork, are of a kind to arouse the worker's interest and diminish his fatigue, and in the end to associate him with the whole production by increasing his responsibilities and grasp of the whole of which he forms a part.'[8]

* See below, Chapter III, p. 59.

We may note that this is not only an example of the *alternation* of jobs but already the beginning of job *enlargement,* a direct method to which we shall return in a later chapter. Furthermore, the teams thus created are necessarily interdependent and come to constitute small workshops, as it were, within a larger organization.

From what we have observed it looks, therefore, as though the spontaneous reaction of certain technicians against the traditional organization of labour and the experiments they have tried, which are a kind of heresy from the orthodox point of view, have mostly led to the restoration of a margin of freedom to the team. It is through the increase of teamwork that these new practices have been able to slip between the meshes of a system rigidly organized by planning departments. It seems as if modern industry were discovering — or rather rediscovering, following Aristotle and certain other writers — the truth that man is by nature a social animal, made to live and work in a community. It follows that he is most likely to make full use of his capacities, and to obtain the best results from them, if he works in a group. Planning seems to be moving towards the idea that, while operational methods should be predetermined in what must inevitably be a most minute way, as should timing, motions, objectives and procedure at all levels, a certain amount of freedom should be left to the team in the apportionment and alternation of jobs, provided they are kept strictly within the unit of organization.

WORKERS' REACTIONS

If certain engineers have departed from the current practice of orthodox Scientific Management for purely technical reasons, it is also clear that the workers' reactions to the usual conditions of work on the assembly line have in many cases influenced them and caused a revision of their opinions. Walker and Guest, in their fascinating study of a great American automobile firm, which they call 'Plant X', have thrown light on these reactions by giving us the results of an inquiry carried out with modern methods and with a good statistical presentation of the principal results.

The workers of Plant X, who were employed on the assembly line according to the classical methods, showed a clear preference for more varied work (85 per cent of the sample). Moreover, when the number of operations contained in a job increased, the worker was more likely to consider it 'interesting' (commentary on Table 6, p. 53). There existed a positive correlation between this number and the verbal expression of interest in the job.[9] Such indications, confirmed often enough by other observers, justify the effort to introduce more variety into working conditions by transfers, rotation and job enlargement, wherever it is made. A revealing sign of the worker's real reactions to the classical assembly line is absenteeism. Walker and Guest, having carefully selected six measurable features of mass-production, show (pp. 120–1, Table 11) that the more closely a job corresponds to these, and in particular the more repetitive it is, the higher the absentee rate. I myself have often pointed to similar facts in relation to labour turnover as well as to absenteeism. For instance, in November, 1948, in the Archer Avenue factory of Western Electric in Chicago, which employs mostly women and girls on conveyor-belt jobs performed at a high speed, an average of twenty girls leave every week; this corresponds to more than 1,000 a year out of the 5400 employed in the factory.[10] In studying the reactions of their sample, Walker and Guest arrive at a similar interpretation. Furthermore, that a correlation exists between labour turnover and repetitive jobs on the assembly line is suggested by the general fact that in the United States automobile plants using the conveyor-belt have the highest labour turnover of all manufacturing industries.[11]

Another proof of the strain created in workers by the traditional methods of Scientific Management is their desire for change of work and for promotion, and the way in which they express and justify this desire. They feel themselves bound, chained one might even say, to their job by specialization, by its minute subdivision and the absence of any special training for it. Their comments are tinged with vexation and bitterness. There is no need to learn how to do such jobs, since they can be performed by anyone after a few days', or even hours', experience. On the other hand, directly they are given something of more scope to do, with a larger number of operations and a change of tasks, something therefore requiring a longer period of initiation, their inferiority complex diminishes and signs of pride in their work appear. This was the case with a certain semi-skilled worker whose job it was to remove dents from hoods. 'Each hood is different for every car,' he said. 'Took me six months to learn it. And it takes years to be good at it.'[12] So semi-skilled workers aim at getting transferred to multispecialized jobs as substitutes or utility men, or to supervisory ones, both of which seem to them a real advance.

In Plant X, two-thirds of the workers belonging to the sample studied wanted to be transferred to some other job in their department. Of the 115, 56 wanted repair or utility jobs, 16 wished to become supervisors and 15 foremen, while the remaining 28 wanted any other production job as long as it was not on the main assembly line. Less than 10 per cent volunteered increased pay as their principal reason for wishing to change. For most of them it was primarily a question of altering the immediate *content* of their job. Many described their aspirations in this way: 'On the job I want, I could do a lot of different things.' Or: 'It would give me the chance of learning more.' Or: 'It would be easier, not so much work.'

The replies to a second set of questions, which were concerned with the desire for any jobs in the plant and not just ones in their own department, showed similar tendencies (Table 10, p. 110). Especially interesting comments from our point of view included the following: 'It's different — not doing the same thing all the time'; 'Can't learn anything ew on the job I have now'; 'It's a little easier and more varied' and the following, which is highly significant: 'On the job I'd like you can see how the whole plant works.' There are seldom any replies suggesting as the reason for wanting to change the desire for a higher position or improved social status. Walker and Guest list as follows, in order of decreasing importance, the kinds of reason given for wanting to change: (1) more variety; (2) pace not determined by a moving belt; (3) more initiative and skill demanded; (4) not as physically tiring; (5) getting ahead.[13]

Let us note that the attraction of greater variety is intimately linked for many workers with the wish to be more closely associated with the planning of their work. They want to have a freer use, in the widest sense of the term, of the instruments entrusted to them. But they would also like to escape from the petty restrictions imposed upon them by planning 'at the top', and to share in the working out of methods. In motorcar factories, during the comparatively fluid period each year when models are being revised, it would be possible to satisfy this wish to a certain extent. Such experiments have given good results. In any case the psychological benefits of teamwork, in which a person can enjoy a certain amount of freedom within his group, are partly to be explained by the desire to participate in the planning of one's own work, a deep-seated and widespread desire which 'Scientific Management' (so-called) has most unwisely overlooked.[14]

VARIETY AND OUTPUT

The empirical resort to such methods as have been described above already implies a recognition by technicians of the grave difficulties inherent in the simplification of jobs, a practice they have been following with much energy and confidence, but also blindly, ever since the beginning of the era of 'scientific' rationalization.* To admit that for many workers the way to obtain a maximum output is either to transfer them from one simplified job to another or to introduce work rotation systematically, is already a reaction against an excessive division of labour. From the technician's point of view, it may even seem a retrograde step, going beyond such methods in the direction of a reintegration of jobs.

Thus both daily workshop experience, and a number of scientific investigations conducted by industrial psychologists, agree that the effects of simplifying jobs, and in particular the set of attitudes we call boredom, can be lessened when some variety is introduced. I have just cited quite a number of cases, taken from observations made in France and elsewhere, in which a regular exchange of jobs

* This energy, confidence, and blindness have also led us to speak of an 'orthodoxy' in the title to this chapter. The idea of an 'orthodox' or 'traditional' type of Scientific Management underlies the criticism levelled at it in the United States by such well-known experts as J. C. Worthy, A. R. Heron, P. F. Drucker, J. D. Elliott, C. R. Walker and many others. Under the influence of Taylorism, which I have examined in detail from the standpoint of the human sciences in another book, principles have spread into current planning practice, and particularly into the sub-division of jobs, which have never until recently been seriously called in question save by the theorists. Those reconsidering them to-day are not in any way seeking to reject *en bloc* 'traditional' Scientific Management, but only to show how it can now (for various reasons) be freed from much dead wood and so be better adapted to answering both the technical and the human needs of modern businesses.

Moreover, consulting engineers on both sides of the Atlantic, uncommitted to any 'orthodoxy', have already seen the point in the daily exercise of their profession: and the experiments and opinions I am here describing can only confirm them in the efforts they are making.

between workers in a team has been spontaneously organized by the engineers without showing any harmful results on the total output or the unit cost. The maintenance and extension of these methods prove clearly enough their practical value.

Since 1924 scientific studies in this sphere have been systematically developed by English psychologists under the inspiration of Dr C. S. Myers, and their results have been conclusive. They were first applied to groups of jobs, such as the packing of soap, the making of cigarettes, the folding of handkerchiefs, confectionery work, etc.[15] These experiments show that the effect of introducing some variety into work depends upon (1) the kind of activity studied, (2) how quickly the changes are made, (3) how long they last, and (4) of what kind they are. These changes must not take place too frequently, so as not to multiply the periods of initiation, which always decrease speed whilst the 'hotting up' process is taking place. But when these precautions are taken, a varied job entrusted to a single person can yield as high an output as when it is given to several semi-skilled workers, sometimes indeed a higher one. This will not seem surprising if one remembers that workers as a rule definitely prefer alternating activities, because they are then not so boring, as we saw in the case of Plant X. Scientific literature is full of observations and experiments on the subject which support this view.[16] The subjective factor has too long been underestimated by technicians, some of whom have now at last discovered that a worker's attitude to his job *also* has quantitative effects upon his output, effects no longer to be ignored.

Even if, therefore, the introduction of variety leads to difficulties in organization and administration, and even if it may threaten the *possible* maximum short-term efficiency resulting from job simplification, in the long run it will produce *real* compensatory gains, when we take into account the loss of output, lowering of morale and refusal to adapt or co-operate which stem from dissatisfaction and boredom. The report of the National Industrial Conference Board on the problem of boredom rightly stresses these practical considerations.[17] This report is one of the signs of a growing awareness, previously unknown, in industrial circles, which were until recently convinced of the advantages of breaking down jobs and of constantly increasing their subdivision. Now, and particularly since 1945, they seem to be gradually realizing its disadvantages. They appear determined to study its effects upon productivity and to decide 'to what extent a consolidation of jobs can in the long run stimulate individual production'.[18]

'DIMINISHING RETURNS'

Scientific circles and industrial experimenters are now beginning to show an interest in variety and transfer, a new standpoint that leads them to consider directly the question of the division of labour and its present-day problems. Nevertheless, it is only recently that these problems have for the first time been studied specifically with the object of enlarging and enriching work itself.

We must not be surprised at the slowness of this development. In practice such efforts have come up against a fundamental obstacle in the case of most American and European engineers: their profound conviction, which it is exceedingly hard to eradicate — it has almost become a dogma — that the new work procedure, which is based upon a systematic breakdown of jobs into their elementary components, is bound to diminish costs and increase output. But different views are now beginning to be expressed by the managers of some large American firms. They have noted a tendency towards 'diminishing returns' where there is an increase in the subdivision of jobs and extreme specialization. Thus, however good the quality of the machines and of the general lay-out by the planning department, bored workers do not produce work of high quality. Moreover, the technicians underline the fact that an extreme subdivision and specialization of jobs often requires considerable investment and technical expenditure.

This new trend of opinion in the United States has been well summed up by G. C. Homans of Harvard University, an observant industrial sociologist, who writes:

> The division of labor makes the cost of work less in human effort or money. For this reason all societies have gone some distance in making their members specialists. From Adam Smith to F. W. Taylor, the uncriticized assumption was apt to be that the further the division was carried, the greater were the savings effected, that the further a job like shoemaking was broken down into its component specialties, and each assigned to a workman who did nothing else, the less would be the cost of making the shoe. Now we have begun to understand that the division of labor, like any other process, has its point of diminishing returns.[19]

How did this point of view come into being in industrial circles in the United States and in Europe, and how has it been strengthened? How has confidence in the inevitable profitability of job simplification been undermined? What facts have shaken it? We must now examine this question more closely.

EXTRAORDINARY CIRCUMSTANCES

Peter F. Drucker was undoubtedly one of the first scientific observers of American industry at the end of the recent World War to take note of this growing trend and to attempt an explanation. Mass-production rests, he tells us, on three principles:[20] the breaking down of a complex skilled operation into its component elementary and unskilled motions; the synchronization of the flow of raw or semi-finished materials with the operator's movements; and the interchangeability of parts. It is the first of these principles which is now disputed. On the 'traditional' assembly line, each elementary motion is performed by a separate worker. The intellectual process of analysis is laid out *in space*, so to speak, each separate step being represented by a separate worker. This method, which is still in fact the basis everywhere of the assembly line, would be the only right one if the work were done exclusively by inanimate and single-purpose machine tools, such as a reamer or a trip-hammer. But mixed up in these strictly limited and differentiated operations we find workers, human nervous systems we might call them, who, while involved in this detailed and rigid organization, retain a certain plasticity with psycho-social potentialities and needs.

During the Second World War, continues Drucker, extraordinary circumstances forced us to realize not only that the orthodox assembly line is not indispensable, but that it is very often a highly inefficient way of applying mass-production principles. We were forced at that time to mass-produce a great many products, such as bombsights, which for technical reasons could not be handled on the orthodox assembly line. In other cases, the then available labour supply made it impossible to use the pre-war methods. Thus engineers were forced to think about the fundamentals of mass-production rather than to copy traditional methods blindly; and the results of this first critical analysis were amazing.

In Drucker's opinion, the traditional methods of mass-production, of which the assembly lines of Ford's factories are typical, produce three results that cause severe disturbances in the worker. The atomization of labour, reducing it to a single move-ment, increases fatigue and leads to physiological and neurological damage, such as nervous tics, headaches, deafness, neuritis. Secondly, the worker is chained to the pace of the slowest man on the line and is not allowed to work according to his personal rhythm;[21] the result is again fatigue and irritability, jumpiness and nerves. Finally the worker, never completing a whole job which he can identify as his own personal product, suffers from lack of interest and a sense of frustration.

The profound resentment felt about this method of work, the reactions and disturbances it causes, of which the first generation of American assembly-line workers, most of them recent immigrants, were seldom aware, tend now to become more and more con-sciously experienced, so that after the recent war the vocational advisers of the demobilized soldiers gave this explanation for their dislike of accepting such jobs.

Drucker's attack on the methods and effects of orthodox mass-production appears to me a little over-simplified and unfair. In particular he does not take into account the efforts made since 1945 by progressive firms in Europe and the United States to improve the comfort of workers through better equipment and through the organization of 'social' assembly lines.[22] These experi-ments, it is true, were limited in number and are still so to-day, so that the picture painted by Drucker remains partly correct. The defects and dangers he enumerates are not necessarily due, he thinks, to the technical principles of mass-production.

> They result, not from its basic concepts, but from the unthinking use of the human being as if he were a machine tool designed for one purpose only. It is on this assumption that the time-motion studies of Taylor, and of speed-up systems, such as that of Bedaux, are based. But, needless to say, this is a gross abuse, or misuse, of that wonderful, multi-purpose tool, the human being; and like all abuse of tools, it results in low productive efficiency and in shoddy work. The traditional assembly line is simply a piece of poor engineering judged by the standards of human relations, as well as by those of productive efficiency and output.[23]

Most fortunately (from this standpoint) the war brought with it immense problems, calling for quick solutions in circumstances which did not allow of the application of the classical methods of Scientific Management. Owing to the need for developing war industries without having regard to orthodox rules, experiments were improvised which were full of practical significance as to the possibilities of job enlargement. I shall deal with them later. For the moment it will be enough to note, as does Drucker, that it proved desirable in many cases to lay out the work in terms of *concept* rather than of *space*. In other words, a whole productive operation remained split up into fragmentary and distinct elements, but instead of each motion being performed separately by one worker, the same worker performed a whole series of operations one after another, according to the analytic chart made out by the planning department.* Thus in Detroit, Chicago, and many other industrial centres, experiments begun under the stress of circumstances have shown that work rotation and job enlargement, together with greater initiative and responsibility and more freedom to apportion jobs inside the team, were profitable in practice and led to an improvement in morale, a matter about which technicians are increasingly anxious and which henceforth they will have to take into account in their economic calculations and forecasts.

Could one expect that the lessons these extraordinary wartime measures taught would be taken to heart and bear fruit after the war was over? Could they, in the midst of the difficulties of reconversion and the intoxications of prosperity, resist the counter-offensive launched by traditional theories? Drucker had no illusions on this subject, and gives us the reasons for his pessimism, the main one being in his opinion theoretical. The principal obstacle to a large-scale application of the new methods to mass-production is chiefly our present lack of a proper theoretical understanding of its principles. 'It is clear,' he writes, 'that Taylor did only the first half of the job when he analysed individual motions. But the second half — the integration of the individual motions into a work pattern — has still to be done.' Nevertheless, he adds, many engineers learned during the war that the new method 'pays' in terms of productive efficiency, and are therefore likely to try it out in times of peace. [24]

* The worker thus becomes multispecialized without the scheme of production and its subdivisions, as arranged by the organizers, being modified in any way. See above, Chapter I, pp. 11–14.

THE LESSON OF SEARS ROEBUCK

A strong reaction against certain aspects of Taylor's theory of Scientific Management also characterizes the position of Mr James C. Worthy. His views are all the more notable in that, after having occupied an important post in Roosevelt's New Deal administration, he has become a highly regarded specialist in personnel problems. Since 1938 Worthy has belonged to the management of the Personnel Department of the famous giant mail order firm, Sears Roebuck & Co., with its headquarters in Chicago. In 1951, when addressing a meeting of those directly concerned with industrial relations, he declared unambiguously that 'our task consists to a large extent in developing a more adequate science of management'.[25] It is significant, he notes, that Taylor and his disciples were all engineers. They dealt with the human problems of management as they had been taught to deal with those of making machines. 'In doing so, they transferred the engineer's way of thinking to a realm in which he has nothing to say, with consequences in certain cases bordering on the disastrous.'[26]

A good example of this is to be seen in Taylor's ideas concerning the functionalizing of work, which are at the heart of his system and have had, as we know, a great influence upon certain recent versions of what is called the 'scientific management movement'.[27] They lead to a splitting up of jobs into their simplest elements and then to a grouping together of similar functions, precisely as would be done if it were a question of connecting up similar machine components. To-day people still believe that this method raises output by its specialization, securing better supervision and more adequate control, while by decreasing the skill demanded of the worker it diminishes the cost of employing him.

Worthy particularly criticizes (as I myself did twenty years ago, not without shocking certain of Taylor's French disciples who have never forgiven me) the way in which Taylor separates planning and execution, entrusting to management, to use his own words, 'all the large mass of knowledge which in the past was in the heads of the workers, and lay also in their physical ability and skill'. The management must think out and plan the work in the most careful and detailed way, demanding of the worker 'not to seek to increase production by his own *initiative*, but to perform punctiliously the *orders given* down to their slightest detail'.[28] This is the cornerstone of the whole doctrine. Worthy quotes the opinion of one of his colleagues, who is also well-known in the United States, Alexander Heron, vice-president of the powerful Crown Zellerbach Paper Corporation, who wrote in 1948 in his excellent book *Why Men Work*:[29] 'We cannot have a really healthy industrial organism, if it is composed of distinct groups of workers and planners. We cannot expect a team spirit among 90 per cent of our personnel if we keep on telling them that their function is to work and ours is to think'.[30]

In his article, which is so rich in material that I wish I could reproduce whole passages from it, Worthy also points to the failure of Taylorian methods to secure the 'participation' of the workers in the life and progress of the firm. There exist in the specialist literature masses of learned pamphlets and addresses explaining how to obtain more effective participation from the worker, more suggestions and so on. That is all to the good, and everyone will agree that such an objective is desirable. But if results are few, it is precisely because the orthodox theory of Scientific Management by its over-functionalism and the practices due to this has *in actual fact* deprived the wage-earner of all means of participating in the economic life of his firm. As long as this is the case, all efforts to persuade him that he can play an essential part in it are doomed to failure. We must begin by giving the workers a 'creative relationship with work'.[31]

This criticism of Taylor and his followers leads Worthy to think that the excessively complicated structure of producing organizations is one of the fundamental reasons for the bad relationship that exists between employers and employees. When we consider the realities of industrial life, we are struck by the lengths to which the specialization of both individuals and teams has been carried: 'One has the feeling that the division of labour has gone wild, and has been carried far beyond what is needed for productive efficiency.'[32]

I shall not dwell upon the functional specialization of administrative units within a firm, which is considered harmful by Worthy but does not concern us here. I shall simply note that he summarizes the general consequences of this phenomenon in the following way: The *size* of the administrative unit has become too great. The work loses all *meaning* for a specialized employee, who therefore comes to have little feeling of *responsibility* for his elementary job. In face of the resultant apathy, managements

increase *supervisory* pressure, but this procedure only creates
tension and active or passive resistance on the part of the employees, and requires an elaborate hierarchy of many supervisory
levels. Each functional unit then retires into itself and becomes
jealous of its own prerogatives, and in consequence all *spontaneous
co-operation* disappears. Among the managers of a firm so organized
this situation causes both overwork and a state of fear which may
develop into chronic anxiety.[33]

The Sears Roebuck experiment and the investigations made by
its Personnel Department (its 'Survey Program', which used two
different techniques; (1) questionnaires having extra sheets for
comments, and (2) unplanned interviews) have shown that both
output and morale suffer where the job is too specialized.[34] On the
other hand, a better attitude to work and much better results are
met with where employees are engaged on more varied jobs (as
salesmen, supervisors or mechanics). The structure of the firm is
not 'vertical' as is that of most large undertakings, but horizontal.
Being less complicated, it secures a maximum of administrative
decentralization and of consolidation of jobs, thus effectively
encouraging responsibility and initiative among its employees.
In an organization as vast and diversified as Sears, which includes
retail shops, mail-order plants, factories, warehouses and offices,
and whose sales department alone contains 110,000 people, 'a
certain amount of specialization is essential, but in so far as possible
it has been kept to a minimum. The policy of our Company
recognizes the definite advantages of the flexible, versatile "general
practitioner" (particularly at executive level) in contrast to the
narrower and less adaptive specialist'.[35]

But surely, it will be said, the high morale of the staff of Sears
Roebuck is not solely due to structural reforms leading to decentralization and multispecialization. It is important to realize here
that this business being of a capitalist type, as all businesses are in the
United States, the integration of its employees into its economic
life as well as their readiness to co-operate has been greatly
enhanced by a system of internal promotion (Reserve Group
Program), about which we cannot speak here, and by the bold
policy of its directors.[36] During the year 1948, for instance, the cost
to the Company of its voluntary contributions to profit-sharing and
various social insurance benefits rose to 50 million dollars. The
whole of its non-wage payments came to more than 84 million

dollars (about £29,000,000). Moreover, the samples of opinions gathered by the 'Survey Program' show that, however important the economic aspect of these benefits may be, their chief significance as regards employee morale is the fact that they afford tangible evidence of the management's concern for the welfare of its employees. 'If they were less substantial,' writes Worthy, 'their value as symbols and as an earnest of management's attitude would be correspondingly diminished.'[37]

A SOCIOLOGICAL INTERPRETATION

It is, we may be sure, owing to such reactions against Taylorian mass-production theories that the after-war experiments I shall describe later were tried out and have since been continued. They implied a presumption which became a certainty, that the division of labour, if carried beyond a certain point, so far from procuring the productive benefits its planners expect, has serious practical disadvantages. G. C. Homans also gives an explanation for the weakening of an opinion so solidly entrenched among the engineers.

I shall not sketch the general framework of sociological theory in which his analysis is embedded, but need only say that in his eyes, in order that a human group, and particularly a group of workers, may be able to survive in its environment, its members must have motives which he calls *sentiments*, jobs to be done (*activities*), and communications (*interactions*) between each other, whether verbal or not. These three things are always mutually interdependent and form the 'external system' of the group, since they are constantly influenced by the environment, there being a continuous process of action and reaction between the group and its immediate surroundings.[38]

From the point of view of the division of labour, we are particularly interested in those actions and reactions which take place between the activities of the group members (their jobs) and the process of interaction, or of communication, if you like to call it so, which co-ordinates their individual operations and directs them towards the creation of a product. In a working group, for instance in a team of five men engaged in installing electrical equipment in a motorcar engine, partial activities give a total result. The scheme of activity therefore implies a scheme of interaction. Any modification in the one is felt in the other, and vice versa. In short, there is a close and mutual interdependence between them.

The classical method consists in dividing up a total unit of work into partial activities, and then in planning a scheme of interaction corresponding strictly to the scheme of activity to be carried out in the shop. The scheme of activity is then the fundamental factor on which the scheme of interaction must be based. This is in fact the way in which the technicians of a planning department ordinarily proceed in firms developing a new mass-product. But it assumes that by analysing the process of manufacture theoretically one can always discover a practical system of co-ordinating the operations. Therein precisely lies the persistent mistake of so many mass-production experts. In most cases, in fact, the two schemes — of activity and interaction — are equally important and should both be carefully studied and compared.

However that may be, it is certain that at the start of the machine age the rudimentary forms of the division of labour were very costly. So people were increasingly led to elaborate schemes of more specialized activities in order to reduce costs in terms of human effort and of wages. So the idea arose and was strengthened that an increasing subdivision of jobs would be accompanied by a proportionate increase in profits.

To-day this dogma is being called in question, and this is how G. C. Homans interprets the moment at which the division of labour ceases to 'pay' and begins to show 'diminishing returns'.

> The division of labor is not something in itself; it always implies a scheme of interaction by which the different divided activities are co-ordinated. The indirect costs of setting up this scheme, including the costs that arise if supervision is inadequate, may offset the direct savings from specialization.[39]

His explanation is interesting. According to it, the reaction against the division of labour is primarily due (at least in appearance) to economic and technical causes. Certain schemes of activity being given, particularly if they imply very specialized operations, it would be impossible for the workers charged with carrying them out to co-operate and communicate properly.

But, it may be objected to Homans, if the technique of the planners 'after a certain point' turns against itself, is it not because it continues to be managed 'to some extent' by those men who have been ordered to apply it in every detail? Behind the economic and technical causes there are others of a psychological nature, which in the course of these pages we have seen and will again see at work; boredom, dissatisfaction, the desire for some form of real training, for variety, for a feeling of achievement. A human group, we are told, is defined by interaction. A, B, C, D, E, F, G, H . . . form a group because A interacts more often with B, C, D, E, F, G, H . . . than with M, N, O, P, Q, R . . . and the same with the other members of the group.[40] But it is surely *psychological* reasons which prevent A, B, C, D, E, F, G, H . . . from interacting within the framework of a scheme of activities too greatly subdivided, and thus, in the case of a working group, prevent them from producing quickly and well. Do we not meet, within our little group, an individual A perhaps, and several others with him, who express in this way their characters, their personal demands, and particularly their need for understanding, for interest, meaning and involvement in their work? Those are exactly the attitudes and aspirations suggested to me by a direct observation of the 'ordinary' assembly-line shop, and more generally of businesses rationalized according to purely technical methods. With this reservation, we must express our gratitude to Homans for an analysis which helps us to understand better the meaning and deeper reasons for the decline in orthodox views which we have been discussing in this chapter.

CHAPTER III

Towards Job Enlargement

A. AMERICAN EXPERIMENTS

As Drucker rightly saw, the Second World War played an almost revolutionary part in the history of the organization of work when, as the result of pressing armament needs, it forced the sudden conversion of American industry to new types of production, often with inexperienced workers. The habits of Scientific Management were upset and experiments were undertaken by engineers in conditions they would never have accepted in normal times.

WARTIME EXPERIMENTS

Thus in the Cadillac factories of Detroit completely unskilled and industrially inexperienced Negro women were employed in making a high precision aluminium part for aircraft engines.[1] Each of them finished a *whole* part, working according to a chart which showed in three parallel columns (1) what to do next; (2) what to look for before doing it (speed, temperature, etc.); (3) what to look for after doing it. The women had only simple movements to make which were easy to learn. In fact, it took no longer to train these women than it would have taken to train them for orthodox assembly-line work. And yet this enlargement of the job, which through its greater variety brought into play a whole series of muscles one after the other, proved its superior value. At the same time it avoided the disadvantages of limited and repetitive activity, so often condemned by physiologists as the major cause of muscular contractions and fatigue,[2] and made possible a personal and varying rhythm of work and the satisfaction of achieving something oneself. The results, from the standpoint of morale and output, were definitely better than those that would have been obtained from the same worker using the conventional assembly line.

After relating this experience, Drucker takes us through two tank-manufacturing plants, which he studied in 1943 in towns of the Middle West, the names of which he is careful not to give.[3] Let us call them A. and B. They were both controlled by the same company, and were identically equipped by the same engineers to produce the same engines. Yet they differed markedly in performance. A., housed in an old ramshackle building, hastily adapted for its new purpose, regularly exceeded its production quota, had a very low labour turnover in an area containing a constantly shifting working population, and had low absenteeism and accident rates with generally satisfactory labour relations. B., on the contrary, whose buildings were brand new and specially built for making tanks, had a productivity one-sixth less than A. The turnover and accident rates were high, the work relations badly strained. Single manipulation was done faster than in A., and yet the end result was a lower total output, a fact which baffled the engineers.

A more detailed analysis of the working conditions prevailing explained this strange contrast. The new plant had been carefully organized according to the traditional methods of Scientific Management, i.e. all the worker had to do was to follow carefully the detailed instruction charts, performing the same operations in the same way all the time according to the minute specifications of the planning department. In the shops the men were silent, their strained looks showing a constant fear of falling behind the speed required. A., on the contrary, the improvised factory, had not had the luxury of such careful preparation. The technical management had only done the overall engineering and planned the general layout of each operation. But the details of execution had been left to the free initiative of the foremen and their teams. Of necessity, and not by deliberate choice, the management did not interfere at this level in the way the work was distributed, and these groups had spontaneously introduced work rotation and job enlargement, concerning which the engineers seemed to be very worried, apologizing all the time to visitors for what they called 'a lack of neatness' in the organization. On the other hand the workers were happy, this fluid situation allowing the groups to work in friendly rivalry. It was quite a time before the engineers of factory A. understood the great advantages of this 'lack of neatness', the surprising experiment they had been unwittingly making; and it was still longer before their colleagues, and even the workmen, of factory B. accepted the facts and drew the obvious conclusions. However, during a later visit a year afterwards, Drucker had the satisfaction of seeing the two factories using the same methods, now consciously applied, with the same success in both.

It was again thanks to the need for a quick transformation of production that an interesting experiment was started in a metal production plant in Michigan, which switched to making carbines for the army.[4] The workmen, who were largely novices, this being their first industrial job, were trained, Drucker tells us, in the following way: (1) the worker was first left alone for a few days on his machine with nothing but the foreman to guide him, to get used to industrial work; (2) then an instructor took him out to a shooting range and let him fire a few rounds at a target; (3) the next step was to take the carbine to pieces, so that the worker could see the part he was working on, and its functions and importance could be explained; (4) he was then given a carbine in which his part was either too small or too big, and thus shown convincingly the reasons for precision; (5) finally, instructor and worker sat down together and planned the worker's own programme — usually by working backwards from the finished product to the semi-finished piece of metal as it came to the worker's bench. Let us note, however, so as to prevent any misunderstanding on this point, that the whole job had of course been thought out in advance by the production engineers and the time-and-motion study men. Nevertheless, the worker was allowed considerable latitude in timing, speed and rhythm, which he could adapt to his own particular case.

The worker thus learnt what his machine was doing and why. His work was no longer something the boss told him to do; it was something he had discovered by himself, so to speak. And at the same time he was given a sense of understanding and of achievement.

Finally, instructor and worker together summarized the worker's conclusions on a chart — and the foreman was not supposed to change anything on this chart except at the request of the worker himself. To its amazement the management found that the workers invariably set higher standards of timing and speed for themselves than the time-and-motion people had worked out for the job, and that in actual practice they even tended to do better than these high standards.

The experiments described suggest that the breaking down of jobs advocated by orthodox Scientific Management prevents the workers from exercising the powers of co-operation, teamwork and solidarity which many possess. Unable to find an outlet for these potentialities, they experience feelings of dissatisfaction, a sense of strain and a more or less conscious inner resentment, the expression of which will vary from one man to another. Furthermore, as the success of the training methods adopted in the carbine manufacturing plant shows, one of the best ways of giving the worker a sense of achievement, of satisfying his need for understanding and for taking an interest in his work, is to associate him closely with its preparation and planning. At the same time output is increased beyond the forecasts made by the technicians. Such methods bring us into contact with one of the main concerns of the Work Simplification movement, still conceived and developed, it is true, from a purely technical point of view by Allan H. Mogensen and his colleagues of Lake Placid.[5]

A PIONEER FIRM: THE I.B.M.

As we have seen in the last chapter, the directors of Sears Roebuck have completely rejected the Taylorian tradition and now base their practice on a new doctrine of work management. Their attempt to enlarge the content of each function is connected with a decentralized structure that encourages the initiative, responsibility and polyvalence of each worker. The firm's great variety of activities and services — it is a half-industrial, half-commercial undertaking — favours a reform of this kind. Job enlargement here is only one element in the whole, whereas the experiments we are now going to describe are based on job enlargement alone and are for the most part purely industrial.

They have been made in the United States at the Endicott factory (New York State) of the International Business Machines Corporation, a giant company specializing in the construction of all sorts of typewriters, meters, time-recorders and calculating, statistical and punched-card machines. Its branches and affiliated firms are to be found in all parts of the world, and to it we owe the first electronic universal calculating machine, constructed between 1938 and 1942 under the direction of Professor Aiken of Harvard University.[6] The I.B.M. has carried out programmes of this type in other factories belonging to it, and in particular in that at Poughkeepsie, also situated in New York State, which has, like the Endicott factory, a staff of about 8,000. Other big firms have followed closely in its steps, among them General Motors, which has worked out a plan of job enlargement in one of its factories, applying it to some of the most repetitive operations. The important public utility firm of Detroit Edison has also introduced it among its office workers, as we shall see later on. So we may say that it now constitutes an important movement, which we cannot evaluate statistically, although its existence has already found an echo in the American Press.

It may be of documentary interest here to reproduce the beginning of an article written by a staff reporter of the *Wall Street Journal*, one of the most widely read organs of the business world, presenting to its readers the job enlargement movement (11 March, 1954):

> *Poughkeepsie, New York.* — A year ago John Nachamkin sat by an assembly line in International Business Machines' plant here, absent-mindedly fastening parts to an electric typewriter frame. To-day his simple task has undergone a profound change, and so has Mr Nachamkin.
>
> He now aligns the parts as well as fitting them to the frame, work previously done by a higher-paid 'final assembly man'. Then he inspects his own work, a job formerly done by a 'process inspector'.
>
> If something mechanical goes awry along the assembly line on which he works, Mr Nachamkin is responsible for trouble-shooting his own two-yard-long stretch of it, work which had been done by a supervisor or even an engineer. To do this he's had to learn how to interpret a blueprint showing the electrical wiring and other mechanical 'insides' of the assembly line.
>
> The process which transformed Mr Nachamkin from a screw-tightening 'robot' into a much more versatile producer is called 'job enlargement'. It means ballooning the worker's present job, making it more varied and interesting, to encourage him to do it better. It means a lot of other things, too, such as switching workers from job to job to round out their factory educations.
>
> Most companies that have tried it say job enlargement has cut their costs, stepped up their output and given their customers a better-quality product. They believe hundreds of thousands of U.S. workers will be exposed to it in coming years.

The original job enlargement plan, which was conceived in 1943 and has since been developed by the directors of I.B.M., aimed at creating a better psychological atmosphere, better morale, among their factory workers. They also expected that this reform would bring about further progress in the organization and operational techniques of the firm. The following remarks are a significant reflection of the state of mind of the leaders of the Company before the plan was put into execution: 'If you take part of a job away from a man, he says to himself, "Why have they done that to me? Don't they think I can do it?" He resents the loss, takes less interest in the Company. Conversely, if you give a man more of a job to do, he says to himself, "They must think I'm good," and he takes more interest in the Company.' 'The men,'* declared another plant executive, 'are usually unhappy about non-responsible, repetitive jobs. . . . All normal men, even those without great abilities, prefer, I believe, jobs which have some skill and significance attached to them.'[7]

THREE KINDS OF BENEFITS

In this connection let us underline the fact that the I.B.M. plan was accompanied by a systematic effort at vocational training, which constituted one of its essential elements and is a condition of its success in other mass-production firms. This training enabled the workers to understand the meaning of their fragmentary operations by placing them in the setting of the whole production process.

Before the introduction of the plan the workers, who had for years been employed upon the same machines, were not allowed to do their own machine-setting and checking up, although they often wished to. In the production shops at Endicott, from which sprang the first applications of the plan, most of the operations were semi-skilled, not needing more than a week's training. A part was lifted by the worker and placed in the machine. The machine was started; a cutting tool or drill did the job on the part. The machine was stopped by the operator and the part removed. All preparatory work, including the setting up of the machine, had been previously done by specialists. We may notice that some of the

---

* As against the women, who generally complain less. This observation is often correct as regards the mere question of fact, but it requires careful interpretation in respect of many different factors, socio-economic and cultural.

semi-skilled workers, including beginners but also some of the veterns who had grown old in harness, suffered from an inferiority complex and thought they were incapable of assuming any responsibilities, and so did not want them.

In the initial phase of the job enlargement programme, care was taken to increase the scope of operations by adding new responsibilities and skills. For instance, the job was made to include tool-sharpening, the setting up of the machine for each new series of blueprints, a knowledge of calibration, of how deviations from tolerances will affect the part subsequently, and, what was no doubt the most important addition of all, the complete checking of the finished part, which meant using test-plate, height gauge and comparator.

The experiment led to the displacement of quite a large number of set-up men and inspectors, whose functions were now included in the 'enlarged' jobs of the semi-skilled workers. They could be immediately found work elsewhere, as the firm was constantly expanding, and that without suffering a reduction in pay: indeed the pay of one-third of them was even increased.[8]

The enlargement of the jobs of the mass of semi-skilled workers, who took over work which was previously the privilege of skilled men, led besides to a reduction in the number of the latter. This was particularly true of the fixed machine-setters, the 'set-up' men, who even disappeared altogether from certain sections of the plant. Thus in the drilling workshop of Endicott in 1943, at the moment when orders were flowing in during the war period, there was one set-up man for every eleven operators. In 1946 this proportion had fallen to one to forty-eight. By 1950 the set-up man had been completely eliminated from the department. A similar development with similar figures took place in the milling department.[9] It is interesting to note that at Endicott since 1950 the former semi-skilled workers themselves do the delicate checking of most of the parts they produce. A double-check remains at their request only for certain complicated jobs where they consider it necessary. At Poughkeepsie, where job enlargement was started later, but where to-day it is an actively pursued policy, the development has been less rapid, although quite definite. In 1946 there were nine supporting personnel (set-up men and inspectors, forming part of the salaried staff paid monthly) for 100 workers paid by the hour: in 1954 this proportion had sunk to 4·5 per cent.[10]

Without entering into the technical details of this systematic and rational development within a great business, let us look at the resulting balance sheet.

On the debit side, we must reckon the increased pay received by the workers as a result of their higher qualifications, and the cost of the additional checking apparatus widely distributed among them.

On the credit side, the following benefits have been noted: (1) a substantial reduction in losses from defects and scrap, thanks to the greater responsibility taken by the individual worker for the quality of his work; (2) a considerable gain in time, the setting up and checking now being done by the worker himself; (3) job enlargement implies more variety, responsibility and interest for each worker, and the thing produced has also gained in importance in his eyes (the British psychologists, as we shall see later, speak of a gain in 'meaning'): for the fractional parts of a product and their importance for company and customer are likely to be of little interest to the 'primary producer', the semi-skilled worker, in the average mass-production unit.

To sum up, the benefits were threefold. From the company's point of view: a better satisfied labour force, somewhat lower production costs, and a higher quality of product. From the worker's standpoint: an increase both in pay and personal satisfaction in the job. From the consumer's point of view, an improvement in the quality of the product.[11]

Furthermore, if we consider an aspect from which no statistical conclusions can be directly drawn, that of human relationships within the company, job enlargement has affected their structure in a far from negligible way, and thereby altered the condition of many workers.

In every department where the programme was installed, one level was suppressed between the management and the worker, that of the set-up men and inspectors. These had been exercising a semi-supervisory role, comparable to that of a 'straw boss'. The framework of communication and interaction had been altered. The foremen, for example, began to discuss their problems directly with the workers, who thus gained in prestige and raised their status. The factory organization became simpler, more informal, better integrated. Job enlargement, through reducing the pressure imposed upon the workers by foreman and inspector, a pressure increased by the functionalism of Taylor and his successors, tended to 'repersonalize' the job and thereby to improve the likelihood of the worker finding personal satisfaction in it.

The job enlargement plan is being extended to the French company of the I.B.M., the principal factory of which is at Essonnes (Seine-et-Oise). It was first applied to the sub-assembly of counters used on tabulators, which had originally been divided among thirteen workers with fragmentary operations. These were semi-skilled men, anxious to procure advancement, who were mostly discontented with jobs of such small interest. These thirteen stages were successively consolidated into seven, and then into four jobs, with the work 'enlarged'. On Saturdays the workers were given theoretical and practical training for six weeks, being thus initiated into technology and the way machines function. Half of them, on a belt containing thirty operators, have become 'O.P.I.'* The results have been excellent. The workers like having fuller jobs and feel themselves responsible to the customer for the unit since they are accountable for its final assembly. A similar experiment was made with the 'sorters'. In this case each workman sets up the whole machine himself, competing with his mates, and the time for the setting up has been reduced by two hours out of a total of about eighteen. The checking is done by a specialist, but even so it is the machine-setter who is responsible for the final check-up. The management proposes to introduce job enlargement in the same way in the case of the assembly of 'verifiers', 'collators', and 'reproducers', instituting 'self-supervision' everywhere and eliminating the set-up man.

DETROIT EDISON

The extreme specialization developed by traditional mass-production methods has not only affected industrial production during the last half-century, but has also profoundly changed the character of office work. So the experiment in job enlargement recently made by the Detroit Edison Company in its Customers' Billing Department is as important for us, and deserves as much attention here as that of the I.B.M. in its factories.[12]

The Detroit Edison Company is one of the largest American firms producing and distributing electricity (utility firms), and

* 'Ouvrier Professionnel de Première Catégorie', i.e. a skilled worker of the lowest of the three classes.

serves an area of 7,500 square miles containing 1,250,000 customers. The employees deal with 35,000 meters on an average per day, and send out and receive the same number of accounts and payments. Each year about 250,000 accounts are closed and 300,000 opened. The firm has therefore a huge accounting department with more than a thousand employees, who have to set-up, keep up-to-date and balance the records of each customer. The bills, made out on punched-card machines, pass from operation to operation, gradually accumulating the necessary information much as a product flows down an assembly line in a factory. Until 1950 the Company's technicians followed classical mass-production methods, simplifying jobs as far as possible, being convinced that thereby they were achieving a maximum output at a minimum cost. In their zeal they had even thought of installing a conveyor-belt to carry customers' records from employee to employee in order to specialize jobs still further.

J. Douglas Elliott, the general manager of the Accounting Division of the Company and one of the chief inspirers of the experiments I am going to describe, stresses the speed with which office jobs (they had been almost like crafts) had been split up into smaller ones, as mechanization and mass-production methods crept into the office in the twentieth century.[13] Old employees, nearing retirement to-day, can still remember how, forty years ago, when the Company was starting, one and the same accountant performed all the operations which to-day are separated. He added up and wrote out the bills, entering them in the main ledger; he collected statistical information, sent out reminders to customers in arrears, and replied to requests for information. Certain of these 'all-round men' even read the meters before coming to the office. To-day the invoicing is almost completely mechanized, as is much of the book-keeping. The rest of the manual operations are highly subdivided, being distributed between meter readers, collectors, tellers, customer-contact employees, telephone inquiry clerks (who are themselves split up into specialized groups), and operators of a whole series of tabulating, punched-card and other machines.

In offices as in industry, notes Elliott, jobs have been made to fit the machines constructed by the engineers and are devoid of interest for the worker. They demand little thought, no initiative and no responsibility in respect either of quantity or of quality. The quantity tends to be determined by the actual pace of the machine and the production schedules of the firm. The quality is checked entirely by specialist inspectors and the final checking is done by statistical processes. Thus the problem of the large work unit, which was often, we must not forget, as tedious in offices as elsewhere, has been replaced by new problems caused by the multiplication of jobs made up of such limited and repetitive operations that they require no real cerebral activity and, when automatic, bring only the medulla into play.

These are of course new problems. At Detroit Edison 'monotonous and uninteresting work is costly to the Company'.[14] In the first place the low morale of employees thoroughly bored with their work results in more absences, complaints, grievances and frustration. The quantity and quality of work also suffer, in spite of, or rather because of, the strictness of the planning. These are in themselves all costly to the Company, but to these expenses must be added others, the cost of rest periods, of music given out on loud-speakers, of decorating workrooms or offices (baptized by the name of 'colour dynamics') which are all ways of alleviating the workers' feelings of boredom and dislike. Their expense is considerable. But when have the technicians, in simplifying jobs and depriving them of all interest, taken these costs into account in making their calculations and forecasts?

Moreover, Elliott observes, we have carried specialization to an extreme without noticing that in the end we create needless operations and on occasion even duplicate them; a rude awakening awaits those convinced that a further division of labour inevitably leads to further economies.

Finally, overspecialization gives rise to another very important source of increased costs to the firm. The potential capabilities of the average worker are not fully utilized. We are very careful to determine the possibilities of our new office machines, which are constantly being made more efficient. But we are far from trying equally hard to evaluate the capabilities of the men and women we employ. To tell the truth, we plan systematically the training and development of our managerial and technical staffs, and, so far as they are concerned, we are aware of the problem of 'full employment' in the individual and human sense of the words. But as soon as we are dealing with workers or employees, we seem to think that they are incapable of doing anything but the extremely limited operations we impose upon them; whereas in fact it is only in a minority of cases that this type of work is not below a worker's capabilities, and can provide him with adequate satisfaction. Elliott here makes a passing remark which, coming from a great 'manager' and technician, conversant with the realities of the business world, has its moving side: 'Maybe this is the area in which we need a little more faith in our fellow human beings.'[15]

In this sense job enlargement, as understood by the directors of Detroit Edison, seeks not only to make labour less monotonous and repetitive, but also to provide the employee with a greater variety of tasks, thus giving him more opportunities for exercising his own judgement and showing his capabilities. In short, its aims as applied to office work are three: (1) to reduce the monotony of jobs; (2) to decrease specialization where it has created duplication and increased costs; (3) to utilize more completely the intellectual abilities and personality of each employee.

Elliott, in giving examples of job enlargement both in the offices and in the power plants of Detroit Edison, stresses the point that these reforms should be introduced not for sentimental reasons but as the result of cool calculation, since they bring economic benefits which the ill-informed find it difficult to grasp. I will list some of them here without going into technical details.

The Customers' Billing Department of Detroit Edison originally consisted of three machine work groups of tabulating-card, key-punch and calculating-machine operators, the work flowing within and between the groups in a traditional production-line fashion. The work was highly subdivided, the morale was poor, the organization was rigid. A complete reform of this multicopier workshop was undertaken and jobs were redistributed, so that each employee was enabled to operate the three kinds of machine, the former categories being consolidated into one in the classification of jobs. In principle the supervisor assigns the work to each employee and there is a rotation of tasks. In fact very often the employees themselves know where they are needed and distribute themselves among the machines of their own accord.[16] Thus, as we saw in the industrial experiments already described, it is a question of allowing a margin of freedom within a team without prejudicing the planning of the workshop or the smooth running of the whole.

In the same way radical changes have been made as regards the staff dealing with customers' records (of which there are more than nine million, about eight per customer). This staff was ultraspecialized, even containing four separate groups of telephonists, each dealing with one particular type of information. After a year's study the Detroit Edison management decided to consolidate similar functions which had formerly been specialized, and to mechanize operations further by the use of electronic equipment.[17]

The information at one time scattered among nine million records is now consolidated on less than 150 reels of magnetic tape. Each clerk is responsible for all work pertaining to a specific batch of accounts. Thus, let us note in passing, the *enlargement* of individual jobs, so far from running counter to work *simplification*, works in harmony with it by promoting, wherever technically possible and psychologically desirable, the *unification* of operations formerly dispersed among a crowd of 'specialized' employees or workmen.[18]

Several of the important reforms introduced by Detroit Edison encourage greater freedom and more complexity in the work of the individual team members, although the team's activity still conforms strictly to the general plan of the shop, which is not in any way altered. Sometimes teams are set up whose members are homogeneous and polyvalent. For instance, the typists in the team which makes out reminders to be sent to customers in arrears have had their jobs enlarged, operating the tabulating machines and having complete responsibility for this section of the accounting department. Sometimes the reaction against overspecialization takes the form of enlarging the work at team level. Here Detroit Edison is following a path which French experts in management have also been taking.[19] A synthesis is made of the activities of several specialized groups, and each of them then assumes the whole of the responsibilities and functions of a sector of which they take complete charge. So at Detroit Edison two teams, each composed of seventeen clerks, look after the accounting machines and the checking and maintenance of the name and address cards for half the Company's customers. Their members are thus promoted to polyvalent activities. Instead of seven job classifications per group, there are now only three. Duplication has thereby been exposed and eliminated. None of the work is any longer behind schedule, nor is overtime required any more. Besides which the general atmosphere has most decidedly improved.

We may also note that job enlargement 'at the bottom' has led to a similar development in the supervisors' functions.[20] Before the start of the experiment they were themselves highly specialized. Many decisions and responsibilities relating to their sector were absorbed and distributed among the Front Office staff and the Customers' Account clerks. Now the supervisors (*a*) hire their own employees, after a first screening of applicants by the Personnel Department; (*b*) prepare their own annual budget with the help of their work groups; (*c*) introduce procedural changes among these, so long as such changes do not affect other groups or run counter to the Department's or the Company's policy; (*d*) are the first to receive the complaints and grievances of their staff.

Their functions have thus been enlarged within a few years. At one time primarily concerned with discipline and reduced to the status of policemen, they have now become 'managers in their own right'. The balance of this five-year experiment is definitely positive, so Detroit Edison believe. Job enlargement has been accompanied by a decrease in the absentee rate and a rise in productivity. Although a great number of the employees and machine operators have been promoted to a higher pay-rate, the general total cost has been reduced. In particular additional help has become unnecessary and overtime has been halved. As regards the 'indirect benefits', resulting from the interest taken by the employees in their work and the improved atmosphere in the firm, their importance, although more difficult to translate into figures, is certainly considerable.

From the examples given it can be seen that job enlargement does not consist in any sense of a return to craft methods. It does not hand over to one workman the complete construction of a complex machine, like an aeroplane engine or a television receiver. We are dealing with a reaction against the excesses of the division of labour, not with a reactionary attitude. It is a question of taking into account a group of facts, some purely technical and others of a psychological and social kind, which have come under the notice of those who organize, direct, staff and observe mass-production processes, and in consequence of restoring to the content of the job, as it is experienced from day to day and month to month by factory worker and office employee, the importance denied to it, or at least ignored, by Scientific Management. Did Taylor, Gilbreth, Gannt, or even, to come nearer to our times, Bedaux, ever consider from this standpoint the number of operations contained in a job assigned to a worker by the planning department? Yet the interest now taken by big firms in job enlargement shows that it can accompany the most careful planning and organization, as well as increasing the individual worker's margin of freedom and general satisfaction.

CHAPTER IV

Towards Job Enlargement

B. BRITISH INVESTIGATIONS

THUS there is a growing interest in the United States in the economic and psychological effects on mass-production of the division of labour. The widespread experiments we have described show how deeply industrialists and specialists in human relations are now concerned about these effects from a very practical point of view. These experiments, however, have no theoretical substructure, although the writings of Drucker and Walker have thrown a clear light upon what has been happening and no doubt have made business men conscious of it to a certain extent. In Great Britain, on the other hand, where up to now industrial experiments in job enlargement have not gone nearly so far, various important scientific investigations have been undertaken since 1948.

EARLIER STUDIES OF UNFINISHED WORK

Before giving these in general outline let me mention certain other inquiries, inspired by Kurt Lewin between the two World Wars, which have been largely ignored by industrial psychologists, although they seem to me of capital importance in work study. I am referring to experimental inquiries concerning unfinished work.

We have seen that in the United States industrial experts, whether scientific observers or those actually engaged in industry, have been driven to concern themselves with the excessive division of labour, which leads to 'diminishing returns' as jobs are broken down and simplified. These economic facts only express quantitatively the subjective reactions of workers performing fragmentary jobs, imprisoned as it were in a narrow sector of production, working on a portion of an object or of a part, which they themselves will never finish, and chained to an activity which is in fact constantly *interrupted* by the minute subdivision of operations. On the other hand, in the workshops of firms proceeding with plans of job enlargement, the attitude of the workers has been completely transformed, because, so it is said, their jobs contain more variety, responsibilities, meaning and interest. They also possess greater scope, the workers being less often interrupted and having more of the feeling that they are finishing the product. As mass-production in a firm gets organized and the substance of the job assigned to a worker and which he has to repeat grows less, the greater becomes his desire for completing a product. Speaking about his experience of jobs broken down by a 'specialization' imposed from above, a worker on an automobile assembly line declared, 'I would like to do a whole fender myself, from raw material to finished job. It would be more interesting.'[1]

The general phenomenon appearing among workers of 'boredom' or 'dissatisfaction', as it is called by factory observers to-day, is the result of many different causes, a complex which has not as yet been properly investigated with the aid of scientific procedures. The studies concerned with the non-completion of jobs, carried out by experimental psychology, do not give a full explanation, which must inevitably have many facets, of a phenomenon in which so many varied elements play a part; but, although they are only laboratory experiments, they do seem to me to throw some light upon many of its main characteristics in industrial life.

With a view to studying and grasping properly the effects of the interruption of a job, B. Zeigarnik has measured its influence upon memory.[2] The subjects of the experiment were asked to perform a series of twenty tasks, such as modelling an animal, threading a string of pearls, or doing a jigsaw puzzle. They were allowed to finish one half of these small tasks, but were prevented by an interruption from completing the other half. At the end of the experiment they were asked to write down all they had done. The facts show that the tasks that were interrupted were remembered about twice as often as those completed, a result confirmed later by memory tests. In other words, when a task is completed it is easy to forget it; but when it is left unfinished it weighs upon the mind and may even become an obsession. In another series of experiments the subjects were left free afterwards to finish what they were doing: they were thus able to dismiss it from their minds, when the differences in remembering disappeared.

Ovsiankina, continuing Zeigarnik's researches, showed that there exists a strong tendency to finish interrupted jobs.[3] When given the chance, the subjects, as soon as they thought themselves unobserved, quickly resumed the task they had had to abandon and finished it surreptitiously. Is this due to the pride one takes in a finished job? It seems rather to come from the need of using up the full 'energy system' formed at the moment of starting a piece of work. These experiments appear to show that when we are harnessed, as it were, to a task, we mobilize a quantity of emotional energy which tends subsequently to be used up. We thus put the whole of our personality into a condition that requires that the task should be completed. This has also been demonstrated by the work of Gordon W. Allport, who suggests that an uncompleted task leaves in the personality a tendency towards fulfilment which he calls 'conative perseveration'.[4]

Other points may be stressed. Work possessing definite outlines, so that its completion is clearly marked, suffers the least from being interrupted. Among the laboratory tasks given to his subjects by Zeigarnik, modelling a dog in clay was a more definite operation than threading a pearl necklace. For the necklace, at the interruption of the work, might be smaller but could nevertheless be considered a finished article. Moreover, the operative is by no means indifferent to the moment when the interruption occurs. Other things being equal, the worker feels more anxious to finish his task when near the completion of it than when interrupted at the start. Similarly, when he is interrupted towards the end, the frustration felt is much greater.[5] The reason for the interruption and its nature may also influence his reaction. Finally, one should not think that everyone reacts in the same way when interrupted. Some resent it greatly, while others seem almost to ignore it. Here, too, the capacity to perform repeated and fragmentary operations differs in each individual. This has been well shown by Wunderlich, who tried to distinguish types of mind by their capacity for absent-mindedness during work without it affecting a series of precise automatic motions.[6] Lewin's school has suggested in this connection a method of vocational guidance which has never been put into practice, so far as we know, while no test of it has been worked out which might be used by industry. Subjects who prove unable to grasp the *internal structure* of a job, the way in which its parts are related to the whole, are comparatively un-affected by the non-completion of a task. So it follows that some workers performing highly simplified jobs that have no meaning for them would feel this desire to finish much less than others and so would be less subject to frustration, dissatisfaction, and 'boredom'. Let us suggest in passing that this may perhaps partly explain a fact well-known to so many industrial observers, in the United States as well as in Europe, that in many cases women are more ready to accept extremely fragmentary work than men.

SIZE OF THE WORK UNIT

In the United States the reaction against the division of labour has particularly affected the workshop, having now assumed a definitely practical character. In England also it has arisen out of the uneasiness and concern felt in industrial circles. One case of excessive specialization is often cited, that of a factory for men's clothing, situated in the Midlands, where the manufacture of a waistcoat was broken down into sixty-seven different operations. Without leading to any large-scale industrial experiments such as those of the I.B.M., the movement there, thanks to financial support from the government, has benefited from a series of inquiries beginning in 1948. These were at first controlled by a Human Factors Panel (a sub-committee of the Committee on Industrial Productivity), which was presided over by Sir George Schuster, and commonly called the 'Schuster Panel'. This ceased to function in 1950. In March 1953, government aid for social and psychological research in industry was brought under the joint control of the Department of Scientific and Industrial Research and the Medical Research Council. Grants of about £100,000 yearly have been administered by two joint D.S.I.R. and M.R.C. committees, one concerned with individual efficiency in industry, and the other, presided over by the eminent psychologist, Sir Frederick Bartlett, with human relations in industry.

The British investigations carried on by the National Institute of Industrial Psychology of London were originally centred round the idea of the 'unit of work'. In fact they had been preceded in England itself by the inter-war inquiries of D. W. Harding, which were concerned with the subdivision of assembly-line work.[8]

Harding had noticed that in increasing the size of the unit of work, for instance the soldering of wires in a wireless set, a better output was obtained and there was greater work satisfaction. The English investigators were particularly interested in the *unit work cycle* (the cycle of operations performed and repeated by a worker for each unit of production) and in the *total work cycle* (i.e. all the operations needed in order to finish a production unit, for instance a reel, a crankshaft or a waistcoat). To these experimental concepts they added that of *batch size* (the number or quantity of units of production issued to a worker — or to a group of workers — or taken from him *en bloc* once his work on them is finished). They thus got to the root of the problems caused by job enlargement, problems which had been approached by the American experimenters in a more directly practical way and from a rather different point of view.

One of the main objects of the inquiry was to study the optimum relationship between the cycle of simplified operations performed by a worker (for instance, in the course of assembling a wireless set) and the whole of the work (the assembly of the set as a whole). They thus hoped to define and indicate the most favourable conditions for both the satisfaction and the output of the worker, a hope, as can be seen, much like that of the American pioneers of Endicott. Out of thirty-five studied, seven firms were chosen for the experiments, which were carried out by the National Institute of Industrial Psychology (director C. B. Frisby). These included factories manufacturing electrical equipment, wireless sets, linen goods, carpets, type moulds and metal tubing, and the experiments were directed by David Cox and Dyce Sharp.[9] More recently D. Cox, assisted by D. Sharp and D. H. Irvine, and with the help of the Medical Research Council,[10] has undertaken a more general inquiry into repetitive jobs and their effect on the worker. These inquiries, the first results of which were published in October, 1953, are also directly concerned with the problems of the division of labour.

The first investigation proposed to start by studying the size of the *unit work cycle* compared with the *total work cycle*, showing its effects on the worker's satisfaction and on productive efficiency. Next it intended to examine the relationship between batch size on the one hand and satisfaction and efficiency on the other.

Since the beginning of the century an increasing division of labour has led to a reduction of the unit of work in many industries. The benefits foreseen are well-known. This splitting up corresponds, it is said, to a constantly increasing mechanization of mass-production. It also permits a 'simplification' of the beginner's training, which is reduced to a mere 'showing how it is done', often taking no more than a few days. Supported by these arguments, the technicians have looked upon small work units as necessarily associated with benefits easily measurable in terms of increased hourly production.

In the long run, however, things turned out to be not so simple. As regards immediate benefits, small work units frequently tend to show disadvantages, which are not so easily measurable and which have up to now only been estimated in subjective terms. In particular they diminish work satisfaction and increase the feeling of 'boredom', of 'monotony'. These factors, which are not visible at first, can influence efficiency in three ways: (1) by lowering the output per hour; (2) by reducing the total number of work hours through a rise in absenteeism; (3) by increasing labour turnover. Their influence upon the hourly output had already been made clear by Harding's investigations between 1928 and 1930.

I shall not concern myself here with a technical analysis of the methods used. Wherever it was possible the investigators resorted to the method of differences, comparing a 'control group', operating with very small work units, with an 'experimental group', working with enlarged units or with a larger batch size. Naturally the optimum conditions for the experiment demanded groups equivalent in ability and experience as well as comparable psychologically in the individual characteristics of the workers. The ideal would have been the transference of the same workers from one team to the other. But this was not possible in practice in any of the firms, owing to the combined opposition of the managements and the trade unions.

It is interesting to note in this connection the su prise shown by the English psychologists at the reception given to their plan of investigation by the sixty-four firms with which they got into touch before beginning their inquiry. They thought that in choosing highly mechanized industries with very simplified jobs they would have the benefit of technical facilities but would meet with difficulties among the managers. In fact the opposite occurred. Many British industrialists and engineers are conscious of the dangers inherent in repetitive and fragmentary jobs, but have come up against technical difficulties in organizing valid and significant experiments, especially in creating a second production line as a control. And the attitude of the trade unions in England did not differ from that of the unions in the United States, which were as a rule understanding and sympathetic, as we have already indicated. Many of the English unions too saw clearly that such investigations, if they had practical results, would halt the tendency towards 'deskilling' caused by the progressive simplification of work.

EXCESSIVE SUBDIVISION OF LABOUR

These experiments, considered by their initiators as 'preliminary explorations in a more or less unknown field', have as a whole proved that many jobs in industry to-day are too highly subdivided for the capabilities and taste of the workers. A lessening of the size of batches undoubtedly improves the output and morale of the still comparatively inexperienced. But it must be noted that many experienced piece-rate workers performing fragmentary jobs, in a lamp factory for example,[11] set an intermediate target for themselves, making up batches corresponding to a certain output and a certain wage-packet. The division of labour by stages, thus spontaneously established, corresponds to a very common tendency, taking a variety of forms among workers in mass-production. We may call it the desire 'to see that one is getting on', and the satisfaction of noting this progress. Conversely, it is the feeling that one is 'not getting anywhere', accompanying highly subdivided and repetitive jobs which are not grouped in any way and so do not hang together and are lacking in internal structure, that saps morale and dissipates motive-power, diminishing both satisfaction and output. Using the terminology of Zeigarnik and Ovsiankina, one would say that the job was always 'interrupted', always 'unfinished'.

Making batches, then, fulfils the piece-rate worker's need for concrete evidence that he has achieved something. When the batch attains a certain size he has a direct sense of accomplishment. But this habit, which is often observed in the workshop, has another psychological basis. A worker receiving a constant flow of parts or half-finished products can make a pile of them, 'build a bank' as the Americans say; for instance, in a motorcar factory where his job is to fit the door handles and locks. He then has the chance of varying the pace of his work within the limits of the assembly line. Walker and Guest when interviewing workers found among those practising this method quite high degrees of satisfaction. Of course, it is only possible where the parts are small in size and is therefore out of the question in the final assembly of a chassis or an engine.[12]

As regards the size of the work unit, the experiments conducted in a factory making wireless sets were particularly suggestive. Having arrived at a certain stage in their inquiry, the investigators studied an experimental and a control group of ten women workers, whose unit of work on the assembly line lasted two minutes. One woman in the experimental group, when her fellow workers for various reasons (personal choice or transfer to other jobs) had left, undertook to perform the whole set of operations herself, a cycle lasting twenty minutes and equivalent to the total of the ten jobs of the control group. There is no need to stress the importance of this experiment, and its phases deserve a brief description. The output of the 'single' worker was at first definitely below that per head of the control group. But at the end of nine weeks it was equal to it, and from the tenth to the twenty-third week higher by 18 per cent. It is to be noted that the quality of her work, at first poor, constantly improved, until it was very definitely above that of her fellow workers who were performing highly simplified operations on the assembly line. Was she exceptional? She was a young woman of thirty-five, the average age of the group, energetic, it is true, and of comparatively high intelligence, but not the highest in her group.[13] Results of this kind, moreover, are sufficiently close to those of the American experiments to be considered reliable.

In a factory making lingerie, studied by Cox and Sharp, a reduction of the size of teams from six to four workers, which is of course equivalent to a definite increase in the work unit, caused output to rise by 43 per cent above its original level. Certain experiments failed because the girls refused to accept larger work units. There were psychological reasons for this, the need for security of pay and fear of not reaching the same output on the enlarged job; but we must also note the influence undoubtedly exerted by the differences of rhythm as between one individual and another which have been so well described in the work of Léon

Walther.[14] The British investigators in assessing and interpreting their experiments have not in my opinion paid enough attention to this important factor.

The size of the work unit has a direct effect upon training. As we have seen, one of the arguments most frequently used in support of the minute subdivision of labour is that it simplifies and speeds up training. But[15] this argument presupposes that the basic operations to be performed are so worked out that each job remains the same whatever alterations the production may undergo. Now this is far from being the case since, according to Henry Ford's phrase, industry must be constantly 'creative' if it is to give good service and be successful. I am reminded of what I saw in a highly rational-ized machine-tool factory situated in a Brussels suburb, where a change in the model of a mass-produced lathe had required several months of readaptation, what was in fact a new training,[16] for the factory hands (who were largely unskilled workers specialized on machines) before normal output was regained. Simplified jobs per-formed by workers without any professional training lead to a lack of flexibility which can be extremely detrimental when production has to be altered or renewed.

Conversely, the English experiments show that workers anxious and able to work on bigger units, and to enlarge their jobs, are those who are in complete command of the smaller unit. It is the inexperienced worker who is frightened of his job being enlarged. But, as we have previously seen in the case cited from a wireless factory, an experienced worker can very quickly learn to do a complicated cycle of operations in a way that is highly profitable to the business.

Here again we meet with the findings of scientific inquiries concerning the problem of unfinished work. Partial knowledge of a complicated cycle provides the human mind with a much more lasting stimulus than the perpetual and routine repetition of an easy task. In many cases therefore it is useful to give the worker a not too simple job, establishing work 'units' which are not too limited but require attention and some attempt to acquire more training or at least more skill in order to obtain greater speed ('speed as a skill'). Thus a stimulus is given, and there is an increase in interest, in the desire to learn, and a latent tension is created which can be beneficial *if it is satisfied*.[17] The semi-skilled worker's training should therefore be a continuous process, starting with the less complicated and going on to the more complex, until a higher limit is reached which corresponds to the worker's capabilities. In other words, many workers gain satisfaction from mastering jobs more complicated than those they had been doing previously, so long as they are not *too* difficult ones. As D. Cox writes, 'Satisfaction with the job may be partly attainable by a steady process of training graded to the operator's capacity, which presents difficulties but ensures that they will be overcome.'[18] These remarks make one think of the phrase coined by an industrial psychologist, which I quoted in the Introduction to this book, 'the man is bigger than his job'.

DIFFICULTY AND MEANING

We have thus arrived at the heart of our problem and I shall now try to indicate some of its main features. From this point of view we may be said to be watching the rediscovery by the mechanized industry of the twentieth century, with its claim to be 'rationalized', of an age-old truth, that work must include the overcoming of difficulties, a truth so often emphasized in relation to works of art by writers on poetics and aesthetics, from Aristotle to Paul Valéry and Alain, as they pondered over the struggle between man and matter and the connection between form and content.

On a mass-production level, industrial psychologists and sociologists have noted that work units which are too small cause boredom, and even a lower output once a batch is finished. That is one of the antinomies of the division of labour. Technicians have carried subdivision to extreme limits, thinking thereby to increase individual output and lower costs. But they have thus reduced work units to such tiny proportions that they no longer correspond to the psychological needs of many human beings, to that latent tension which requires difficulties to overcome and wants to *master* a job, having therefore to *struggle with it* to some extent. What they have done, in fact, is to introduce into big business conditions that lower output, instead of increasing it indefinitely and almost inevitably, as they had expected.

From a psychological standpoint job enlargement presents another feature, i.e. the *possible* growth in the meaningfulness of a job. For a series of motions does not *necessarily* gain increased significance, where fractional production is concerned, through an

extension of the unit work cycle. Here are a few examples taken
from experiments made by industrial psychologists. To file and
clean die-castings in an engineering workshop gives a worker less
satisfaction, even when the job cycle is enlarged, than to polish a
flat surface. For, in the latter case, he can see the *finished* results of
a personal action, whereas in the former his job has floating
contours and must always be recommenced.[19] During his 1931
experiments Harding had arranged for ten wires instead of two to
be soldered in the assembly of wireless sets, and both output and
satisfaction had then increased. But in 1950, on an assembly line
where radio headphones were being made, eight of the girls out of
a team of twenty refused the chance of doubling their work unit.
This consisted at first in the soldering of seven elements and the
fixing of a few others, and occupied two minutes in all. In Harding's
experiments,[20] job enlargement had for the worker a sense of
qualitative change. Instead of soldering wires she was making 'part
of a wireless set'. For the girls making headphones, on the contrary, doubling the job did not add to its meaning in any way but
only made it more complicated, so that it needed more remembering. Hence the negative attitude of so many of them. Nevertheless,
experiments of this kind are incomplete if they are not accompanied by a programme of vocational training within the firm, by
means of which the workers may come to understand the technology lying behind the idea of enlarging work units. It is to this
policy that the success of job enlargement in the I.B.M. factories
was mainly due.

These experiments have also shown that the control of quality is
very far from suffering from an enlargement of the semi-skilled
worker's job, in spite of the belief of the supporters of the traditional methods, who have even sought to make this one of their
main arguments against any attack upon their doctrine. At Endicott, as well as at Poughkeepsie, the supervision of quality has
gradually passed out of the hands of specialized inspectors into
those of the workers, who have been promoted to more complicated and skilled work. When we visited the factory at Essonnes
(the French I.B.M.), we noticed similar facts. In the English
experiments, after a short period of adaptation, the output of the
girls whose 'units' were increased surpassed in both quality
and quantity that of the women engaged in more simplified
jobs.

LESSENING CONSTRAINT

Finally, among the satisfying features of job enlargement let us not forget the increased freedom allowed to the worker who deals with a number of work components. First comes the possibility of varying the order in which the operations are performed. This depends upon the way production is planned and is not always possible. But in such a case the worker can at least vary the size of the batch of objects passing through his hands, i.e. he can change his rhythm, a form of freedom found among certain assembly-line workers, who from time to time speed up their work and 'get ahead of the belt', in order to give themselves a breathing space, enabling them afterwards to work for a few moments with less strain. When the 'unit' has not been oversimplified, the worker can vary it in this way at regular intervals and change the phases of his work. For instance, in making electric fans he can fit one apparatus completely and then pass on to the next, or he can fix the feet to a batch of two dozen fans and then perform another operation on the same set, and so on. Vernon, Wyatt and their collaborators, during a series of inquiries into the comparative effects of varied and uniform work (1924–37), recommended, among other things that repetitive jobs should be alternated about every two hours.[21] Now the increase of the 'unit', by allowing the worker to vary his work within the enlarged job, keeps the advantages of work rotation and also gives the job a little interest and meaning, which it often completely lacked before.

Certainly, constraint in varying degrees enters into all types of work, and certain psychologists, such as L. S. Hearnshaw, have even considered its presence the chief criterion of whether a human activity can be classed as 'work' or not.[22] Nevertheless, Cox notes at the end of his inquiry (1953), 'Repetitive work often appears to be organized so that this element of constraint is greater than it need be, and the evidence of this study suggests that such unnecessary constraint is resented — and alternatively, that any relaxation of it is appreciated.'[23]

Here are to be found the psychological roots of the satisfaction derived from a change of job. A first breach is made in the constraint imposed upon the worker, a constraint which the main systems of 'Scientific Management' have tended to increase up to the present day. During the British investigation subjects were suggested to the workers interviewed; the one to which reference was most often made was that of changing jobs. The comments were as a rule favourable, the girls giving as their subjective reason for liking to do so the fact that it reduced boredom. In the same way, the particular form of transfer found in job rotation was approved (by a small majority) because of the greater variety of work it made possible. Change of jobs and work rotation provide an *indirect* form of job enlargement, which appears to many industrialists and technicians less subversive than procedures derived from the principle of job enlargement itself. The group of jobs thus performed by the worker provides him with work of greater scope and variety, even if each job in isolation possesses no greater meaning or interest. Being able to vary his methods allows the worker a certain amount of freedom, not implied by systematic work rotation. But rotation does introduce variety and lessen the feeling of constraint.

This shows, be it said in passing, how rudimentary still is our way of selecting the semi-skilled worker, the *ouvriers specialisés* of France, *angelernte Arbeiter* of Germany, and *operai comuni e manovali specializzati* of Italy, the proportion of whom employed to-day in large industrial firms throughout the world is very considerable. It is often thought sufficient in factories to distinguish between team work done on the assembly line and jobs performed on so-called 'individual' machines. In fact, a distinction should be made within these between different types of jobs which require different characteristics and capabilities. A real vocational selection should take into account: (1) the *time* taken by the work unit; (2) the margin of variation possible in the *order* of operations (variations of method); (3) the margin of variation in the *place* occupied by the worker, i.e. his possibilities of movement while working; (4) the measure of variety possible in the use of *materials*. To these four factors mentioned by Cox and Sharp, we may add a fifth: the possibility of varying the *pace* of working, its rhythm. A comprehensive study of jobs from this standpoint would enable us to adapt them better to those performing them, and would lessen the tremendous amount of dissatisfaction, boredom, constraint and resentment which they cause among so many workers to-day.

CHAPTER V

Durkheim's Theory

CONTEMPORARY FORMS OF THE DIVISION OF LABOUR

IN THE course of this book I have outlined recent developments in the specialization of industrial work, and have shown the growing anxiety felt by technicians concerning industrial practices which have long seemed inseparable from it. I have also analysed the main experiments, undertaken in spite of a current of opinion that is still strong, aimed at preventing the worker from being 'bigger than his job', as happens in so many occupations to-day.

Taylor, 'the father of Scientific Management',[1] whether he wished to do so or not, by his time-and-motion studies and use of the stop-watch and by the role he assigned in the firm to the departments concerned with the planning and distribution of work, originated a movement which has developed rapidly and inevitably since his day. In 1893, the very year in which Taylor in Philadelphia decided to devote himself to spreading his beliefs as a 'consulting engineer specializing in the systematic organization of workshops and in costs' (that was how he described himself on his commercial visiting card), Émile Durkheim, who was almost his contemporary, being born two years later and dying two years after him, published in Paris his famous book, *La Division du Travail social*, which remains even to-day the product of the most vigorous mind that has ever worked on this great problem. So at this point it seems essential to turn back to this classical work and to consider it from our present point of view in the light of certain twentieth-century developments of the social phenomena he discussed.

CONDITIONS OF ORGANIC SOLIDARITY

According to Durkheim the division of labour is a fact contained in the very evolution of life. He reminds us already in his Introduction that for biological philosophy, which, inspired by Herbert Spencer, was then in vogue, the more specialized an organism's functions are, the higher is the place it occupies in the animal scale.[2] This is therefore a phenomenon which has its roots in an infinitely remote past, going back to the appearance of life on this earth. Our societies seem to follow a movement that affects the whole of the living universe.

According to a principle adopted by Durkheim as his point of departure, and which is found throughout his book, the division of labour is essentially a source of solidarity. 'The division of labour presumes that the worker, far from being hemmed in by his task, does not lose sight of his collaborators, that he acts upon them and reacts to them.'[3] Thus from the very start he considers as pathological all forms of the division of labour that fail to lead to solidarity. Indeed, it is in a chapter of Book III, devoted to 'Abnormal Forms', that we find his main discussion of the division of industrial labour and of the problems we are considering here.

In any division of labour, when the different functions are not in harmony, it is because 'they are not properly regulated'.[4] The division of labour when thus devoid of co-ordination is 'anomic'. In this category is included any case where it fails to produce social solidarity. We shall then have to discover the reasons causing it to 'deviate from its natural direction'. In the summary of this chapter made by Durkheim himself we can see particularly clearly the way in which his thought moved. In the 'normal' division of labour the functions are in harmony. If this harmony is absent, it is because these functions are not co-ordinated or the co-ordination is poor. The division of labour is then 'anomic'. Hence there arises for Durkheim the need for co-ordination, which is the 'normal' result of the division of labour. Hence, too, his nostalgic longing for the guild system, which he attempted to justify in the long Preface added in 1902 to the second edition of his book.[5] One can say without misrepresenting him that he saw in 'division of labour' and 'co-ordination of functions' synonymous expressions. To prevent 'anomie', he declared, 'the solidary organs must be in sufficient, and sufficiently prolonged, contact. This contact is the normal state'.[6]

According to these principles, then, there is a state of the division of labour that should not be upset or made to deviate from its normal, beneficent course. Job specialization, which was the contemporary form of the division of labour and had begun to penetrate into the larger firms in Europe as well as in the United States at the time when Durkheim was writing his book, was for him a pathological condition, showing the *'anomie'* resulting from the lack of a proper co-ordination of functions. Auguste Comte saw in phenomena of this kind, which his genius, we may add in passing, had intuitively discerned in the first industrial revolution of the nineteenth century, a necessary result of the division of labour as soon as it had attained a certain stage of development. For the creator of positivism all specialization, when carried too far, ends in disintegration. Comte was pessimistic as to the future of what he called 'the fundamental redistribution of human labour'. It leads, he thought, to dispersion, if 'individual divergences' are not compensated by 'a permanent force or discipline able to eliminate, or at least to keep constantly in check, their discordant effects'.[7]

Durkheim did not see the future of the division of labour in any such dark colours. Unlike Comte he thought it naturally implied solidarity, not disintegration. But, for that to be so, all the conditions needed for solidarity would have to be realized, which meant primarily that 'a co-ordination, determining the mutual relationship of functions, would need to be adequately developed'.[8] According to him, and here he agrees with Taylor, if the division of labour is to show all the beneficial effects it should, the way in which the elements necessary to one another should work together as a rule must be 'predetermined'. In this sense Taylor's system with its 'Thinking Department' and functional foremen, enveloping the worker in an eight-fold network of controls, would have seemed to him quite satisfactory. However, and this is a paradox which shows already how abstract his standpoint was, he would have been obliged to condemn as 'abnormal' the effects of the system on the attitude of mind of those subjected to it.

If we look a little further into the implications of his doctrine, we will notice that in 'normal' conditions the functional rules, so to speak, 'express' organic solidarity and inevitably accompany it. They 'emerge from the division of labour' and are, 'as it were, a prolongation of it'.[9] All they do is to translate it into a tangible and definite form, within the framework of a given situation. Elsewhere, however, Durkheim deplores the lack of co-ordination, 'which prevents a regular harmony of functions'.[10] This is a remarkable contradiction in the work of so eminent a logician.

Actually, in order to explain the anomic forms of the division of labour, and particularly those due to the evolution of industrial production, he usually invokes the idea of faulty co-ordination. Industrial life to-day, he says, presents new conditions; there is an expansion of industry along with an expansion of markets, mechanization creating a strain upon the nervous system, the separation of the worker from both his family and his employer, 'regimentation'. The changes caused by these revolutions in industry have been so rapid that 'the interests in conflict have not as yet had time to achieve a balance'.[11]

'ABNORMAL' FORMS OF THE DIVISION OF LABOUR

Durkheim therefore was not blind to the debasing effects of industrial specialization. He does not deny their existence but declares that they do not necessarily result from the division of labour.

The worker, it is often said, is 'reduced to the role of a machine'. It is worth while quoting Durkheim's comment on this statement in view of its penetration and up-to-dateness, particularly if one remembers that it was written by an armchair scholar at a moment when large-scale mass-production had scarcely begun in the United States.

> In fact, if [the individual] does not know whither the operations he performs are tending, if he relates them to no end, he can only continue to work as a matter of habit. Every day he repeats the same movements with monotonous regularity, but without taking any interest in them and without understanding them. . . . One cannot remain indifferent to such a debasement of human nature.[12]

Having in passing discarded the sham remedy of a 'general education', which for him is incapable of overcoming the evils of an anomic division of labour (and here one sees dawning in his mind the impending disappointments connected with the experiment of popular universities), Durkheim resumes his argument and involves himself once again in the wheels of his system.

Such facts, he continues, exist. They are incontestable and much to be deplored. But it is not true that they are an inevitable result of the division of labour which produces them only 'in exceptional and abnormal circumstances'. It is not necessary to temper this division with its opposite (a 'general education') for it to develop without having these disastrous effects upon the worker's mind. 'It has only to be itself, to let nothing coming from without *denature* it; that is enough.'[13]

This then is the ideal framework for what Émile Durkheim considers the normal conditions of the division of labour. When they are realized, the individual is no longer imprisoned in his specialism: instead, he is in constant contact with the workers in charge of the functions next to his, being aware of what they need, of any changes taking place in their work, and so on. The real, the 'normal', division of labour implies that the worker is not turned wholly inwards, concerned only with his job, but remains looking outwards on those around him, influencing and being influenced by them. Because of this he also knows that his activity has an aim and perceives at least its general outlines.

What Durkheim says on this point is very vague, and one can rightly doubt whether a worker's labour is necessarily full of interest and solidarity simply because he realizes that 'his actions have an aim beyond themselves'.[14] One can also question whether this vague motivation is enough to make him regard a fragmentary and uniform activity in a completely different light. Nevertheless, in stressing that a very specialized job can be transformed in the eyes and minds of those who perform it by its being linked to the work around it and having a clear purpose of its own, Durkheim strikes a very modern note, which is not alien to Marxism. Between the two World Wars, at a time when the industrial psychologists of Soviet Russia were preoccupied with these problems, they adopted a point of view (reinforced by the observations they made in shops and factories) which would have delighted Durkheim. For they declared that 'the integration of the worker in a socialist society' gave to the fragmentary tasks he was called upon to perform, even to assembly-line work, an entirely different character from what they would have had in a capitalistic business.[15]

It is particularly interesting to notice that Durkheim included among 'abnormal' forms of the division of labour cases where the job content was excessively reduced by specialization, that is to say precisely those cases which have so enormously increased in number, since his death in 1917, as a result of the 'rationalized' industry of the present day. 'Solidarity is very closely related to the functional activity of specialized parts. . . . Where functions languish, however well specialized they may be, they are badly co-ordinated and do not properly feel their mutual interdependence.'

He remarks further in this connection that the primary concern of an intelligent and experienced manager should be to 'suppress useless jobs, to distribute the work so that each individual shall be sufficiently occupied, thereby increasing the functional activity of each worker'. These are perfectly correct principles of action but much harder to carry out in a factory or office than Durkheim seems to have thought.[16]

But Durkheim goes further and brings in the idea of the *continuity* of labour which, he thinks, can be connected with the degree of functional activity, a decrease in this making it discontinuous. Conversely, an increase will at once cause greater solidarity, since an organism's functions can only become more active by becoming more continuous;[17] a statement proved false by the actual development of industrial work in the twentieth century. Durkheim admits that, in businesses where jobs have been subdivided and the content of the worker's activity has consequently been reduced to below what it would 'normally' be, the different functions are too discontinuous to be adjusted or co-ordinated with one another. However, Scientific Management since Taylor has had as one of its essential principles that of introducing into the workshop, together with an extreme subdivision of operations through time-and-motion study and stop-watch timing, a rigid and detailed co-ordination of jobs by means of 'instruction charts', 'dispatching' and 'planning'. All forms of mass-production afford examples of unfinished operations in which functional activity is greatly reduced but which nonetheless are continuous and co-ordinated. This does not mean that they give rise to any organic solidarity in the sense intended by this great theorist of modern sociology.

Division of labour and continuity are in fact often accompanied to-day by a decrease in the content of each unit of work performed by the 'semi-skilled worker'. The reduction in the hours of the working day and the changeover from extensive to intensive pressure, to an intensification of work, were analysed by Marx in some classic pages of *Das Kapital*. He showed how this development leads to a more intensive effort on the worker's part and at the same time to a 'filling up of the "pores" or gaps in the working day'.[18] Taking into account the capacity for individual effort, which varies inversely with the length of time during which it

needs to be exerted, we can see that there is an optimum length for
the working day by which the maximum daily output will be
secured. This has been shown by psycho-physiological researches,
particularly those carried out directly after the First World War by
the Industrial Fatigue Research Board in England.[19]

The stop-watch procedure of Taylor and his successors also
aimed at securing immediate efficiency by ferreting out unnecessary delays, those 'idle periods' which are only another name
for what Marx called the 'pores' or 'gaps' in the working day.
The *intensity* factor, which has never ceased to grow in importance
in 'scientifically managed' industrial plants, escaped Durkheim's
notice. Therefore he failed to see that the intensity of highly
simplified operations increases with a deterioration in the functional activity of the worker. Here we must take note of a serious
confusion of terminology. The worker performing the kind of
operations we have been describing is said to possess a 'specialized
skill', corresponding to a functional activity as understood by
Durkheim. A workman fitting a few screws and bolts on an
automobile chassis, a girl punching a hole in the face of a watch —
always the same one — by means of a tool, has no 'special skill'.
It is not a skill at all, but rather a dexterity due to neuro-motor
co-ordination, which in the long run causes automatism and
routine. This activity is not the application to a job of a polyvalent
or basic training. It has no connection, for instance, with that of a
specialized mechanic on a machine cutting gear-wheels, and still
less with that of a laryngologist or a nerve surgeon. I shall return to
these problems later, only noting here that the intensity and
continuity so generally characteristic of rationalized production
to-day are often accompanied by a debasement of the functional
activity of the worker considered as an individual. If we abandon
all theoretical preconceptions and watch the division of labour as
practised every day in our factories and workshops, mines and
offices, it is far from showing the features — or the virtues —
attributed to it by Durkheim.

AN INADEQUATE DOCTRINE

We now see some of the limitations of this doctrine, apparently
so compelling and watertight, which attempts, unlike the other
parts of Durkheim's great work, to coerce rather than to persuade.

Had he lived, in order to maintain the purity of his theory of organic solidarity, he would have been obliged to consider 'abnormal' most of the forms taken by labour in modern society, both in industry and in administration, and even more recently in commerce (I am thinking of the American supermarkets).

If the 'normal' division of labour presupposes that the worker is linked with those around him, constantly aware of what they are doing and of changes in their jobs, that he is in fact connected with them by functional and mutual influences, then we must leave out of it by definition most of the semi-skilled jobs that are actually performed to-day in offices, industry, commerce and even agriculture.

Mechanization and rationalization, inspired by the engineer's almost mystical belief in the value of specialization, have strongly emphasized this process during the last half-century. For Durkheim, haunted by memories of the great epoch of the guilds, and convinced that 'the absence of all corporative institutions creates in the organization of a people like ours a void, the importance of which it is difficult to exaggerate',[20] the introduction of a co-ordination and regulation of functions would allow a 'liberation' of the solidarity inherent in the division of labour. Elsewhere, as we have noticed, he seems to think that it would be enough to eliminate the circumstances distorting it in order to enable the division of labour to regain its natural virtues. All this, it must be admitted, seems very abstract, and remains in spite of its logical form vague and elusive, something that is rare with Durkheim. In fact, if highly subdivided jobs are to have meaning restored to them, certain conditions must play a part which Durkheim has failed to take into account: in particular, economic and social equality must be accorded to the worker, making him a full member, with equal rights, of the community to which he belongs, so that the more or less conscious feeling, which is almost universal in France, that his efforts are not fairly remunerated, that he is being 'exploited', may be removed, and he may be encouraged to attribute quite a different value to the work he does, however fragmentary it is.

But even this is insufficient. There are many jobs, created by the division of labour in its present state of development, which an impartial observer, not blinded by mere theory, can hardly consider as leading in themselves to solidarity. A sense of solidarity is quite incapable of transforming the microscopic nature of tiny work units, if they are the only jobs allotted to the worker and he is chained to them for weeks, for months or even years. One of the discoveries made simultaneously in the twentieth century by science and industry (and that is why I have stressed recent investigations and experiments) is that we must advance beyond the mere division of labour. The present reaction against job simplification, the multiplication of experiments with transfer, work rotation, and even job enlargement, show that the division of labour is not necessarily a good thing in itself; also that it would be too easy a solution to our problem to treat as 'abnormal' the vast majority of its effects upon our technical civilization.

Most of the examples used by Émile Durkheim in thinking out his system were derived from his own speculations, and were actually unrelated to the concrete facts of industry, administration and commerce. Therefore his theories, which were far from corresponding to concrete reality at the time he conceived them, have diverged still further from reality since. Technology, born of the constant progress of the physico-chemical sciences, has played a part in this. The intense and varied development of mechanization lay outside the scope of his ideas. . . . Workers on the assembly line are not engaged in 'ephemeral combinations' or 'particular exchanges'.[21] The fragmentary tasks they perform are continuous and proceed from simple to complex, being carefully planned and co-ordinated by the engineers of planning departments. And yet by themselves they in no way create a network of permanent connections, an 'organic solidarity' in Durkheim's sense of the words.

REALITY TO-DAY AND DURKHEIM'S CATEGORIES

In fact, apart from any preconceived ideas, the phenomena of solidarity appear at this present stage of industrial development in forms quite foreign to Durkheim's categories, so long at least as we restrict our observations to capitalist enterprises.

First of all we must take note of the interdependence required by the technical organization of production, that is by rationalization and by the way in which jobs are split up in workshops, offices and modern firms with large shops and warehouses. The girl who spends the day in fitting hands to a watch depends upon the other workers who make the holes in the watch face; the member of the bacon-factory team who links the sausage depends upon the other member who fills the skin. In their turn the man putting on the anchor or the hairspring and the man separating the finished sausages both depend upon the workers preceding them, and so on, up to the last finishing touches and the packing of the product.

This interdependence is to-day a feature of most types of mass-production, which is commonly characterized by groups of machines working in cycles. But it is also present, although less apparent, in jobs performed by those working on so-called 'individual' machines, such as presses, drills and slotting machines, which are connected with operations carried out in other parts of the factory by other machines.

This mechanical type of solidarity is the most visible one, being, as it were, written into all mass-production operations, the distinctive feature of which is precisely this passing from the simple to the complex in a continuous manner. The Germans call such work *Fliessarbeit*, 'flowing work', and the Russians *nepririvnii potok*, the 'never-ending stream'. The workers themselves are knit into a whole in which each job is an element, and the jobs are fitted into one another like the parts being manufactured or assembled. There is no question then of a solidarity born of similar segments, as in Durkheim's 'mechanical' solidarity, but on the contrary of very different segments which, even when taken all together, do not lead to 'organic' solidarity.

This stage of development implies therefore an interdependence due to the way production is materially organized. The 'scheme of activity', to use G. C. Homans's terminology, then determines the workers' 'scheme of interaction'.[22] Similar examples are to be found in the co-ordinated tasks of multicopiers as well as among the clerks and salesmen of big administrative and commercial firms. How far can this technical interdependence go by itself towards creating a sense of moral interdependence? And under what conditions can it do so? As far as I know this question has never been scientifically studied. Such an inquiry would probably disclose considerable differences in different cases. My own factory experiences and the opinions of workers and of participant-observers incline me to believe that mechanical interdependence does not necessarily cause moral solidarity. Many other factors must be taken into account, the chief one being the structure and quality of the technical organization itself. If this is faulty, if, for instance, the flow of raw materials or of finished products is ill-sustained, the close dependence of one job upon another will often cause irritability and a state of nerves and may set one worker against another. But if the organization is good and the job of each worker is suited to his capabilities and personal rhythm, if further-more the workers can see each other (*Uebersichtlichkeit*),[28] and, finally, if the speed of the flow has been correctly calculated, mechanical interdependence may lead to a growing sense of moral interdependence.

But social solidarity, uniting the workers and making them feel indispensable to one another, bound together by common interests and a common aim, is quite another matter and much more than such interdependence. Here we must distinguish between two kinds of solidarity, both found in real life to-day. There is the firm's unity, which brings together all the personnel of a business or a factory, of a big store, a workshop or a mine, and so causes a group-solidarity *within* the firm. And there is the unity of the workers as wage-earners, linking them to other wage-earners *outside* the firm, to the employees, miners, etc. of other firms. This latter is what Marxism, with its theory of social 'classes', calls 'class solidarity', making of it through the 'class struggle' the chief cause of all political and social movements and the main instrument of its revolutionary dynamic. This, too, is the form of solidarity which constitutes a common denominator underlying different types of trade union action, however great their differences in theory and in practice.

In a capitalist firm of the traditional kind, where the workshop personnel and office staff are almost wholly composed of workers or employees without any share of responsibility for the running of the business or say in the distribution of its profits, the measure of solidarity within the firm is often very small. The worker or em-ployee is hardly *integrated* in the business at all. *Esprit de corps* is weak, and the workers are 'uncooperative', to use an American expression which has a depth of meaning for us. The powerful 'industrial relations' movement, which has been continued to-day under the name of the 'human relations movement', aimed precisely at increasing this spirit of co-operation, this moral solidarity, within the firm, by introducing more and more con-siderations of a psychological kind into the scientific management of labour. It has achieved appreciable results already in the United

States and in certain European countries, but very few so far in France. I have made a study of these elsewhere, and have proposed a distinction between *centripetal* movements, tending to increase the internal solidarity of the firm as a whole, and *centrifugal* movements aimed at weakening it.[24]

The solidarity of the workers, on the other hand, is not confined to the framework of a particular business. It unites the workers on the basis of their similar situation as producers and of the similar conditions under which they live and work. It will, of course, vary in strength and character according to distinctions of training and occupation, and as the result of differences in union membership, in race, national origin and religious belief. Nevertheless, if we take the example of a team of one hundred men and women, working on an assembly line and making alarm clocks in a big factory, it is not the interdependence of the operations imposed on them by the division of labour that leads to a feeling of moral solidarity, and creates a network of lasting relationships within this human group. It is not their technical status, in principle at least, but their social status that gives rise to this feeling, their daily awareness of their common situation in regard to their employer (the owner or his representatives), and in general within the society of which they form a part.

This was the type of solidarity that Georges Navel rediscovered in his workshop when, after having fled from factory life and earned his living on the land and in the building trade, he got himself admitted by means of false certificates as a fitter-mechanic for a trial period in a big automobile firm.[25] While he was at work, feeling anxious and 'rusty' because of his long absence from the shops, a fellow of his own age came up and encouraged him, bringing him tools and an electric lamp so that he could see more clearly, as well as ensuring that he had begun his work correctly. This active form of solidarity has clearly nothing to do with the division of labour itself, any more than that of a shop steward who encouraged and reassured Navel, when the trial period was long past, telling him he would nevertheless be given a job on simpler work. We should here explain how it is that the solidarity of the workers leads to the organization of trade unions, which is in fact one of its aspects. So long as it does not disappoint them, trade unionism is for many workers not only, or even essentially, a defence of their interests but rather a visible expression, a concrete symbol, of solidarity, of a network of human relationships within the industrial jungle.

We have left Durkheim's categories far behind; according to them, solidarity was the very essence of the division of labour, spreading around it, wherever it was allowed to take its 'normal' course, 'a natural harmony of functions', due to the co-ordination implicit within it. Moral solidarity is, in fact, closely dependent upon the structure of society and the relationships between producers to which this gives rise.

Among workers in particular firms, let us add, there often exist forms of solidarity based upon race or religion, such as those uniting North African workers in a large factory in the Parisian suburbs, or the negro workers employed by firms in Chicago or Detroit, which produce separate groups that tend to be absorbed in the solidarity of trade union action. These movements have no connection with the division of labour but originate mainly in a common state of mind, which was Durkheim's definition of mechanical solidarity in society as a whole. This type of solidarity prepared the way, through the similarities it implied and the sympathies it evoked, for organic solidarity.[26] But workshop experience tells a very different tale, and one sees how difficult it is, when confronted by the realities of the contemporary world, to apply Durkheim's terminology in view of the many confusions to which it tends to give rise.

One of these is that the solidarity of the workers, expressed in their daily behaviour in the shops and on a wider scale in their struggle through the trade unions for an improvement in living conditions, might itself be called in Durkheim's language a form of 'mechanical solidarity' defined in relation to a group of producers united by a 'state of mind'. But this would still mean, if we insist at whatever cost on retaining the doctrine, that the reality is different from the theory. For recent technical developments in this case, contrary to Durkheim's prediction, would not only have hastened the specialization of functions but would also have increased enormously the sphere of mechanical solidarity and not that of organic solidarity, even in its 'anomic' form.

In his essay on 'Theories concerning the Division of Labour', which was published in *L'Année sociologique* in 1903, C. Bouglé, later one of the leaders of the French sociological school but then a young disciple of Durkheim, clear-sightedly insisted on the conditions which were necessary if the division of labour were really to produce the beneficial effects on society described by Durkheim. In the course of a detailed analysis he states that 'from Durkheim's defence of the division of labour one gains almost as pessimistic an impression as that given by its socialist critics'.[27] He notes in particular that, if it were to have all the good results suggested, each worker would have to be free to choose his functions. But such a choice is surely a rare privilege in society to-day. If there is no correspondence between occupation and capabilities, he continues, if large numbers of people are constantly repelled by the work they have to do each day, 'if their work is their deadliest enemy', specialization has failed and no co-ordination is possible. A dangerous atmosphere of discontent ensues, which is still further aggravated when society does not provide equal opportunities at the start of life but gives to some a broad, prolonged and cultured education, and subjects others from childhood to intensive manual work, forcing them to accept any kind of a job, to acquiesce in any kind of demand, just in order to make a living. 'Here again it is constraint and not spontaneous freedom that controls the relationships to which the division of labour gives rise, producing in consequence a state of war, whether latent or declared, instead of a state of social peace.' In other words, 'the division of labour fails to reap its harvest of solidarity in all spheres'.[28] For it to be able to do so, a certain juridico-economic environment is needed, a certain social structure, in default of which it may end in antagonism instead of unity. During the half-century following the publication of this essay the forms taken by specialization in our technical age have only increased the gulf that exists between the ideal results of the division of labour as Durkheim conceived them and its actual consequences as observed in our societies to-day.

CHAPTER VI

The 'General Practitioner'
The 'Specialist' & the 'Specialized'

I. POLYVALENCE AND SPECIALIZATION

Thus the specialization of functions in many spheres of human activity, above all in the economic one, has followed a very different course from that predicted by Durkheim. Jobs have been broken down into small work units, their operations being performed with every modern technical device, i.e. by mechanical equipment which is constantly being improved through an increase in speed, efficiency and precision. The workers, well trained in these simplified operations, perform them almost perfectly. Industrial psychologists have come to consider the abilities thus shown — in particular manual dexterity and speed (speed as a skill)[1] — as distinct forms of skill, corresponding to different capabilities in different individuals. Moreover, if we compare the quality of work done by a specialized worker on one of these fragmentary jobs with that of someone with a polyvalent or craft training, a 'general practitioner', the advantage lies very definitely with the former. When, for example, in one of the great slaughter-houses of Chicago, a member of the production line preparing pigs goes sick, his place is taken by a substitute, a utility man. He may be a polyvalent pork-butcher, professionally trained, an 'all round man' in his trade, as they say in the United States, where he is becoming rarer and rarer. He knows the whole work of the preparation room where the pigs are cut up, but his performance in a specialized team — for instance, in one preparing hams on a conveyor-belt — is slower and less accurate than that of men who, following the instructions of the motion-study department, have learnt to perform only one single operation. This fact has been frequently observed and I have verified it myself in many French firms engaged in the most varied branches of industry, in engineering, shoemaking and textiles, and organized on mass-production lines, whether using the conveyor-belt or not. Shop foremen and personnel do not as a rule like being sent men with a polyvalent training to take the place of specialized workers. Conversely, such men do not like this type of work, which is for them just a provisional makeshift or, if they cannot find other and more suitable employment, a harsh necessity.

Specialization, which we will consider for a moment as a whole, has incontestable advantages and corresponds to a natural development that it would be absurd to deny or to wish to reverse completely. Only theorists far removed from reality would think of such a thing. It is to be found, we may note, at the manual level in all occupations, even in those forming part of a highly developed technical or scientific training, in what the Anglo-Saxon countries call the professions such as dentistry and surgery. Let us take the case of a dentist. There exist in New York and other large cities in the United States dental clinics consisting of groups of specialists. Some of these do only fillings, others only extractions, and others again only fit dentures and artificial teeth, and so on. In the opinion of eminent French stomatologists, who have nevertheless remained general practitioners themselves and continue attached to the unity of their profession, this system has the advantage of giving the public the help of specialists who perform each of these operations more skilfully than the average general practitioner. However, let us point out that among its disadvantages there is the fact that a man who extracts teeth day after day all the year round, and does it very well, is liable not to worry very much about the presence of a few teeth more or less in a mouth. The mis-adventure of a passing traveller who wanted an aching tooth examined and, after an anaesthetic, was presented with three or four on a plate, is revealing. In the next room or on the floor above, it is true, a colleague of the tooth-extractor, equally proficient in the converse operation, is ready to equip the toothless jaw with a set of new teeth 'more handsome than nature had provided'.

The decline of the general practitioner in surgery and the rapid progress of a very advanced form of specialization during the last twenty years deserve a study to themselves. But this would be out of place here nor should I be competent to undertake it. Medicine offers another field of observation from this point of view, since the objective techniques of analysis and examination now occupy an increasingly large place in it. Medical specialization is a difficult problem and produces varied and contradictory results, as Dr Henri Péquignot has very clearly shown in an excellent essay.[2] But there is no question of condemning it and still less of wishing to put the clock back in ways which might be more or less efficient. 'Medicine is becoming increasingly an agglomeration of techniques, forming a whole much larger than any one person can absorb, learn or use,' writes Dr Péquignot, and he adds, 'There is no truth, no practical efficiency, no care for quality, if we ignore these techniques — and still less is there likely to be any technical progress.'[3]

THE 'SPECIALIST' AND THE 'SPECIALIZED'

But the comparison I have just sketched between the polyvalent practitioner and the specialist deserves a more thorough discussion.

In fact the development of labour to-day provides innumerable examples of occupations being broken-down into a variety of specialisms. These show characteristic features so that one can distinguish several distinct types.

Let us take the housepainter's trade. The painter-craftsman, or general practitioner with a polyvalent training, will paint a sign, or imitate marble or the grain of wood, with less speed, regularity and accuracy than a 'specialist' painter. On the other hand, the non-specialized painter-craftsman will take a shorter time than the lettering specialist in doing his usual job, i.e. in redecorating a house.[4]

A basic knowledge of his trade is indispensable to the specialist painter in learning his specialism, just as at another occupational level a basic knowledge of his profession is essential for the dentist if he is to become an expert in filling or in extracting teeth. The same is true for a doctor if he is to set up as a heart specialist or as an endocrinologist. On the other hand, no such basic knowledge is necessary for a 'specialized' worker; for instance, for a man whose specialism lies in his ability to cut off the left ham of a pig on the preparation line in a bacon factory. To be trained to the trade may even constitute a technical and psychological handicap, since the general practitioner is less apt to execute the standardized motions required by such a job with the maximum speed and accuracy, as well as less ready to accept and put up with such a job in the long run. Here an essential difference appears between the *specialist* and the *specialized* (semi-skilled) worker.

The basic trades tend, throughout the growing scale of their complexity and of their technical and scientific implications, to be increasingly split up into specialisms. This is as clear in the case of a fitter at one end of the scale as it is in that of a doctor at the other. The size of the polyvalent sector of labour decreases as our social and economic life alters with the industrialization and urbanization of the rural areas, where up to now its place had been considerable.[5] The mechanic, an 'all round man', able to repair a whole engine, to sharpen and set his instruments accurately himself, as well as to manage a variety of machine tools, would only continue to exist, for instance, in garages in small towns and villages. In the extreme case, the basic trade would only be learnt as a *means* of specialization, a change which would completely alter the way in which it is taught and transmitted. This seems to be the direction in which medicine is already heading in France, where students with only twenty-four 'credits' may enter for specialized certificates even before they have become doctors.

If the basic profession or trade is threatened as such by specialization, one finds at the other end of the scale that simple repetitive jobs, such as are performed by a significant proportion of semi-skilled workers in all branches of industry, no longer form a part of any basic trade. In engineering, for example, the manufacturing operations performed by a worker on a machine are mostly determined by the machine's actual structure, by the mass-production procedure and methods of assembly carefully worked out by the engineers of the planning department. In the same way, in the assembly of wireless or television equipment the delicate operations of connecting and fitting the parts are not, properly speaking, an element in any basic trade. They are combinations of tiny operations conceived as functions of a line of manufacture carefully planned by the technicians of the firm.

We are thus led to make a clear distinction between the relationship of the polyvalent general practitioner to the *specialized* (semi-skilled) worker, and the relationship of the general practitioner to the *specialist*. These relationships, however, are comparable on one point at least. The general practitioner is inferior to both the specialized worker and the specialist in their particular specialisms but superior to them when given a job dependent upon his basic trade.

Now that we have reached this point it might be as well to reread the famous pages which F. W. Taylor devoted in his *Principles of Scientific Management* to the specialization of workers trained according to his methods.[6] The worker, conforming to Taylor's rationalized programme, must obey the instruction sheets minutely elaborated by the planning department. These sheets determine time-and-motion, tools and proper speeds and depth of cut. The single foreman is superseded by eight different men who act as agents for the planning department between the shop and the office and form a network of experts, teaching and supervising the workmen. 'What I demand of the worker,' remarks Taylor,[7] 'is not to produce any longer by his own *initiative*, but to execute punctiliously *the orders given*, down to their minutest details.'[*]

Elsewhere he writes:

> When through all of this teaching and this minute instruction the work is apparently made so smooth and easy for the workman, the first impression is that this all tends to make him a mere automaton, a wooden man. As the workmen frequently say when they first come under this system, 'Why, I am not allowed to think or move without someone interfering or doing it for me!' The same criticism and objection, however, can be raised against all other modern division of labor. . . . And it should be remembered that the training of the surgeon has been almost identical in type with the teaching and training which is given to the workman under scientific management. The surgeon, all through his early years, is under the closest supervision of more experienced men, who show him in the minutest way how each element of his work is best done. They provide him with the finest implements, each one of which has been the subject of special study and development, and then insist upon his using each of these implements in the very best way. All of this teaching, however, in no way narrows him. On the contrary he is quickly given the very best knowledge of his predecessors; and, provided (as he is, right from the start) with standard implements and methods which represent the best knowledge of the world up-to-date, he is able to use his own originality and ingenuity to make *real additions to the world's knowledge, instead of reinventing things which are old.* In a similar way the workman who is co-operating with his many teachers

---

[*] The italics are Taylor's own.

under the modern scientific management has an opportunity to develop which is at least as good as, and generally better than that which he had when the whole problem was 'up to him' and he did his work entirely unaided.[8]

This attempt of Taylor to liken the worker specialized by Scientific Management on a standardized operation to the surgeon-apprentice is, however, exceedingly weak. The student of surgery during his long training is actually in constant contact with trained surgeons and their assistants, all experienced people, teaching him how to use instruments and doing operations in his presence. This real instruction continues for many months and years. Furthermore, his specialism is based upon a complete series of medical studies, ending in a doctor's diploma, and is therefore founded on a scientific education of a general kind. The worker, on the contrary, who is 'specialized' so as to perform a series of fragmentary operations on a machine according to the instructions of a planning department of the Taylorian kind, can be 'taught' in a few days. When he can execute these operations correctly, 'his vocational training,' so writes Gilbreth, Taylor's faithful disciple, 'is finished, whatever his age.'[9]

The 'specialized' worker, besides, is hardly in the same situation in relation to the foremen who instruct him on behalf of the management as the young surgeon is to the professors and heads of the clinic. The latter, if they are worthy of their job, aim at making the advice they give to their students live and bear fruit. They try on every occasion to connect it with the student's theoretical knowledge of anatomy, normal physiology and pathology. Do we find any equivalent concern in the training given to the specialized workman? Indeed, is not one of its essential objectives, trumpeted abroad on all sides as one of the main merits of such a system by the defenders of Scientific Management, the effort to *reduce* to a minimum the time needed for training? Is it not, also, a most improper confusion of terms to talk of instruction in both cases, when Taylor's 'specialized' worker is drilled rather than instructed?

Finally let us note that Taylor in his day knew only surgeons of the general practitioner type. Nowadays we must go farther and, as Pierre Naville has rightly said, consider the moment at which specialization occurs: 'In fact the scope of a specialism varies according to whether it is learnt before or after the acquiring of a more general competence.'[10] Thus a surgeon who has had a general medical and surgical training and then specializes in lung or nerve surgery, a heart specialist, or, in the industrial sphere, an engineer who has gained a diploma at a technical college and then specializes in certain types of textile work or in internal combustion engines, are specialists in a very different sense from a 'specialized' worker, who has only passed through the ordinary state school and has never had a cultural education or been trained to a trade.

In fact it is again only through a confusion of terms that we can speak of specialization in both cases. We lack a broad, concrete 'phenomenology' of specialization as it exists to-day in our technical civilization. For the limited purposes of our discussion at any rate, we propose to distinguish the *specialist*, the (superficial) reduction of whose sphere of activity is based upon a previous professional training of which it is the prolongation and crown, from the *specialized* worker, who carries out a fragmentary job into which he is initiated (in the case of the semi-skilled worker it is one wholly concerned with motions) without having received, or usually receiving later, any general training such as would form a background explaining or illuminating his 'unit of work' by connecting it with the whole process.

However, we must be careful not to present an idealized picture of the specialist or to exaggerate the virtues of his kind of specialization. It is not possible to maintain that the specialist always adds to the skill and knowledge common to all members of his profession certain other special skills derived from further, narrower practice. The specialist fitter of stamping dies loses the knack of handling a planing machine or a time-recorder. The young doctor who specializes at, or even before, the end of his studies, quickly loses his previous general skill in medicine; and an electro-radiologist would be very embarrassed if, after a few years, he had to diagnose and care for someone with a liver or eye complaint. This is not said in order to lessen the distance between the specialist and the specialized worker but is meant to point to the fact that specialization, even when preceded by a general training, today implies, and will increasingly imply, a choice. In fact in the two cases specialization has quite a different psychological value. In the one the whole person is involved in the job; in the other, reduced as it is to a fragmentary activity without any general background or occupational training, there is no such involvement at all, still less any development of personality.

II. SOCIAL UNITY AND INTEGRATION

Such are the main lines along which specialization seems to be developing to-day. Taking these facts as our starting-point and recognizing the real advantages of specialization wherever it occurs, it is for us now to try to define the conditions that will help us to meet, by-pass or overcome its equally real dangers.

Let us first consider the collective influences exerted on the worker by the society of which both he and his firm form a part. Among the influences capable of transforming the value of specialized jobs in the eyes of those performing them, of transfiguring them to a certain extent and for a certain time, is the degree to which the worker or employee is integrated with the aims of his community, the extent to which he accepts the objectives of the collective whole in which he lives and works.

This theme was one of the *Leitmotivs* of Soviet industrial psychology during the period of the first five-year plans. About 1930, I. N. Spielrein, I. M. Bourdiansky, S. Gellerstein, W. Kogan, A. I. Kolodnaya, and many others, declared that very specialized jobs, even the elementary operations of the assembly line, possessed an entirely different psychological meaning and colour for the Soviet worker taking part in 'socialist competition', working in an enterprise belonging to the whole community, knowing that its profits would go to the whole community, than for a worker doing the same jobs in the factory of a capitalist country.[11] I shall not here discuss the problem of how far a very fragmentary job, in itself entirely devoid of meaning and interest, can be subjectively transformed in the worker's mind through his relationship to his firm and to the society of which it is a part — the problem, in other words, of deciding on the basis of actually known facts whether the technical conditions of labour are completely contained in its social conditions whatever the social régime and the relations it has established between producers. Let us note, moreover, that in the present state of our information from Soviet sources, it is impossible to judge how far the very specialized jobs performed daily in the U.S.S.R. by millions of workers and employees really acquire more scope and human value and give greater satisfaction owing to the framework of social institutions in which their work and firm are integrated.

It is nonetheless true that the factors referred to above have a real influence, and that the comments made contain as a whole a large element of truth. They are confirmed besides (in very different conditions and ways, it is true, from those which I myself observed in the U.S.S.R. during the period of the first five-year plans) in those undertakings in America and Europe where various methods, such as participation in management and in profits, workers' social clubs, etc. have been tried by intelligent and venturesome directors, securing from their workers a high degree of support for the firm's objectives.[12] Special mention must here be made of the successful French experiments, in producers' co-operatives, or communities of work, the best known of which is Boimondau at Valence. There is no doubt that the disadvantages of highly specialized jobs are lessened when the worker considers himself well paid and feels himself a member of democratically run industrial group, offering him the means of self-expression and chances of promotion, in a relaxed and confident atmosphere.

There are no ideal examples of this, but even those imperfect ones to which we can point in France, in a capitalist economy, show how important a part is played by the relations existing between the worker and his firm in lessening the harm done by highly specialized work. Thus, there is no doubt that a job takes on a sense of greater value in the worker's mind when he feels himself in sympathy with the aims of the community as a whole, and not just with those of his firm. Therefore, when a considerable proportion of the working population of a capitalist country contract out of it because of their conviction that they are being exploited, any attempt to overcome the harmful effects of specialization is rendered vain in advance.

DUAL TRAINING

There is another collective factor, the influence of which may be decisive, that of education. Can society transform its school and university system, at the present stage in the development of the division of labour, so that it may protect both child and adolescent against the dangers of specialization, may even perhaps give them the means of controlling it?

A dual training, both general and technical, in the whole of a particular trade is certainly a good means of preparing the worker for transfer from one specialized job to another or for rotation between them, should he not be able to find any employment corresponding to his qualifications as a general practitioner: as mechanic, housepainter, carpenter, etc. It opens his mind as well as widening his occupational horizon, avoiding or lessening the risk of his becoming a 'robot' reduced to a few psycho-motor automatisms.

I have often heard industrial directors and technicians, and recently a manager of our S.N.C.F.,* although it is not a mass-production enterprise, criticize certificates of vocational aptitude, the way in which they are organized and the tests they include. Let us agree that a certain number need reconsideration and that an occasional reclassification is necessary in order to keep up with technological changes in production. But these criticisms are also levelled at the whole apprenticeship system in France, at its dual character, by which our technical education attempts to link together cultural and vocational training, at what they call its too broad and general scope. These critics seem blinded by the growing expansion of the area of specialization and the corresponding lessening in that of general functions in which the skilled worker can take immediate part and make full use of his 'systematic and complete' training. The situation is complicated so that at the moment these criticisms appear superficially justified. Even though the 'global' ideas of technical education in France may seem in some ways out-of-date today in relation to technical developments, in others paradoxically they are really more up-to-date than would be a more highly specialized training. This is clear in view of the tendencies towards job enlargement, transfer and work rotation to which we have referred. These cannot fail to grow in the near future so that in this sense, and without either party always being aware of it, 'modernity' is not on the side on which it seems to be at first sight.

POLYTECHNICALIZATION

In the sphere of education there exists a much more ambitious view which would lead to a radical reform of the social structure. This is the idea of 'polytechnicalization', which Marx, developing the conceptions of socialist workers and thinkers in France,[13] made one of the main sources of the humanization of labour in a classless

* *Société Nationale des chemins de fer.*

society. Any detailed exposition would be out of the question within the space at our disposal here; we will deal with it, however, in relation to the functional specialization of jobs.

Marx, watching the developments of the first industrial revolution within the framework of a capitalist economy, had already clearly seen and denounced the effects of what he called 'professional idiocy'. He described forcefully the appearance in the factory of the semi-skilled 'detail' worker, his superiority in the short run over the specialist or polyvalent workman and conversely the physical and moral damage he was bound to suffer sooner or later. 'It is clear,' he writes, 'that a labourer who all his life performs one and the same simple operation converts his whole body into the automatic, specialist implement of that operation. Consequently, he takes less time in doing it than the artificer who performs a whole series of operations in succession.'[14] Moreover, while eliminating the manufacturing division of labour from a technical point of view, mechanized big business changes the extensive magnitude of the working day into an intensive one, shortening its hours but filling up its 'pores',[15] or gaps, in a closer and more intense fashion. Marx notes in relation to manufacture:

> An artificer who performs one after another the various fractional operations in the production of a finished article, must at one time change his place, at another his tools. The transition from one job to another interrupts the flow of his labour, and creates, so to say, 'pores' or gaps in his working day.[16]

These 'pores' contract and tend to disappear when he is fixed all the time to the same operation. Mechanization, by an intensive development of the means of production and of their rational use, reduces the hours of work but at the same time causes a greater strain on the worker by 'more closely filling up the "pores" of the working day'. One sees how the actual conditions in which specialized workers do their work can affect the development, and even the balance, of the personality.

One can also see how they contribute to enlarge the gulf that separates the 'intellectual' from the 'manual' worker. This separation, which Marx considers inherent in capitalist society, can only be abolished by socialism, which should make that one of its first objectives. Let us recall a famous passage in *Das Kapital*:

From the Factory system budded, as Robert Owen has shown us in detail, the germ of the education of the future, an education that will, in the case of every child over a given age, combine productive labour with instruction and gymnastics, not only as one of the methods of adding to the efficiency of production, but as the only method capable of producing fully developed human beings.[17] [Thus] recognizing variation of work as a fundamental law of production, and so the fitness of the labourer for varied work and the need for the greatest possible development of his varied aptitudes, it becomes a question of life and death for society to adapt the mode of production to the normal functioning of this law.

In this way the working class will achieve through the conquest of political power the final aim of socialism, which, on the plane of human personality, is in Marx's eyes 'to replace the detail worker of to-day, crippled by life-long repetition of one and the same trivial occupation . . . by the fully developed individual . . . to whom the different social functions he performs are but so many modes of giving free scope to his own natural and acquired powers'. This complete transformation would be accomplished by the 'introduction of technical education, both theoretical and practical, into the popular schools'.[18] Engels, in his *Anti-Dühring*, echoes from his own standpoint his master and friend. The new society, delivered from the chains of capitalism, will give rise to 'a race of producers with an all-round training who understand the scientific basis of industrial production as a whole, and each of whom has had practical experience in a whole series of branches of production from start to finish'. Thus each will be able to work according to his own inclinations and capabilities, thanks to a 'polytechnical' education responsive to the community's needs; for 'industry, systematically controlled by society as a whole in the public interest, requires human beings with harmoniously developed capacities, capable of finding their way about within the whole system of production'.[19] Let us note that this was still Stalin's objective in 1952, when, in his reply to Yaroshenko, he names among the three fundamental conditions for the transition to communism:

a real transition, not a mere verbal one: the securing of such a cultural advance in society as will enable all its members to develop their physical and intellectual powers harmoniously, so that they may receive a sufficient education and become active agents of social progress, being free to choose their work without being chained for ever to one predetermined occupation on account of the present division of labour.[20]

For a long time Marx thought that the citizens of a socialist society could become 'fully developed individuals' in and through their work; individuals for whom, as he wrote in his *Critique of the Gotha Programme*, productive labour is the 'first necessity of life'.[21] This was perhaps an essentially political doctrine — an 'exoteric' doctrine as it were — a weapon to reinforce his criticism of capitalist society and drive the proletariat towards self-education. In any case the theme of the multispecialized worker as an 'ideal type' runs through most of his writings.

However, by the end of his life, when he was revising the third volume of *Das Kapital* (published in 1894, after his death, by Engels), his attitude had changed and his whole emphasis was upon the 'realm of freedom', which, so he declares, 'only begins, in fact, where that labour, which is determined by need and external purposes, ceases', lying 'outside the sphere of material production proper'.[22] Marx saw from the start of the second industrial revolution that in the conditions to which it was leading the reduction of the working day and an active use of leisure would become of fundamental importance as a means of safeguarding the individual and his development. Faced by the *necessity* of a severely limiting and highly developed specialization, evident at all levels of skill and in every occupation, and as such inseparable from technical progress no matter what the social structure; faced, too, by the fact that modern industry, including that of the first collectivist state, is being increasingly penetrated by an ever more elaborate scientific organization, would Marx, we may well wonder, had he lived a century later, have continued to regard as the final aim of communist society — as his 'ideal type' — the individual who attains *in and through his work* an integrated and polyvalent development thanks to the various specialisms which are the 'different and successive forms of his activity'?

ITS VICISSITUDES, VALUE AND LIMITATIONS

Polytechnical education, taking its inspiration from the ideas of Marx and Engels, led to important discussions and experiments in the U.S.S.R., particularly between 1930 and 1936 at the beginning of the era of the five-year plans. These arose from an attempt to combine an initiation into the technical and organizational principles of a planned economy with manual work and scientific and literary studies. These efforts, and the discussions which went with them, aroused keen interest in intellectual and especially educational circles in the West. Elsewhere we have described the principal stages in the growth of this type of education. It started with the Work School (*trudovaya skola*), which was still permeated with the idea of craftsmanship, and became a useful foundation for multispecialization and in any case for any change of work.[23] Such training was certainly well suited to a time in the industrialization of Soviet Russia when, particularly during the first two five-year plans, massive displacements of workers from one branch of production to another were constantly taking place, as well as transfers within firms the techniques of which were often at first very backward. Moreover, the very principle of polytechnical education was a denial of the theory still permeating the works of certain industrial psychologists in the West, that there are individual aptitudes which determine once and for all the occupational career of the adolescent.

The decisions of the XIXth Congress of the Communist Party of the U.S.S.R., held in October 1952, announced the introduction of polytechnical education at the same time as the generalization of the *deciatiletka* (the extension of the second degree of education from seven to ten years), which was to take place from 1955 in the big towns and from 1960 throughout the whole of the Union. All schools were to benefit from these important reforms. In the information published on this subject it was said that 'experiments in polytechnicalization were made during the years following the revolution' and 'are being renewed to-day on a large scale'.[24] In fact they were not called experiments at the time when they were carried out but were part of an essential doctrine, formulated in a decision made by the Central Committee of the Communist Party of the U.S.S.R., dated 5 September, 1931, and constituting a part of Soviet law. They were developed by certain specialized institutions, such as the Institute of Scientific Research for Polytechnical Education, which was directed by the intelligent and active S. Gaissinovitch. In August 1932, a decree of the Central Executive Committee (T.S.I.K.) had announced a major reform concerned with the prolongation of school life and the development of the new culture based upon productive work.[25] It established a 'third degree' of education, the *deciatiletka*, extending from seven to ten years the educational period for young people if they should decide not to enter a factory training school at the end of the *semilietka* (the second degree of seven years' education). As a result of its remarkable experiments which I was able to observe on the spot between 1932 and 1936, Soviet polytechnicalization had at that time attracted world-wide attention among those concerned with the problems of a new humanism in our industrial age.

The schools I then visited near Moscow and Leningrad were perhaps exceptions. Subsequent events at any rate have proved that polytechnicalization was much less solidly rooted in theory and in practice than I then thought. Its 'rebirth', proclaimed by the decree of October 1952, with its most discreet references to former experiments, shows that it must have undergone a severe crisis, the causes and character of which it is not easy to discover. An article by S. G. Shapovalenko, corresponding member of the Academy of Educational Sciences of the R.S.F.S.R., which appeared in the review *Soviet Education* in November 1952, throws some light upon the subject. In the years following the historic decision of 1931,

> polytechnical education in the elementary school was reduced in practice to a sort of apprenticeship, to the establishment of primitive carpentry, locksmith and engineering shops in the schools. In these craftshops the pupils did not receive any proper idea of the present state of industrial production, based as it is upon advanced techniques. In consequence the People's Commissary of Public Instruction, on the direction of the Central Committee of the Party, did away in 1937 with 'Work Study' as a school subject. But he did nothing to strengthen the polytechnical aspects of the courses dealing with the principles of science, i.e. mathematics, physics, chemistry, biology, geography, and industrial and artistic design, so that polytechnical education failed to progress during the following years.

This explanation is curious when one remembers the facts. In contrast to certain craftsmanship doctrines of the Work School (*trudovaya skola*), the decisions of 1931-2 as well as the activities of Gaissinovitch and his Institute, inspired as they were by the famous saying of Lenin's widow, N. Krupskaya, 'vocational training should go from the head to the hands', laid the greatest stress on the need for close links between manual work and scientific knowledge during the school course.[26] The direction given by V. M. Molotov to the XVIIIth Party Congress of March 1939, is so general and vague that it leads one to think that nothing then remained of the former discussions and experiments and that a start was being made again from zero: 'In view of the large number of boys and girls who finish their education in the middle school and who, in most cases, then go to work in factories, it is absolutely necessary that they should receive at least some preparation for their future activity before leaving school.'

The coincidence of dates leads us to suppose that the crisis of polytechnicalization in the U.S.S.R. was linked, like that of industrial psychology, with the vast purge undergone by Soviet institutions between 1935 and 1939. The war intervened before any practical result could follow a new effort. The XIXth Congress, while restating the decision of August 1932, extending school life from seven to ten years, included in the programme of the five-year plan the following recommendation:

> In order to raise the status of general education in socialist schools, and to enable pupils leaving the middle school to choose their careers freely, it is desirable to begin introducing poly-technical education in the middle school, and to take measures for the establishment of a general polytechnical education.

To clarify the background of the new experiment in poly-technicalization let me quote the declaration made in November 1953, by J. A. Kairov, then Minister of Public Instruction in the U.S.S.R. It is singularly vague, and indeed less advanced as regards the connection between theory and practice — a fundamental point in multispecialization — than the official tests of 1931–2. 'Polytechnical instruction,' says the Minister, 'which will be given in the course of education in the lessons on physics, chemistry, biology, mathematics, geography and drawing, will help to raise the standard of work by enabling pupils to understand how the sciences are applied in industry and agriculture.' Polytechnical instruction will definitely replace the bookish lesson and will allow a larger place for intuitive education. Pupils will do practical work in the shop. 'Finally, labour problems will remain the central concern of teachers and of all Public Instruction personnel.'[27]

In an article which seems poorly informed as to what was done between the two wars in this sphere, N. Dombre tells us that the courses in mathematics, physics and chemistry will be connected with practical work in the school laboratories and workshops.[28] An important place will be rightly given to drawing, 'that international language of technology'. The practical work will be completed (as it was between 1932 and 1936 in the 'Z.O.T.' circles, Young Engineers' Clubs, and 'Children's Technical Centres',[29] etc.), by work in engineering, chemistry, photography and radio-telegraphy. The teaching of biology will also be accompanied by practical work on school farms. Visits to production centres, factories, and machine and tractor stations, given up, we are told, fifteen years before, will be started again. Pupils must not be 'passive spectators' (when was it suggested they should?) but active observers, making plans, sketching machines, and drawing up lists of output, etc.

As Luigi Volpicelli, professor at the University of Rome, remarks, one is surprised to see the leaders of the U.S.S.R. bringing up once again for solution, as though they were new, problems which Soviet education had made the centre of its practical reforms nearly thirty years before.[30] It is true that thirty years are not a long time in view of the immensity of the task. Moreover, French experiments made on a modest scale with 'educative manual work' show the difficulties encountered in our own country by efforts derived from a similar inspiration. Let us hope that the advance of the Soviet régime towards a climate of greater freedom, such as is especially needed in education, will allow these fine possibilities to be realized and so help in the solution of one of the gravest problems facing our technical age.

Whatever may have happened to the experiments to which it led in the U.S.S.R., there is no doubt in my mind that polytechnical education is on the right lines and puts into the hands of young people powerful weapons to help them guard against the dangers of specialization. If it is completed by a liberal, intelligent and generous policy in connection with the use of leisure, to which point I shall return later, such an education may constitute one of the surest ways of neutralizing the harmful effects of the division of labour in the industrial era through which we are passing.

Without any growth in the individual personality during leisure hours, however, it will be no panacea in itself, as Marx seems for a long time to have thought. Can it bridge the cleavage that exists between the intellectual and the manual worker? Technical evolution, and particularly the development of automation, is of course intellectualizing a growing number of industrial occupations, and is thus moving in this direction. However, if an adolescent has done various types of manual work at secondary school for a few years, even in a collectivist state, and has then worked with machine tools and done odd jobs on a farm or on a tractor station, becoming finally a bank clerk, a lawyer, a doctor, or even an engineer, is that really enough, with nothing else to keep him in contact with manual work, to bridge the gulf separating him from mechanics, miners, and agricultural labourers, who work only with their hands, and whose labour is not itself enriched by a complementary training and active leisure pursuits? A long process is clearly required and we ought not to underestimate its complexity and difficulties. A piece of self-criticism published in the *Komsomolskaya Pravda* on 17 July, 1953, reads: 'There are students among us who believe that a real gulf separates an engineer's job from that of an ordinary workman, and who look down on the practical producer. They believe that it is exclusively the engineer's job to make the calculations, and the worker's to carry them out.'

III. POSSIBILITY OF INTELLECTUAL REVALUATION

To overcome the dangers latent in specialization remedies of a different order are required, which will affect the actual content, the internal organization and the structure of work. Their full effect, moreover, is often prepared by, is even strictly dependent upon, the existence of a polytechnical training; the remedial effect is not the least merit of such training. Thus we return to the proposals we have already made recommending regular transfer, work rotation and, wherever possible, job enlargement.

Transfer and rotation are *indirect* ways of increasing the scope of a worker's or employee's functions and of widening his occupational outlook. Transfer is a simpler method of securing variety of work, but rotation may sometimes be preferred, just because it can be allowed for in planning and be made a part of the programme, thus avoiding improvisation and sudden alterations. It has its natural place in mass-production, and workers, moving from job to job according to a well organized plan, can gain a view of the whole process of manufacture or assembly, and thus rediscover, strung out not in space but in time, the *unity* of which technology has deprived their work by breaking it down into fragments. Work rotation, combined with classes in the factory itself intended to help the worker to understand the place of the product, a magneto, say, or a condenser, in the resulting whole, and to grasp its technical aspects, can effectively lead to an intellectual revaluation of labour. The status thus acquired by the worker is different from that of the polyvalent artisan or craftsman but not necessarily inferior to it in the resultant possibilities of involvement, personality development and satisfaction.

I shall not stop here to consider the question of job enlargement, as I have already discussed its value and limitations, and in particular those factors limiting the scope of its application. But I must once again stress the fact that all the measures hitherto mentioned, if they are actually going to overcome the deadening effects of specialization and give a new value to semi-skilled labour, must be accompanied by a vocational education which will integrate these specialized jobs into a single whole, providing the worker with an elementary knowledge of mathematics, the physical sciences, and drawing and technology, such as will enable him to *understand* what he and his fellows are doing — and so to control it.

This intellectual revaluation seems all the more possible to-day in that it corresponds to two modern occupational trends. One is the disappearance (with the advance of automatism) of a certain number of fragmentary and repetitive jobs which keep the worker chained to the technical demands and pace of the machine; the other is the appearance of new functions concerned with maintenance and repair. This development is not only clearly visible in technically advanced countries as well as in the most modern firms, but is as apparent in the great motorcar industry with its special 'transfer' machines as it is in power plants, automatic glassworks, oil refineries with modern equipment, and so on. The specialized workers in many firms, as we noticed in Detroit as early as 1948,[31] now form a nursery of machine operators.

The directors of the Renault concern, we may note, set up in 1952 in their Billancourt factories sectors of production including under one management a group of manufacturing plants with their corresponding planning departments, a reform which deserves special mention.[32] Is this attempt to unite at the top the planning and execution of work, which ever since Taylor have been so radically and 'rationally' separated, to remain only an episode without further developments? Or will it be reproduced by other firms and be repeated lower down the scale at shop level, thus reinforcing a movement that is making for a more intellectual type of work and is being encouraged by such reforms in Scientific Management as that of Work Simplification? It is too early to give an answer. But the movement exists and has been well described in John Diebold's book *Automation*.[33] Thanks to the growth of automatism, which is constantly being increased to-day by the use of electronic devices, production will not eliminate man as many over-anxious and ill-informed prophets have too quickly declared; but, while freeing for less tedious work those I have called elsewhere the 'stop-gaps' of mechanization,[34] will continue to employ a large and *relatively growing proportion* of skilled workers, whose jobs *can* be given much more value by the knowledge, care and responsibility they require and the status thereby implied.[35] Thus the maintenance staff needed even in an automatic factory dealing exclusively with the standardized exchange of faulty parts and not with their repair would remain considerable.

If we concern ourselves only with recently observed facts, we can see that a certain number of jobs are being upgraded, i.e. that there is a tendency to raise their intellectual and moral status in the firm. 'Automatism,' writes Mr Eugene Staley, 'will mean that human labour in advanced technicological societies will be used less and less for the repetitive functions involved in feeding work-pieces through machines and assembling them into finished products. Labour will be more and more "upgraded" into the kinds of functions performed by the engineer, the designer, the production planner, the skilled maintenance and repair man, the organizer or manager.'[36] Without fully subscribing to such a glowing picture of our industrial future, in which no shadows appear, let us recognize that the 'possibility' he describes is not wholly Utopian. From the standpoint we are taking here, the desire to link the revaluation of specialized labour with vocational training can find new and valuable support in his views.

Transfer, rotation and job enlargement are then measures applicable in the present state of production techniques wherever overspecialized jobs continue. Conversely, wherever these techniques allow of automatic working, the problems of specialization cease, since all human intervention is suppressed in the actual work of execution. Automatization, or, as it is now being called on all sides, 'automation', reduces the sector of overspecialized jobs at certain points. But, and this is what most advocates of automation do not see, this sector is constantly being added to, and the sector containing global and complex jobs is constantly dwindling, as these jobs get broken-down into more simplified operations. So far as I know no attempt has yet been made to evaluate statistically the relationship between these two inverse movements, an evaluation by branch of industry and by country which it would be difficult, though not impossible, to undertake. This relationship varies in different places and at different times, reflecting the technical development of a particular industrial community at a given moment. It has a higher absolute value, for instance, in the United States than in Italy or Brazil. But it does not help us much to suppose that in a land with a highly diversified economy such as France, in which the proportion of medium or small firms with out-of-date equipment is high, the phenomenon of job specialization is increasing, although its rate of growth has already passed its maximum.

We have described *collective* remedies for the harmful effects of specialization and have suggested measures *within* the field of work itself which might militate against them. The functional unity of the human personality suggests that we should now turn our attention to life as it is lived apart from work, and inquire whether leisure, or 'free time', does not offer ways of minimizing these dangers and even of solving at a deeper level the problems we have been discussing here.

CHAPTER VII

Leisure and Dissatisfaction with Work

L ET ME remark, to begin with, that the term 'leisure' requires to be used with all sorts of reservations. There is a distinction, indeed sometimes a contradiction, between what the word and its etymology suggest, with their aristocratic overtones and flavour of passive enjoyment, and the immense scope and extraordinary variety of what individual members of our industrial societies do outside their 'working' activities, which depends upon geographic, social and economic factors and constitutes one of the most striking phenomena of the present day. The reasons for my mistrust of the word will gradually, I hope, become clearer in the course of this discussion, which will propose more adequate terms and concepts. Since present-day language offers us nothing else sufficiently direct and simple, I shall use the word to begin with as a makeshift. It will allow me at any rate to suggest to the reader a new outlook from which to regard the problems of specialization and its future.

ONE AND THE SAME MAN

The foregoing facts and inquiries cannot be fully grasped or understood, if we fail to relate the phenomenon of job enlargement which I have been describing to certain general trends observable to-day in the development of leisure activities. For the fact is that many people in many very different countries and environments are employing their leisure in diverse ways in an attempt to realize the potentialities left unused by their work. 'A man is not one person at home and a different person at his work, *he is one and the same man*. He projects his personal worries, frustrations and fears on to his workplace, and vice versa from workplace to home.'[1] Many needs, for interest, for meaning, for a sense of participation and of achievement, left unsatisfied by the rationalized jobs performed in factory, office, mine and workshop, together with the latent tensions caused thereby in many people's minds, maintain their pressure after work and influence the way in which people spend the constantly increasing hours of leisure provided by the progressive reduction of working time. This does not of course explain all the characteristic features of leisure activities, which vary enormously in form and content according to region, tradition, cultural pattern and socio-economic level. It would be a mistake here, as it always is, to single out only one factor and make of it the sole explanation of such diverse and complex phenomena.[2]

Nevertheless, so great to-day is the increase in active leisure-time pursuits and in the search for structured, responsible and finished activities, that we are forced to connect it with the contemporaneous development of the bread-and-butter jobs performed by a very large section of the active population of our industrial societies. I have drawn attention in other studies to the growing use of leisure for art and craft hobbies, for model-making and a whole gamut of 'subsidiary' activities, which are pursued either spontaneously or because of the encouragement they receive for various reasons from the state or from large private firms in countries as different as England, France, the United States, Poland, Czechoslovakia and the U.S.S.R.[3] As regards the last named country, our information about the organization and comparative importance of the different leisure-time activities of the workers remains insufficient. But it seems clear that the phenomena of 'subsidiary' activities are also to be found in an economic and cultural framework very different from our own, and possess a greater importance there owing to the wide opportunities for technical training and advancement offered by that country.

We must also notice that in competitive societies such as the United States and other highly developed capitalist countries, where the technical atmosphere is overpowering and consumers are subjected to the everpresent, dynamic forces of publicity, the fragmentation of labour does not always cause the worker to seek leisure activities of greater scope in order to compensate for his frustrations.[4] It may tend instead to disorganize the rest of his life and to arouse aggressive tendencies and outbursts of savage self-assertion through indulgence in all kinds of stimulants, in alcohol, in games of chance or luck,[5] or in habits or bouts of 'conspicuous consumption', brutal amusements like 'stock-cars' and mass-spectacles disguised as 'sport' or 'artistic' events, boxing, all-in wrestling, speed racing and crime and horror films. It is especially in this way that certain American observers with something of a psycho-analytical bias interpret the unnatural week-end behaviour of semi-skilled workers who, caught in the authoritarian wheels of rationalized industry, work all the week, as on the assembly lines of the great motorcar factories of Detroit, at fragmentary and cramping operations.

Other people stress the growing effort to escape after work is done. According to Daniel Bell, one of the most clear-sighted of the younger industrial sociologists in the United States, this escapism is even a characteristic of the American worker to-day. He writes

> The worker becomes bored, absent-minded, accident-prone, or he retreats from reality, engulfed in a myriad obsessive reveries. The big lure among the workers remains the hope of running one's own business, of 'being one's own boss'. The possibility of leaving the shop forms a staple topic of conversation on the job, states one observer who worked on a plant.[5]

'SUBSIDIARY' OR 'ESSENTIAL' ACTIVITIES?

But the main form taken by this desire to escape after work hours is 'a desperate drive for leisure'.[7] While the engineer or industrial magnate, indeed anyone working in one of the liberal professions, will in many cases be entirely absorbed by his work, the worker is not, and so reserves his best efforts, his energy, for what he will do out of working hours in his 'free time'. In the United States an average week's work, which was 70·6 hours in 1850, dropped to 40·8 hours in 1950, while the week-end is now usually two complete days, and a seven-hour day seems already in sight. The worker seeks to regain in his leisure hours the initiative, responsibility and sense of achievement denied to him in his work. In the last ten years there has been a 'fantastic mushrooming' of hobbies, of arts and crafts and of all sorts of free-time activities, such as photography, pottery, electronics, radio, etc., in what Erich Fromm has called, contrasting them with the 'press-button' services of automatic machines, 'do-it-yourself' activities.[8] Bell adds this comment, which fully supports the interpretation of these facts that I have suggested elsewhere: 'America has seen the multiplication of the "amateur" on a scale unknown to previous history. And while this is a positive good, it has been achieved at a high cost indeed — the loss of satisfaction in work.'[9]

It would be a mistake to think that such things are typically American and only characteristic of workers in the most highly industrialized country in the world. The equivalent is to be found in other less technically developed societies, such as England and France.

In England there is a well-marked development of hobbies among workers and employees occupied in rationalized jobs, as is shown in the multitude of clubs created by those employed in big firms and in the exhibitions they organize.[10] 'What is your hobby?' asked a notice put up by one of these firms which I visited near London. Many workers are so absorbed in their hobbies, for instance in dog-racing, model-making or football pools, that it interferes with their work and reduces their efficiency. This is often the case with workers who get no satisfaction out of their industrial occupations. 'Perhaps', writes Ferdynand Zweig in his vivid little book, *The British Worker*, 'most men believe that the function of a job, even an interesting job, is primarily to provide money for the comforts, amenities and pleasures of life'.[11]

One of the comments most frequently heard from the workers about their hobbies is that they give them 'something they like doing', something 'in which they feel free', free above all to choose what they will do as well as the place and moment at which they will do it. English workers have a variety of hobbies, manual occupations being preferred to cultural ones of course on account of the general environment in which they have been educated and the absence of group stimulus. It is true that instrumental music, choral singing, amateur dramatic clubs and art societies including drawing, painting, sculpture, engraving and especially photography, are not uncommon. But the English workman's hobbies are mainly those we find among the working-class of other countries too, i.e. carpentry, the making of toys, of model aeroplanes, wireless sets, engines, etc., leather and tin work; we must also add gardening and the breeding and care of animals of all kinds, which is a characteristic of English society in general. British investigators stress the great interest in and even love for animals shown by the workers; only a systematic inquiry would elicit to what extent this characteristic is linked with certain forms of industrial work. At the end of his chapter on this feature of English working-class life Zweig writes: 'Hobbies probably express a man's whole personality more truly than work itself does, because he works through necessity, but follows his hobby through choice. Hobbies,' he adds, 'try to bring colour into the dullness of our industrial civilization. Repetitive jobs are inevitable, but satisfying hobbies can counteract the effects of an over-mechanized life.'[12]

In France, although this sphere has not as yet been systematically studied, we have made similar observations in the case of both factory and office workers. As regards office workers, an investigation carried out by Henri Colas among the employees of a big Parisian bank confirms the importance of 'escape' activities during leisure hours.[13] Pierre Louchet, too, has undertaken a valuable inquiry into pigeon-fancying, which is the favourite leisure pursuit of the coalminers of Northern France. His study showed significant differences between the attitudes of the surface and of the underground workers.[14] An investigation conducted by P. Fougeyrollas at Malakoff (Seine) on a sample of 300 couples legally married or living in a 'free union', also contains some suggestive facts about the way in which the attitude towards leisure pursuits varies according to social, occupational and family ties.[15]

In Belgium, where 'subsidiary' activities abound among the workers, I noted during a visit the following sections listed in the catalogue of a big exhibition organized by the workers and employees of the large steel firm Ougrée-Marihaye at Liège: Photography, Pen and Ink Drawings, Water-colours, Charcoal Drawings, Linocuts, Paintings, Mechanical Drawing, Architectural Design, Decorated Objects, Metalwork, Bookbinding, Embroidery, Weaving, Dressmaking, Crochet and Knitting, Model-making (aeroplanes, motorcars, boats, machines), Woodwork, Sculpture.[16]

WORK AND FREE TIME

The variety of objects upon which so many men and women in our industrial societies expend their energies during leisure hours leads one to associate with them the idea of *activity*. This is why in former studies I have proposed calling them 'active leisure-time pursuits'. But this is still an inadequate description. The workers insist, as we have seen, and they are excellent judges in this matter, upon the *freedom* these pursuits allow in contrast to the constraint of their bread-and-butter jobs. A true leisure activity is one freely chosen and pursued at the moment and in the way desired by the individual concerned, who expects from it satisfaction and even a certain inner growth. This is well seen by I. Meyerson, who in his definition of work insists on the 'constraints of the material and of the human environment'.[17] L. S. Hearnshaw stresses the same point when he declares that the 'characteristics of constraint, obligation and discipline are the very essence of the meaning of work', a view which he has repeated with certain modifications in a more recent article.[18]

I agree, but with one important reservation. In the daily life of many men and women with small or medium incomes their wage-earning occupation is not the only compulsory activity. There are other kinds of duties caused by economic needs, which eat into their 'free time', such as supplementary work, including paid jobs belonging to the 'first' or 'second' trade or profession, performed in France as *travail noir* (black work) by employees who succeed in augmenting their main income in this way. Then there are the domestic chores of women, who in working-class homes are often helped by their men folk.[19] There is also the utilitarian side of the craft work or small manual jobs performed at home, and there is even a utilitarian aspect to the study courses, taken in the evening or at week-ends, which lead to professional examinations entitling the worker to an increase of pay and status in his firm. To be complete we should in many cases add to this list the time absorbed by family obligations and duties which are forced upon the worker and are neither chosen nor desired. These cannot be called 'active leisure-time pursuits', since they contain elements of constraint or at least of mere passive acceptance.

Work and *non-work*, as we must call it if we are to recognize its complexity[20], are thus connected by mutual influence. I will leave aside the influence exerted by the structure and nature of non-professional activities upon the character and content of the paid job, an excellent field for research with which I am not concerned here. Instead, I shall examine in this and the remaining chapter of this book the general influence of professional work upon 'non-work' activities. This to-day seems to be one of the major results of *industrialism* in the widest sense of the word, using it to include all its technical, economic and psychological ramifications.

An investigation carried out on a sample of 819 French workers and employees in 1953 by J. Dumazedier showed that, whereas the majority of them still thought of 'leisure' as merely 'time', more than a quarter already considered it as an activity. Not one of them, we may note, thought of leisure as a 'state'. Instead, nearly all defined it by contrast with the occupations of daily life. About 50 per cent spoke of these as 'necessities and duties', among which were counted, apart from work, the various kinds of activity previously mentioned. If we examine the analysis of their budgets and expenditure made in the course of different studies, we can usefully class 'non-work' activities under four heads: activities due to (1) economic needs; (2) social obligations; (3) family duties; (4) recreative and cultural needs.[21] By reducing hours of work, industrialism tends in the social conditions of to-day not only to increase 'free time' but also to reintroduce a certain number of constraints into these hours of leisure. This may also be said to be true, *mutatis mutandis*, of all societies in which industrialization is proceeding apace, including the U.S.S.R. and the 'people's democracies', where other forms of constraint, political, occupational and cultural, reduce the free time available to many workers. At any rate, if we are to avoid the dangers of a contradiction in terms, we must restrict the words 'free time' to those hours during which the worker is free from the above-mentioned duties and can exercise choice, thus both expressing and, if he has the capacity and the means, developing his personality.

DISSATISFACTION, HABITUATION, ESCAPE

Thus, quite apart from work itself, the influence which industrialism exerts upon the behaviour of masses of individuals is multifarious and intense, and results in certain definite social phenomena of a collective kind. On the basis of the data we have brought together here, let us recall some of the explanatory hypotheses suggested in the course of this work.

The 'scientific' organization of labour, or Scientific Management, by increasing the separation between planning and execution and establishing a rigorously centralized, 'vertical' and authoritarian administrative structure, has made it difficult, often indeed impossible, for many semi-skilled and unskilled workers to secure promotion within the firm. This blockage of mobility, which leads to the abandonment of any real hope of advance, seems to me to have had a very definite influence upon the behaviour of many people in their 'free time'. In some cases the impossibility of showing any personal characteristics during work creates a more or less conscious feeling of dissatisfaction, about which more later, causing a more or less marked state of depression as well as a continuous nervous strain.[22] In other cases it encourages aggressive tendencies out of working hours, an ungovernable thirst for self-assertion, shown, as I have already stated, in eccentric ways of using leisure, in a passion for gambling and for games of chance, like that of 'numbers', so common among the semi-skilled workers in America, or in the astonishing infatuation for football pools among British workmen. A certain number of leisure activities might more generally be interpreted as attempts to compensate for what is lacking in working hours. So I suggest that there is a close connection between the non-involvement of the personality in the fragmentary jobs required by factory and office and the need for self-expression which is equally excluded from the various duties of everyday life. A systematic study from this standpoint should be undertaken of hobby clubs and circles, which are constantly increasing, both as independent 'voluntary associations' and as part of the life of industrial and even administrative firms. If carried out by teams of industrial and social psychologists and sociologists, such a study, I believe, might prove extremely valuable.

Among the various psychological aspects of this opposition between work and non-work activities, we should at least notice here contrasts in the sense of time. Industrialism, dominated as it is by the desire for speed and output, has increasingly introduced into work activities a 'time technique', which seems to be experienced differently by different individuals. The life of pre-machine civilizations was characterized by what Lucien Febvre, in his *Problème de l'Incroyance au XVIe siècle*, called 'floating time, dream time', based upon natural rhythms. Recent studies of half-rural and half-industrialized communities in France report on the difference in sense of time between industrial and rural workers living in the same geographical environment. In the same way ethnographers, when investigating the process of industrialization of so-called 'primitive' peoples, in negro Africa for instance, have noted their reactions to the introduction of an idea of time completely foreign to them.[23]

On the whole, modern working conditions in factories, offices, etc., appear to many of our contemporaries as the source of an oppression of spirit, to the challenge of which non-work activities constitute a reply. If we follow up this idea, we may be able to understand better the tremendous urge among all classes to 'return to Nature' during the intervals between work, whether long or short, at week-ends, or during vacations, and the increasing success of holiday camps with the rise in the average age of campers. This, too, suggests the way we should regard certain tendencies shown in hobby activities, i.e. as reactions against being machine-paced and organized from above, against standardized and ready-made objects, against work on the assembly line, in the stubborn pursuit of self-fulfilment in finished and meticulous art and craft work freely executed according to a personal rhythm.

In an intensive study of a community we can see and understand how people react to dissatisfaction in their work by watching how they behave during leisure hours. But industrial psycho-sociologists have also tried to study the subject directly by sample inquiries and participant observation. There are many scientific publications concerned with this question, not all of which are of equal value. Morris S. Viteles has made a shrewd analysis of this literature in his *Motivation and Morale in Industry*, while C. Wright Mills, in his book on American white-collar workers, has noted that the expression of work satisfaction varies according to occupation and professional level. It is less frequent, for example, among office workers (42 per cent) than it is among managers (74 per cent), among the semi-skilled (48 per cent) than among the skilled (56 per cent).[24] Erich Fromm, who quotes these figures, remarks very rightly that they are only derived from the conscious expression of dissatisfaction and would certainly be much lower if the unconscious depths were taken into account.[25]

There are in fact different mental levels at which this dissatisfaction remains unexpressed. First, in our competitive and conformist societies, where people apparently happy and contented are often considered 'well-adapted' and 'successful', while anyone expressing dislike of his job is regarded as a 'failure', many of those who feel dissatisfied hesitate to admit it even to themselves, much less to others, owing to the pressure of public opinion.[26] There are besides some people who not only are not ready to admit this dissatisfaction to themselves, but declare and believe themselves to be happy or satisfied in their jobs without being so in reality. Moreover, psycho-analytical experience has shown that the feeling of work dissatisfaction, or even of unhappiness, may be deeply repressed, as it can also be in marriage, many couples refusing to admit either to themselves or to others how ill-assorted they are and what a failure their married life has been. Nevertheless, in spite of verbal expressions of satisfaction, signs noticed by the analyst, such as dreams, nervous strain, insomnia, general fatigue, high blood pressure, ulcers, or other psychosomatic symptoms, may reveal the existence of these unconscious feelings. How many of the 74 per cent of managers, who in the inquiry referred to declared themselves satisfied with their work, would, if carefully examined, show symptoms of this kind? And would there not be even more cases among the workers and employees who gave affirmative replies to this question?[27]

I have myself been struck, when studying firms, by the answer often made about their assembly-line work by people who, during their first few months, had shown signs of restlessness and distress. They then settle down and refuse to run any risks or to gamble by changing their work in the factory or looking for another, more interesting and better paid job elsewhere.[28] They say they are 'satisfied', as did a woman worker I questioned in a watch-making factory in the Bernese Jura. For years she had been drilling the same hole at the same spot in the watch face; yet she refused to make the least change and would not even drill another hole in the same face. This is far from being exceptional. The desire for routine work, the 'habituation', to which such cases point, has a variety of causes into which we cannot enter here. But, clearly, the expression of satisfaction that accompanies it may often cloak an unconscious feeling of dissatisfaction, colouring the whole of life both at work and away from work. Moreover, if, as Fromm notes, the restlessness shown by a large labour turnover is a sign of dissatisfaction, conversely the steadiness due to this habituation is just as much a symptom of the same thing.

Work dissatisfaction, whether conscious or not, has a lasting and manifold influence upon the way in which life is lived apart from work. This is shown in the efforts to escape to 'subsidiary' activities. Now all escapism, the psychologists say, is behaviour of a more or less neurotic kind, accompanied in different ways by repression, partial separation from reality, frustration, and even sometimes by aggressive tendencies. When someone feels the need of escaping from his work, it is because it no longer plays the vital part in his life it should, as an outlet for his deeper needs or as a balancing factor in his personal development.

However, there are different ways of escaping during leisure hours — two opposed types of activity. At one extreme, there is the behaviour called 'killing time', and, at the other, genuine active leisure pursuits. 'Killing time' is a general feature of behaviour found among the masses in our technical civilization. The means of passive enjoyment are constantly being increased and new ways found, ever more artificial, hollow and mechanical, of 'having fun', of 'amusing oneself'[29] — a range infinitely varied according to income and taste. They are all ways of forgetting oneself, one's emptiness and extreme boredom, whether one is aware of it or not, to which work dissatisfaction has greatly contributed. The mad search for 'fun' may be a sign that someone is frustrated in his work and seeks compensation for it in the only ways that are *possible for him*. Let us not forget in any case that in our great industrial centres the cultural institutions available to the workers and which they are capable of using are very meagre, if not almost non-existent. We must take this fact into account when seeking to understand the way in which they spend their leisure (and still more when attempting to judge it) quite apart from any attempt to encourage popular education. Let us note in passing that in all the major languages a need has been found for an expression denoting this 'killing of time', such as the French *tuer le temps*, the German *die Zeit todschlagen*, etc. In the technical societies of capitalism the 'alienated' human being is unhappy. 'Consumption of "amusement" serves to repress the awareness of his unhappiness. He tries to save time and yet is eager to kill the time he has saved.'[30] Dissatisfaction with his atomized work is in my opinion one of the chief features of this alienation.

But it is also this that impels people towards an active use of leisure, which is one of the higher forms of escapism since it involves the personality more fully. But even in the case of those who find a partial means of self-expression and self-fulfilment in in such pursuits, it is nonetheless true that their working life is effectively sacrificed, being an empty and wearisome burden they carry on their backs. One can say therefore that such leisure pursuits are not a healthy way of achieving a balanced development of the personality but only a makeshift, unavoidable at a certain stage and in certain patterns of technical civilization. Thus, although these forms of escapism are more successful, they too in the psychiatrist's eyes are pathological in character.

THE LIMITS OF 'AUTOMATION'

Here the fervent adherents of 'automation' would be tempted to intervene, declaring that we are overestimating the importance of these points. The facts we state, they say, may of course be quite true and real, but they will soon be out-of-date. Automation will suppress most fragmentary and repetitive jobs and so increasingly alter the data of the problem. Moreover, the jobs that remain will be intellectually revalued and upgraded by being enlarged, a process the importance and possible benefits of which we have already underlined.

It is quite true that not only are advances being made in automatic working — this is one of the most striking features of our time — but also that automatism, when complete, tends to eliminate all simplified jobs, which then become mere 'stop-gaps' in mechanization, as I recently called them.[31] They would be operations still provisionally entrusted, for technical or financial reasons and often for both together, to nervous systems of flesh and blood instead of being performed by mechanical and electronic systems, by 'metal limbs'.

Automatism has upset all former technical qualifications. Some are suppressed, others transferred, and there are new creations, which give a new status to those engaged in such occupations, since they require attention, and sometimes initiative, as well as almost always responsibility. This increase of responsibility, say the directors of the Union of Automobile Workers (U.A.W.-C.I.O.), does much more than compensate for the reduction in physical effort and manual skill that is required.[32] This is the sector of 'automation' which has at the moment captured the interest of a large number of serious observers, technicians and specialists. During recent years it has also given rise in Europe as well as in the United States to a whole journalistic literature, which has become a fashionable craze, being fed by speculations derived from cybernetics, many of which are quite devoid of any scientific basis. I shall return to this in the final chapter. It is the fate of all great movements of ideas to become the fashion and have a halo thrown around them, and those of our time have suffered badly in this respect. But this is not the fault of their originators, and we cannot in all fairness attack Bergson or Freud for all the exaggerations of their doctrines to which their success has given birth. As regards cybernetics to-day, however, we must recognize that the reckless way in which some of its pioneers, and particularly Norbert Wiener, have rushed into the social and economic spheres, has encouraged the misleading ventures of certain of its commentators and adherents.[33]

We do not wish to underestimate the capital importance of this widespread movement towards automatism, or the way in which it is bound to affect the future of our industrial societies and enhance the dignity of the producer as a human being. Nevertheless, we must face the realities of to-day and remember that the sector of automatized work is still far from predominant, as I have already indicated in my preface.* Of course I am not blind to the forces that make for a growing introduction of automation into more and more branches of industrial activity, administrative and commercial, or to its financial and technical advantages. But the factors offsetting this are equally powerful. These new techniques require new resources, resources in money and materials (capital, special machines and equipment) and resources in human beings, specialists, skilled foremen, executives and technicians. In no country can we hope to build up either of these at any given speed, nor can the adoption of the new techniques be imposed upon producers and administrators at all levels, or upon the trade unions either, without arousing forces of inertia, or even actual resistances, commensurate with the magnitude of such a technical transformation.

THE LIMITS OF JOB ENLARGEMENT

Job enlargement on the other hand is far from providing, either immediately or in the near future, a universal solution of the problem, and this for a combination of reasons which can be easily grasped. Let us consider the case of International Business Machines. In discussing its experiments Walker did not conceal the fact that a number of favourable conditions were here found together. The product was of high quality, complicated and

* Cf. pp. xvi–xvii.

delicate, and there had been a previous selection of staff. A technical training could also be given within the business itself, and in consequence there was an encouraging possibility of promotion. Finally, and this is an essential point, the industry was expanding and so capable of absorbing immediately all 'displaced' employees.[34] Without this last condition, job enlargement would have been strongly opposed by the trade unions. Their agreement was conditional upon a whole series of previous guarantees, which convinced the workers that there was no question of any form of rationalization that might be opposed to their interests, such as is only too often the case.

Walker, taking everything into account, estimates that in the United States at the present moment job enlargement would be materially and morally beneficial in certain companies only; the jobs of some 500,000 workers might be affected.[35] That is a very small number compared with the 27·8 million (1950) engaged in mines and in industry in the States, among whom there are 11·7 million employed as semi-skilled workers and 2·8 million as labourers. It is true that the same trend exists in many firms where the directors have come empirically to the conclusion that changing tactics and ending the splitting-up of jobs makes 'things go better'. But they do so without being aware of the broader implications and human import of what they are doing, and without therefore taking full advantage of its beneficent effects.

Thus the sphere to which job enlargement is applicable at the moment is small in comparison with the numbers employed in industry. However, we must not forget that this new conception can also be of value to large sections of the 'tertiary' services, to those employed in offices and administrative work. Large companies, in which the staff is mainly composed of clerks, warehousemen, salesmen and delivery hands, have begun to apply it seriously, as we saw in the case of Sears Roebuck, the giant mail order firm, whose structure and significant experiments we have already described on the basis of the comments of James C. Worthy, manager of their Personnel Department.[36]

A TECHNICIAN'S UTOPIA

Thus, regard to the actual facts does not allow us to share the optimism of those who see in 'automation' and job enlargement a way of eliminating or revaluing all simplified and downgraded jobs in the near future, and thus involving the personality of all producers in their everyday work and enabling them to find satisfaction in it.

Such, however, is the belief of Peter Drucker, as expressed in his book *The Practice of Management*,[37] which also contains a masterly critique of orthodox Scientific Management as well as a lucid account of its decline. Drucker is an enthusiastic supporter of 'automation'. The 'new technology', to use his expression, 'will employ more people, and above all more people who are highly skilled and highly trained'.[38] Just as mass-production has had the effect of increasing most rapidly the numbers and proportion of the class of skilled and trained employees (this seems to us a very disputable generalization in the light of many statistical studies); and just as the unskilled labourer of yesterday has become the semi-skilled machine operator of to-day, that is 'a man of higher skill and education, producing more wealth, earning a vastly higher standard of living'; so, at this new stage in technical progress and thanks to automatism, industry will require more and more skilled and highly trained men — managers to think through and plan, highly experienced technicians and workers to design the new tools, to produce them, to maintain and direct them. Indeed, the major obstacle to the rapid spread of 'automation' in all countries will almost certainly be the lack of trained men.[39]

We are not at all unmindful of the immense *possibilities* of the 'new technology'. But we must know whether we are describing a glorious world of the future in which all problems are solved, including the social ones inseparable from a full utilization of technical progress; or whether, within the framework of the realities of to-day, we are trying to suggest ways by which millions of human beings can feel themselves to be human and can be recognized as such, gaining more genuine satisfactions and greater human dignity. Some optimists prefer to make lyrical guesses as to a far-off future rather than to observe things strictly as they are to-day. Drucker, at the beginning of a chapter in which he sketches what should be the 'human organization for peak per-formance', declares without more ado that this is the heading of a 'Manifesto'.[40] He is quite right; for the conditions he postulates in order to make a fragmentary job into an 'integrated whole'[41] are far in advance of the real situation, at a time when assembly line work is constantly on the increase in countries of the most diverse structure, and the end is not in sight. To say that every individual job 'must' constitute a distinct stage in the process of manufacture, and to add that its rhythm and speed 'must' depend exclusively upon the man doing it and not on those who precede him, is to cross out with one stroke of the pen the hundreds of thousands of jobs with a compulsory rhythm which have to be performed to-day, i.e. the huge family of machine-paced operations of which the assembly line is only one particular species. To maintain that work should always encourage and direct personal development, failing which it falls short of the full use of man's specific qualities and powers,[42] correctly states an ideal. But it should be compared with the actual social, economic and technical conditions of production in our industrial civilization. Here again we meet with the Utopian conception (which will one day become a reality, I agree, but when? and as the result of what long series of social adjustments?), according to which, thanks to the 'new technology',

> nobody will 'tend' machines; the semi-skilled operations servicing the machine will be performed by the machine itself. As a result, the worker, instead of being paced by the machine, paces it. He will determine what it does and how well it does it — by setting it, directing it, and maintaining it. His control is complete, and, because the production process is integrated, the way each man controls his own job shapes the performance of the entire operation.[43]

Moreover, within the framework of automation, what the enterprise must demand of the worker is to direct his efforts *willingly* and *entirely* to the goals of the group of which he forms a part. 'It cannot aim at acquiescence. It must aim at building an aggressive *esprit de corps*'.[44] From this point of view the worker or employee takes responsibility at every moment: for it is he who in fact controls and determines the quality of the whole process through the way in which he does his job and maintains his technical equipment. His contribution to the enterprise becomes thereby something infinitely more complicated than what orthodox Scientific Management since Taylor has been content to call 'a proper day's work'.

That is all very well, and once again constitutes an ideal we must strive to realize with all our might and main. But how can anyone fail to see that, *behind the technical presuppositions* upon which alone our mystical prophets of 'automation' insist, particularly the training of highly qualified staffs for direction, control and supervision, there are *social* conditions of vital importance without which the new technology can only be of value in a very limited number of cases? Walker, in studying the I.B.M. experiment in detail, was more clearsighted when he stressed the favourable factors which led to its success. The leaders of the American trade unions, on their side, insist with the utmost vigour upon getting guarantees, failing which they refuse to agree to a policy of automation. Among the chief of these are the re-employment, wherever possible within the enterprise itself, of all 'displaced' workers (which presupposes expanding industries), the retraining without loss of pay of semi-skilled workers whose jobs have been suppressed, an effective and universal system of pensions with a lowering of the pensionable age, the general introduction of a 'guaranteed yearly wage', and an increase of unemployment pay.[45] Drucker glosses over the existence of these problems,[46] and in this book never faces them directly.

The effects of automation form one massive economic whole, requiring in fact, if they are to be absorbed and humanized, planned decisions together with a re-examination of the system of free enterprise. Besides the very important measures just mentioned, there are others, needing proper co-ordination, which are inconceivable without the regular intervention of the State and a radical reform of social institutions.

If automation is to be widely introduced and have a beneficial effect, so its theorists tell us, a higher professional training must be given to many grades, and technological knowledge spread throughout the working-class, so that each function may be intellectually revalued and integrated as a whole. This requires a complete reform of our school and university system, something which private firms cannot undertake even if they wished to, however powerful they may be; it also implies that the whole of society should take a decisive step forward and remodel its institutions. Moreover, it is clear that the profits derived from 'automation' must be redistributed as fairly as possible throughout the population, so that its increased purchasing power should be able to absorb the increased mass of products thrown on the market by the 'new technology'. Last but not least, who can believe that in a

capitalist system of economy all the workers will 'willingly dedi-
cate'[47] their moral and professional powers to an enterprise which
does not fully associate them with its technical direction and the
distribution of profits, to any enterprise, that is to say, which has
not become structurally *their own*?

So, in spite of all Drucker's intelligence and vigour, I see in
certain of his prophetic theses a new form of what I recently
proposed to call the 'technician's Utopia'.[48] It is not his attitude
towards the possible developments of automation that is in itself
Utopian, for these developments may very well be of overwhelming
importance for mankind's future in industrial communities. What
is Utopian is to imagine that the realization of this magnificent plan
depends exclusively upon technical conditions, and to overlook the
importance of the social and human context in which automation
is developing. Only such a schematic view can possibly lead one to
think that job enlargement and 'automation' will eliminate all
forms of 'atomized labour' in the very near future.

While we must be on our guard against a dangerous mystique,
whose obvious weaknesses only reinforce by way of reaction the
obsolete ideas of Scientific Management, we can nevertheless see
in job enlargement a very important turning-point in our technical
civilization. The subdivision of jobs, constantly on the increase
during the development of the machine age from the end of the
eighteenth century onwards, will in future appear, not as a one-way
process of unlimited duration, but as a transitory form of labour,
and often a pathological one, if we consider it in relation to some of
our deeper human needs.

THE CRISIS OF POLYVALENCE

At the beginning of this book I asked whether the new techniques of production had not caused a crisis affecting the craftsman,
the polyvalent producer or 'general practitioner', in all spheres.
Is he to disappear and to be replaced by all sorts of specialisms?
And in the realm of mind is the philosopher destined to remain the
last and only representative of an all-embracing activity to which
nothing human is alien? Even in philosophy specialization has
made many inroads since the time of the great encyclopaedic
followers of Descartes, the most accomplished of whom was
Leibnitz. 'Synthesis as a specialism', which was demanded by

Auguste Comte,[49] is still valuable in the natural sciences to-day for a grasp of the whole and a co-ordination of problems. But it certainly no longer has any standing in the human sciences or in the promotion and application of the techniques of politics, economics, industry and administration. It seems true that poly-valent activity to-day is passing through a crisis long ago fore-shadowed by the advance of the machine age. At the same time we are watching a series of regroupings due to a complicated dialectic. There is the consolidation of fragmentary operations in apparatus possessing a variety of implements, such as we see in many modern machine-tools. Then there are the recombinations spontaneously made as the result of the development of techniques in supervision and maintenance. And lastly there are systematic regroupings, such as those resulting from job enlargement.

But this new movement, although it is bound to spread with the progress of automatism and the appearance of new functions, is neither a general solution nor a panacea. It cannot cover all sectors of economic life in the ever-changing realities of production to-day. Moreover, job specialization, which results from a search for ever-greater efficiency, speed and precision, has by no means lost its original momentum. Its impulse continues and cannot but con-tinue. For anyone unwilling to delude himself, to become engrossed in dubious speculations about a distant future or to be involved in an all too fashionable craze, it must seem highly probable that for several generations yet there will remain a multitude of jobs in which the worker can find no outlet for his tastes, his deeper wishes, or his personality. Even a radical reform of society, even the collectivization of the means of production and the integration of the worker into his firm as a full member with equal rights, will not endow such work with the scope and interest necessary to make it the centre of his life and a means of self-fulfilment. Thus every-thing points to the growing importance of leisure time for the humanization of our technical civilization.

CHAPTER VIII

Milestones, Problems and Possibilities

THIS STUDY, which is concerned only with the recent development of a few aspects of the division of labour, does not in
fact allow of any dogmatic conclusions. Nevertheless, the
reader would undoubtedly feel frustrated if before the end we did
not take a broader view and relate our experiences to some of the
important problems which face technical civilization to-day or are
likely to face it in the near future.

I. A HYPOTHESIS: THE DISPLACEMENT OF EQUILIBRIUM

Before the era of intense mechanization in which we are still
living, whose beginning was marked by the patents of James Watt,
we may consider European society, the 'Christian civilization of
the West', as a balanced system. Technical progress there was, it is
true, as recent historical studies have demonstrated.[1] But the
alterations to which it had given rise since classical antiquity were
relatively slow, nothing like to-day's violent and massive changes.
Since the beginning of the last century this system has seen an
enormous advance in the natural sciences and in their application
to everyday life, the one constantly stimulating and increasing the
other. This advance has completely revolutionized the means of
production and the conditions of life of hundreds of millions of
people. It has split up the traditional trades, many of which had
remained almost unchanged from ancient times, it has accentuated
the division of economic functions and has disseminated automatic
processes of an ever more refined character. It has in short introduced into this system, which has been hastily extended to other
countries and other continents, a disturbing factor of enormous
range, of which the increasing fragmentation and overspecialization of jobs, our main concern in this book, is only one of the
elements.

In the physico-chemical sciences the famous laws of Gibbs, Van't Hoff and Le Chatelier inform us that a modification of any one of the conditions determining the chemical equilibrium of a system causes a reaction leading to a variation in the opposite sense to that of the external condition which was modified.[2] In other words, when a system of this kind is properly balanced, a modification of one of the factors maintaining the balance causes a displacement of the system, tending to lessen the effect of the disturbance. We certainly do not want to compare the whole of a complex civilization to a system of molecules, but it is possible to suppose that similar reactions may take place in a social environment, and to notice that this law of the displacement of equilibrium describes a process of the same order as the feedbacks studied by cybernetics. So, in the case of the 'system' formed by our technical civilization, one would expect that, from the moment when the drive towards specialization attains a certain degree of range and intensity and thus modifies the whole pre-existing state of equilibrium, a counterbalancing displacement will occur and tend to lessen the effects of the disturbance. Are we not then observing, in the mid-twentieth century, the first signs of this counteraction shown in the increasingly marked propensity to extend the scope of jobs, to recombine and enlarge them? If so, we are witnessing the birth of an already deep-rooted movement, aimed at lessening the violent effects of work specialization of all kinds — effects constantly on the increase and tending to upset the balance of society. In the same sense the forms of specialization, considered by Durkheim as 'abnormal' manifestations of the division of labour, will have to be subsumed in, and explained by, one general law of the displacement of equilibrium. In the course of the next few decades we shall be able to judge whether or not this movement making for job enlargement and consolidation really corresponds to a widespread and deep-rooted reaction, such as is suggested by the hypothesis we have just put forward.

Moreover, the idea of counteraction which is implicit in the Van't Hoff-Le Chatelier law, may itself be interpreted in the classical terms of Hegel's dialectic. Actually, in generalizing the definition of a feedback and applying it to all forms of servo-mechanism, the cyberneticians see in the phenomena in this vast field a process with three phases. What is a servo-mechanism if not a device (James Watt's fly-ball governor was one of the first mechanical models) by means of which a variation in an effect, going beyond certain definite limits, leads to a counteraction and a variation in the cause, which in its turn changes the variation of the effect? The passage from system A to system C through system B, due to the mechanism of self-regulation, may be considered as an attempt to secure a new equilibrium or synthesis at a different level. There is thus a never-ceasing and contrasted evolution, action leading to reaction, *according to a threefold rhythm*.

Such a scheme, it may be worth while to note in passing, is also to be found in the biological doctrines of Bergson. Although at the end of *L'Évolution créatrice* he severely criticized the philosophy of Spencer, who was content, he says, 'to reconstruct evolution with fragments of the evolved',[3] Bergson was himself influenced by Spencer's thesis that biological evolution has proceeded from the homogeneous with its unspecialized functions to the heterogeneous with its more and more specialized ones. So we find in his interpretation of biological and social phenomena the idea of reciprocal action, of a 'balancing' between unity and homogeneity on the one hand and multiplicity and heterogeneity on the other. This can be seen, for instance, in the following passage from *L'Evolution créatrice;*

> So, among the dissociated individuals, a single life goes on moving: everywhere the tendency to individualize is opposed and at the same time completed by an antagonistic and complementary tendency to associate, as if the manifold unity of life, drawn in the direction of multiplicity, made so much the more effort to withdraw itself on to itself. A part is no sooner detached than it tends to reunite itself, if not to all the rest, at least to what is nearest to it. Hence, throughout the whole realm of life, a balancing between individuation and association. Individuals join together into a society; but the society, as soon as formed, tends to melt the associated individuals into a new organism, so as to become itself an individual, able in its turn to be part and parcel of a new association.[4]

If this to and fro movement, in the form Bergson gives it, takes place primarily between individuation and association, it is its likeness to the dialectic of the homogeneous and heterogeneous that is of interest to us here. The history of labour, as we have stated elsewhere, shows a similar kind of 'balancing' movement between activities, which are sometimes complex and sometimes simple, running alongside a parallel development of implements.

Economic life was controlled by the artisan's methods of work long after the coming of industry and the beginning of our industrial revolutions, and these methods survived until quite recently in the polyvalent training and manual skill of many of the craftsmen in industrial workshops. Job specialization has now substituted for them the highly simplified operations described in this volume. We have thus seen that for some years past there has been appearing — as the result of a feedback circuit as it were — a growing number of complicated industrial and administrative jobs, in which a new consolidation of functions and of their corresponding aptitudes is taking place at a different level. But does this synthesis, which, to use Hegel's term, 'transcends' (*aufhebt*) the contradiction between the polyvalent artisan and the specialized worker with his fragmentary jobs, really take place at a 'higher' level? Or is it only on a different plane, and in different socio-technical conditions? Can one say that the worker supervising a very costly Giddings-Lewis reproducer represents a higher form of industrial activity, a group of tasks on a higher level, than those of the artisan? This would scarcely seem to be the case if we consider only the psychological nature of the aptitudes brought into play and not the worker's responsibility for the material objects used. However that may be, a new synthesis has been made on another plane and in another historical and cultural context.

II. FREUD AND THE PSYCHOLOGICAL FUNCTION OF WORK

The concept of equilibrium, which we have borrowed from a physico-chemical model to explain the transformations undergone by specialization in our technical civilization, is to be found in another form in Freud. He uses it in connection with work in a context strictly limited to the individual, as one would expect from him.

The notion of work, like so many other equally complex ideas, is ambivalent, or even polyvalent. Among the many inner contradictions characterizing it, one of the chief is the antithesis between freedom and constraint. Psychologists to-day have rightly seen, as we have already pointed out, that all activity subsumed under the idea of work implies a special element of pressure, of constraint.[5] This aspect of the definition of work is of growing importance in an epoch like our own, when producers at all levels, wage or salary

earners, engage in so many varied 'subsidiary activities' apart from
their job — activities differing from work precisely in the fact that
the element of economic pressure and institutional constraint is
absent, and choice and chance determine what they do.

This general statement is true enough, and we have seen how
valuable it has been in clearing up certain confusions by making an
overall distinction between work and non-work so that we may
consider more closely the 'free time' sector of life. It is, nevertheless, too superficial a distinction and does not explore deeply
enough the essence of so-called work activities to enable us to
understand the part they play in relation to the individual personality. In fact, very often when the personality is involved and
co-operates, work itself is something very different from, and more
than, compulsory activity undertaken for purely practical ends.
It may then constitute an important factor making for equilibrium
and development of the individual. Through it he comes into
contact with real life and in particular with the whole gamut of its
social and economic groups, from the small workteam to society as
a whole, passing through workshop, firm, and trade or professional
union, to name but a few stages.

This was acutely felt by Freud, when, at the end of his life, in one
of his last books, *Das Unbehagen in der Kultur*, he explained the
role played by work in the individual career and stressed its
importance as a balancing factor. It matters little that we may not
be ready to accept Freud's theories as a whole (I myself do not) and
refuse to consider the idea of the *libido* as a general explanation of
work attitudes. There remains his central thesis, which he outlines
as follows:

> Stressing the importance of work has a greater effect than
> any other technique of living in binding the individual more
> closely to reality; in his work he is at least securely attached to a
> part of reality, the human community. Work is no less valuable
> for the opportunity which it, and the human relations connected
> with it, provide for a very considerable discharge of fundamental
> libidinal impulses, narcissistic, aggressive and even erotic, than
> because it is indispensable for subsistence and justifies existence
> in society. The daily work of earning a livelihood affords especial
> satisfaction when it has been freely chosen, i.e. when through
> sublimation it enables use to be made of existing inclinations, of
> instinctual impulses, hitherto repressed, or more intense than
> usual for constitutional reasons.[6]

It is true that Freud rightly restricts the sector in which the ✓
balancing virtues of work have full play by observing that they
afford 'special' satisfaction to those who have been free to choose
their own careers in relation to the whole of their tastes and
capabilities. Certainly many highly unsatisfactory jobs exist to-day
in all human societies, as they have always existed, in the Middle
Ages, not to go farther back than that, as well as during the
manufacturing era and the cruel rise of industrial capitalism. There
are low paid jobs, performed under unhealthy conditions, in bad
physical and moral surroundings in town and country, mines and
ports, where workers, poorly fed and poorly housed, are constantly at loggerheads with those who employ and control them.
These jobs by no means correspond to the kind of work which
Freud is describing when he refers to its beneficial effects on the
individual psyche. But here again we must beware of generalizing
and simplifying too quickly. It is not uncommon to find work-
people who have had to give up rough, hard and fatiguing jobs
owing to illness or old age and who yet look back on them with
regret, quite apart from the loss of wages and companionship, and
are drawn to revisit their old haunts in spite of a past so full of evil
memories. It is astonishing what attachment people sometimes feel
for the mines and building yards, the big industrial factories and
large administrative offices in which they have worked, notwithstanding the physical and moral conditions under which they have
suffered for so long.

Without entering on a philosophical discussion we ought at
least to point out here how Freud, by using the idea of *work as a
balancing factor*, fits into his system the fundamental role it plays
in the life of the human species, while reducing it to the purely
individual level. If work can play the vital part in many people's
lives rightly assigned to it by Freud, it is because it is an essentially
human and creative activity, the very activity that distinguishes
man as *homo faber* from every other species of animal and which
has raised him above the others. It is by work that man with the aid
of constantly improving tools changes his environment and as a
result may change himself — for better or for worse! It is work
that raises man, as soon as he produces his own means of sub-
sistence, above biological time and gives character to human
history, of whose movements it is at once the explanation and the
underlying cause. As Marx says, 'By thus acting on the external

world and changing it, man at the same time changes his own nature.'[7] It is not surprising that an activity which is essential as a determinant of species as well as in the history of human societies should be just as essential a determinant for the individual microcosm, enabling him to understand his successes and his failures, his own individual history.

III. SOME EFFECTS OF LOSS OF WORK: OWING TO UNEMPLOYMENT

The extraordinary importance of the part played by work in the life of the individual can be empirically confirmed by observing how men behave when deprived of it. We have already made a cursory reference to the case of those who have retired or are unemployed. Recent studies by industrial sociologists have begun to throw light on their behaviour, and so, without being able to go into detail here, I should like to look more closely at the facts.*

To understand properly the effects on an unemployed person of losing his work, we must remember first of all that in every type of job unemployment hits the less skilled first,[8] i.e. precisely those who are least able to adapt themselves to a new situation and most liable to feel insecure. Loss of work is often preceded by a period of anxiety, an anxiety which is aggravated when it occurs. The unemployed person shows signs of an emotional instability which increases more or less rapidly and intensely in accordance with his occupational history and the successes or failures he has previously experienced during his working life.[9] Various American and British investigators have studied the stages of behaviour through which men commonly pass when they lose their work, although of course there are many individual differences which they have noted. It has been observed generally that after a first period of shock, when the personality resists and remains almost unchanged, there comes a second in which there is a more or less active search

---

* Let me also remark in passing that on rereading case reports, some made at the end of last century by Freud, and others quite recently by certain of his followers, I have noticed that many of their patients seem to lead an idle life, enjoying an income large enough to relieve them of any need to work and indeed of any object in doing so. I have therefore wondered whether, even according to Freud's own hypothesis, this 'deprivation of work-activity' does not actually play a more important practical part in the origin of some neuroses than many psychoanalysts seem ready to admit.

for work, the worker's demands constantly decreasing until a paid job of any sort would be accepted. Finally a stage of depression ensues. The loss of the settled framework provided by a job and its daily routine, combined with a decreased awareness of the passage of time and a kind of apathetic attitude towards it, unite with family complications to produce in the unemployed man a growing inferiority complex as regards the members of his family and particularly his wife and children.[10] As an American said to a social worker:

> What do you think all these things do to me? They certainly don't add to my self-esteem, to my happiness. At times I boil inside, but most of the time I feel licked. I never imagined that the peace of my home and my control over my children depended upon my job. Why, the job just rules your life.[11]

Freud has rightly seen that work connects the individual with the human community. But it is paradoxical that he has nowhere declared that work is also one of the most active ways in which the individual is linked to the family group, forming in many cases its indispensable cement without which both the group and the individual become unbalanced and disintegrate. French observers agree on several of these points with the American investigations. Loss of work, while constituting a social setback for the unemployed person, also produces after a while a 'toxic condition' requiring complete readaptation. A long period of unemployment is in truth a threat to mental health.[12]

OWING TO RETIREMENT

The study of the psychological aspects of the loss of work owing to retirement has not as yet led to any systematic investigations, notwithstanding the growing interest in Anglo-Saxon countries in problems of 'ageing', and the achievements of gerontology in France. The development of social and demographic conditions, the effects of technological progress (automatism), and the human wastage occurring in certain occupations such as mining, combine in the long run to cause a continual increase in the number of people retiring from active employment and a lowering of the age at which this occurs.

The factors involved are of different kinds and are connected in

many different ways, so that their effects are still further complicated. In France, where they have been clearly analysed by teams
from the *Institut national d'Études démographiques*, they certainly do not all, or always, point in the same direction.[13] Nevertheless, if we take into account the increase in the average
expectation of life, the changes in birth and death rates and the
occupational spread of the population according to age, and
remember that the growth of automatism, according to the most
favourable view, will not increase the number of available jobs (not
to mention what Alfred Sauvy rightly calls the 'economic Malthu-
sianism'[14] of France), we can foresee that, in many fields of employment, competition will grow keener and keener and there will be a
more and more pronounced tendency to lower the age of retirement.
Similar predictions are being made in quite a different economic
and demographic context by reliable American observers.[15]

Psychological reactions to retirement differ greatly; they depend
upon the character of the work previously done, upon whether the
worker wishes to retire or not, and whether he is or is not prepared
for it. There are also other factors; the likelihood and possibilities
of part-time work, the scope of his 'subsidiary activities', his
family ties, and the material conditions, particularly housing,
produced by his retirement.[16] How do those who have retired
regard their previous place of work and former colleagues? Some
American inquiries report that they appear indifferent to them.
But these studies deal with workers of foreign origin, comparatively
recent immigrants, whose job was their chief, and sometimes their
only, link with American society. Once they lose it, they fall back
upon their family and their original ethnic community.[17] There is
no doubt that attitudes vary according to type of employment, and
other investigations suggest, for instance, that those retiring from
occupations in which little skill is required, who have been
restricted to simplified jobs without much interest, are particularly
addicted to hobbies, as though seeking in them more responsibility
and greater satisfaction than they had had during their working
life.[18]

But the most telling fact in my opinion is one brought out by
Jean Daric in his fine study of the problems of ageing.[19] The death-
rate of people of advanced age who are still at work is no higher
than that of those who have retired. English statistics, which are
more detailed than the French on this point, even suggest that the

death-rate is distinctly higher among those who are no longer working.[20] The abnormally high mortality occurring during the year following full retirement also illustrates very clearly the force of the psychological shock caused by the sudden cessation of working life at the end of a career. It is one of the great *rites de passage* connected with human life. Jean Daric quotes the conclusions of Toulouse, Carlson, Lewis and Kardiner in support of his views, reminding us how closely the biological and psychological factors are interwoven. He writes:

> The biologists realize that the whole process of ageing is much less marked where each of the different faculties (physical, intellectual, temperamental) ages uniformly. The sudden ending of the activity connected with one or several of these faculties leads to a distortion which speeds up this whole process of ageing. To grow old properly one should grow old uniformly. This is true physiologically, but still truer perhaps psychologically. A breach of continuity between two different rhythms of life, and the realization that one is no longer socially useful, which does not come so long as one is working, are therefore a disaster.[21]

This explanation of the vital part work plays in our lives completes rather than contradicts the Freudian interpretation of work as a 'factor of equilibrium'.

WORK AND MENTAL HEALTH

The importance of the role of work in the psychological balance of the personality has also been confirmed by certain recent experiments. In fact I do not hesitate to say that they completely upset our ideas of hospital psychiatry and of how mental illness should be treated. I shall only touch upon them here in so far as they throw light from another angle on the general problem of labour in our technical age.

They actually concern this problem very directly and in a variety of ways. First it is becoming more and more apparent that the growth in the number of mental diseases can only be explained by certain features of our industrial civilization and of its increasingly artificial, powerful and widespread *technical environment*, the influence of which is growing ever more prevalent, varied and compelling. Statistics provided by the World Health Organization, although far from exact, except for certain countries such as the

United States and Sweden — we must also be careful not to over-simplify such complex problems as that of suicide — suggest that the mental health of highly industrialized countries has greatly deteriorated.[22] Half the hospital beds of the United States are occupied by mental patients, and during the Second World War 17·7 per cent of those not accepted for the American army were refused owing to psychopathic disorders or deficiencies. The United States devotes more than a thousand million dollars yearly to the treatment of the mentally sick, four people out of every thousand being in institutions, with a record of 5·5 per thousand for the State of New York. Highly industrialized nations, like England, France and Holland, also show disquieting figures for such hospital patients, which reach about 2·5 per thousand. A comparison of the rates of suicide and alcoholism show that these four countries also have the highest rates for both, the United States and France having respectively the highest and second highest rates for alcoholism and the fifth and sixth for suicide. The very clear relationship that exists between the two series of rates as a whole makes it impossible to doubt that these are, generally speaking, symptoms of a lack of mental balance in the populations concerned.[23]

Between the two World Wars it had already been noted by Maurice Halbwachs that the increase of material prosperity in Europe had been accompanied by a growing number of suicides.[24] Psychiatrists do not hesitate to-day to attribute this directly to the new environment created by our technical civilization.

In such surroundings, writes Dr Paul Sivadon, the new relationships set up between the world and man 'sometimes develop too quickly to be incorporated in the nervous systems of the weaker members of society. Thus at times contact is broken, the gap between the world and the individual is increased, and dissociation, in fact alienation, may appear'.[25] Along with changing conditions of work during the last hundred years has gone an 'increase of implements and machines which have formed a screen between man and his natural surroundings'. Reminding us that for these natural surroundings a 'technical environment', as we have called it, has been substituted, Dr Sivadon adds: 'Those too immature to be able to keep in contact with the real world through this screen can only preserve their mental balance by means of satisfying human relationships.'

Other authors, such as Russell Fraser,[26] have stressed the spread of neurosis among industrial workers, and have described the way in which it makes its appearance. Our technical age, as it is developing at present, seems to make too many demands upon the most complex and delicate functions of the personality, subjecting the means of adaptation to too severe a test. Many people called 'normal' conceal their lack of adjustment beneath all sorts of escapism, of 'fun' and 'amusement', such as are to be found everywhere in city life. Or, if they still know how to, and are able, to unbend far from the madding crowd, they take to camping or a nomadic existence, relaxing on the beaches or in the mountains, where they can live in a more primitive way. Thus they allow their higher, more recently developed and more labile functions to lie quiescent for a time. But not everyone succeeds — far from it — in making up for the absence of satisfaction in work, for the ever-recurring strain of the environment, the fatigue, boredom and many minor upsets that are due to it. How many of our contemporaries, gradually worn out by this strain and by their vain efforts to escape from it, are finally numbered among the neurotics who in a real sense 'find it difficult to live' in an alien civilization, whose maltreated and unhappy 'stepchildren', to use Karen Horney's vivid word, they become![27]

These 'asylums', constantly filled to overflowing with new cases (about 5,000 in France every year, 1,000 for the Seine Department alone), which like a tidal wave threaten to engulf them, are the direct heirs of the old 'Bedlams' and continue their disastrous mistakes. In these 'madhouses' of France and England with their padlocked cells, from which only one per cent of the chronic psychotics who have been incarcerated in them for more than two years have ever any chance of escaping,[28] new curative methods of treatment have been developed by pioneers using work techniques. Though still mere islands of hope, they have, wherever introduced, increased the cases of cure or improvement by 40 per cent. Of course there were workshops for mental patients in certain asylums before, and such still exist. But there is a world of difference between the methods we advocate and the often brutal enforcement of manual labour, intended as a discipline rather than a cure, such as they prescribe. Occupational therapists consider these survivals, which are valueless when not harmful, as dangerous caricatures of the new methods. Work as planned in the new way is accepted, and often indeed desired by the inmates, and forms part of a truly therapeutic communal life. It is gradually made more complicated; special materials are selected, and it is performed with a sense of its social value, being paid for as such. The whole is run by a specially trained staff, able to give each patient, treated as an individual and not as a case, a sense of security and confidence, and seeking to rebuild for him a system of human relationships as well as providing for him, if he feels the need, means of plastic and symbolic self-expression (bulletins edited and printed by the patients, dramatic work, drawing, painting, etc.).

The most remarkable example of this in France is the establishment run by Dr P. Sivadon and his colleagues at Ville-Évrard (Seine et Oise). Its success would have led to the creation of a whole network of similar institutions in France, if in this field as in others a scientifically conducted experiment could have easily overcome intellectual and administrative habit and made up for the absence of bold planning and lack of funds.[29] I have visited curative centres of the same kind abroad, among others the Saint-Willibrord institution at Heiloo in Holland (Dr J.-P. de Smet), and the workshop organized by the Unit for Research in Occupational Adaptation at Banstead in Surrey, England, under the direction of the Maudsley Hospital, where Doctors J. Tizard, N. O'Connor and G. M. Carstairs have also obtained striking results.[30] One should see the state of schizophrenic, paranoid and other chronic psychopathic patients, herded together in crowds in centres where they vegetate, full of anxiety or completely crushed, facing from morning to night their insoluble problems, or silently locked in their own inner hell, having, as one of them, an English working man, confided to a psychiatrist in my presence, 'clearly nothing to say to oneself any more'; one should compare the condition of such people with that of their fellows, who, with the extra space and money provided, have been released from all this and been given workshops where they can start on light work in small groups, for which they are paid and whose organization is flexible so that they can build up social attitudes once again and acquire human relationships and interests, and a sense of responsibility. Thus they are able to regain contact with their material and moral surroundings, and learn to restructure and readapt their personality to a world they can assimilate, before being returned (with the necessary precautions) to the one which has so cruelly maltreated them.

I cannot here attempt any psychiatric description of these experiments, nor give in detail the complicated biological, physio-therapeutic, psychotherapeutic and sociotherapeutic techniques of which these methods are composed, differing as they do of course from one specialist to another. What matters to us is that here again we have found in the domain of mental pathology the great principle which stresses the vital importance of work in maintain-ing or restoring the balance of the personality. There are, it is true, harmful forms of work in a technical environment, which gravely impair the psychic equilibrium of millions of men and women in our industrial societies, although of course there are many other causes, individual and social, which form a complex of which we are well aware. But work as part of a new therapeutic whole enables us to deal with this dramatic process of mental decay, helping many patients to rebuild their personality, giving them back a satisfying life in a society they are able to serve instead of being a charge upon it, indeed one of its heaviest and most terrible burdens.

IV. ONE SPECIALIZED WORKER AMONG MILLIONS

In the course of previous chapters I have often referred to the results of inquiries, made among anonymous samples of workers, which have been statistically evaluated. This process is justifiable when it is a question of scientific studies undertaken with the necessary care and caution in order to secure an overall view apart from any particular behaviour. Nevertheless, it seems worth while to illustrate these investigations, when we have the chance, by reporting a concrete case, the evidence of a particular person. So I shall use a workman's report as a significant document character-istic of a whole group, of which it is a striking and individual expression. I do not regret having in a former work discussed at length a book by a working man, Georges Navel, whose narrative gives us a real insight into the inner attitudes and feelings of many French workmen.[31] An interview recorded in 1954 by Robert H. Guest, from whose important book, written in conjunction with C. R. Walker, I have already quoted, is much more limited in scope, but merits a careful analysis to enable us to grasp and understand more fully in their day-to-day actuality the worker's reactions to the specialized jobs of 'mass-production'.[32]

Joe, an American workman, is thirty-six. He is married and the father of two children. He earns about eighty dollars a week and will soon have paid off the mortgage by which he is buying his own home.

In 1940, hearing that a big motorcar firm needed semi-skilled workers for its assembly line and was offering high wages, he had the good fortune to be taken on. Having had some electrical training, he hoped, no matter on what job he started, to work his way up to a skilled post. He was made a spot welder on the front cowling. The work was very simple: at the end of a week he had learnt it all. Soon the war came, from which Joe returned to his factory in 1946. He then tried to get into the Maintenance Department as an electrician, but there was no opening, and he had to go back to the assembly line, the 'iron horse' as it was called in his plant; since when he has stayed on it.

His job is to weld the cowl to the metal underbody. 'The jig is all made up and the welds are made in set places along the metal. Exactly twenty-five spots.' The movement of the belt is strictly timed. He has one minute fifty-two seconds for every set of weldings. Every day he has a ten-minute breather in the morning, half an hour for lunch, and a few minutes stop in the afternoon. 'The cars differ, but it's practically the same thing. Finish one — then have another staring me in the face.'

There is no way of getting even ten seconds ahead. One is always running after the belt. Joe doesn't like working on it. 'No one,' he said, 'likes working on a moving line. You can't beat the machine. Sure, maybe I can keep it up for an hour, but it's rugged doing it eight hours a day, every day in the week all the year long.'[33] Joe has only been shown his corner of the factory, his segment of the line. In twelve years of work he has almost never seen a finished car roll off the final assembly line.

What he thinks about the time-study experts aptly fits those shops where, in accordance with the principles of authoritarian Scientific Management, everything is laid down for the worker from above.

> It's easy for them time-study fellows to come down here with a stop-watch and figure out how much you can do in a minute and fifty-two seconds. There are some things they can see and record

with their stop-watches. But they can't clock how a man feels from one day to the next. These guys ought to work on the line for a few weeks and maybe they'll feel some things that they never pick up on the stop-watch.[34]

Joe hasn't yet been worn down by mere habit. He feels, and clearly expresses, the tremendous gap there is between the job he is compelled to do in the factory and the work he would like to have. Everything is minutely calculated. 'You go by the Bible.' And yet, Joe observes, there are a lot of little things you could tell 'them' which might be useful, but 'they' never ask you. 'They' have a suggestion system, but the 'fellows don't use it too much because they're scared' (and this is a fear I constantly came across when investigating the workers' reactions to technological changes) 'that a new way to do it may do buddies out of a job'.

That in general outline is the work as Joe experiences it day after day. And yet he longs to do something in which he could really show his abilities, free his 'occupational potential', where he would have the feeling of accomplishment and of pride in work well done. 'I'd like a job,' he said, 'where you feel like you're accomplishing something and doing it right. When everything's laid out for you and the parts are all alike, there's not much you feel you accomplish. The big thing is that steady push of the conveyor — a gigantic machine which I can't control.'

'You know,' he added, 'it's hard to feel that you are doing a good quality job. There is that constant push at high speed. You may improve after you've done a thing over and over again, but you never reach a point where you can stand back and say, "Boy, I done that one good. That's one car that got built right." If I could do my best, I'd get some satisfaction out of working, but I can't do as good work as I know I can do.'[35]

Does Joe at least enjoy all those things which shrewd and wide-awake firms provide in the United States and elsewhere for their semi-skilled workers? Pleasant, well-lit and well-ventilated work-rooms, a guarantee of security, canteens, medical services? Oh yes! And Joe thinks that these conditions are all good in his factory, and that in this respect the company has done all it can. He is even allowed, if he hurries up with his twenty-five weldings, to speak to his neighbour. Is then the recent attempt to reform Scientific Management in the name of 'human relations', and to provide agreeable and social surroundings for factory work, capable of altering completely the feelings a worker has towards his job, of transforming its contents in his eyes? Joe's reply to this question is categorical, and its pathetic simplicity will move millions of other workers all over the world.[36] 'But you know,' he said to the interviewer, 'it's a funny thing. These things are all good, but they don't make the job good. *It's what you spend most of the time doing that counts.'**

Joe has few chances of promotion. Everybody produces about the same amount and earns the same wage. The work is so simple that there aren't many rungs in the firm up which to climb. In the factory itself the only 'opening' possible is to become a foreman, and that is a rare one. The firm reserves 'good places' for brilliant young men with degrees, smart College boys whom it engages and trains specially for such posts.

At this point in the story Joe's wife intervened as the result of a question from Guest. Throughout the interview, Joe appears as an excellent representative of many of his contemporaries, chained as they are by their needs (often created artificially for them by their environment) to a type of work they dislike and find it hard to put up with, 'enjoying' the fruits of our technical civilization and at the same time suffering from its effects. For Joe is also mentally a victim of his job, a potential neurotic, near to the point where he would add one more to the ranks of the 'unfortunate children' of American society. 'Often,' said his wife, 'I wish he'd get another job. He comes home at night, plops down in a chair and just sits for about fifteen minutes. I don't know much about what he does at the plant, but it does something to him. Of course, I shouldn't complain. He gets good pay. We've been able to buy a refrigerator and a TV set — a lot of things we couldn't have had otherwise. But sometimes I wonder whether these are more important to us than having Joe get all nervous and tensed up. He snaps at the kids and snaps at me — but he doesn't really mean it.'[37]

Such is Joe's condition, such his attitude and his reactions. He is but one 'semi-skilled' worker among many others. He despises his job, but does not dare to 'run the risk' of leaving it on the chance of getting something different and better. So he is bound, or rather chained, to his firm by the advantages of seniority and a pension to come, but above all by the certainty of a wage which enables him to be one of the innumerable consumers of the 'goods', such as a

* My italics.

refrigerator or a television set, which our technical civilization provides. It sells them comparatively cheaply, but the price paid by Joe and his like for their production is a high one, as can be seen from the interview just recorded.

V. THE CHIEF SIGNS OF ALIENATION IN WORK

That the case of this American workman, Joe, is not a special one is shown by numerous observations and by the analysis of sample cases similar to the one in which he took part. Barring a few differences due to career and character, the experiences of many of his fellow workmen resemble his own. The deeper levels of personality find no outlet in their work, which has become something quite foreign to them, so that in relation to it they are 'alienated'. In no sphere is this concept of 'alienation' (*Entfremdung*), which Hegel made the centre of his system and Marx revived, more applicable than that of man's work to-day. I shall now make a list of the main symptoms of this alienation as I have observed them in relation to the highly specialized jobs whose outlines and development I have been attempting to describe.

First, the work is *depersonalized*. Scientific Management as applied to mass-production has constantly tended to simplify and standardize jobs and to reduce the hierarchy of skills along with the scale of wages. This last process, we may note, has been encouraged in many countries by trade union action, which has been mainly concerned with improving the lot of the majority of union members and raising the wages of the lower paid. In most cases semi-skilled workers, whether men or women, have no hope of promotion in the shop itself save by becoming foremen, or perhaps multi-specialists, and there are at present few of these. Advancement means escaping from their work and transferring to a repair or maintenance post, or becoming a storekeeper or office-worker; but such openings are hard to come by and relatively rare.

Every day the semi-skilled worker sees many tasks almost identical with his own, neither better nor worse. Of course, anyone daily engaged upon such jobs will find that at times they present a different aspect, that there are inner variations. We are well aware of these, and studies of them have been made by various industrial psychologists.[38] Yet, however important these are to the worker and whatever their effect upon his attitude and reactions in the factory, he knows well enough that in the management's eyes such differences are minute, indeed negligible, so that he feels he is an 'interchangeable' unit. Thus he gets the sense of being anonymous, a mere cypher among a mass of other workers. This feeling is reinforced by the absence of any real participation in the business, since he neither shares in its decisions nor is given any responsibility. I shall return to this point later. This sense, moreover, is increased by the almost complete absence of personal relations with the executive staff, except for his immediate superiors, team leaders and foremen, and by the fact that the pay packet he receives at the end of the week or the fortnight is almost or exactly the same as that of all his fellows.

Along with this depersonalization, to which the semi-skilled worker is subjected, caught as he is in the strait-jacket of orthodox Scientific Management, goes the feeling that he can never complete any job, can never stand back and say he has achieved something himself and has done it well. Occasionally he shares a collective sense of pride, as when, for instance, his firm has put out a new and successful model. I have observed signs of this while listening to workers from certain big French firms discussing among themselves in front of the stands at the Motor Show. But such cases are in fact rare under present social and economic conditions, and they cannot make up for a sense of accomplishment, of having achieved something, such as might be frequently felt while at work in the factory itself.

All these features of alienation are intimately connected, overlapping and reacting upon one another. A depersonalized job, always incomplete, is also one that *lacks the sense of participation*. The most conscious theorists of Scientific Management, as well as its empirical popularizers, have tried to plan the carrying out of jobs so that the deeper capabilities and needs of the individual shall not be called into play. This is true in the most different spheres of activity, in industry, commerce and administration, and is to be observed in all continents, as much in 'underdeveloped' countries as in highly industrialized ones. The separation between planning and execution, a principle constantly applied because considered indispensable to technical progress and high output, is paid for by the non-participation of the individual in his work. But, to quote a famous American industrial relations specialist, one who has most clearly seen and denounced the terrible mistake of this point of view, 'Filling a space in the factory or office with his physical body, making motions designed by the minds of others, applying physical strength, or releasing the power of steam or electricity, are not in themselves contributions of the essential abilities of human beings'.[39]

These abilities are definitely excluded from the jobs performed day after day and hour after hour by the worker, who has no possibility of participating in them psychologically, morally or socially. On this point the methods of Scientific Management and the conclusions arrived at by the human sciences concerned with labour are completely at variance. The technician, looking upon man as a mere tool, seeks ways of having everything prepared for him in advance so that he can work as rapidly and effectively as possible. Psychologists and sociologists, insisting that man has a fundamental need to participate in the work he does, recommend that it should be organized in ways that would involve and develop and expand his personality as far as possible.

One of the principal causes of modern man's alienation lies in the absence of conditions of work allowing him to satisfy the deeper needs of his nature. We have already given many instances of this and have pointed to a solution *on the technical plane*. This would take into account both the reasonable requirements of planning and the fundamental needs of the personality. It would plan the work systematically at different group levels, beginning with the small team and ending up with the undertaking as a whole, and would maintain within each group the maximum of freedom and flexibility, its members being able to distribute and organize the work among themselves and take into account each person's capabilities, tastes and need for involvement.[40]

On the social plane this need of participation would find its expression and satisfaction in having a share in the running and direction of the business. Various ways in which this can be done already form a part of the history of industrial relations to-day, thanks to the pressure of the trade union movement. But the institutions that exist, such as the French 'Joint Production Committees', do not function in such a way that the mass of workers feel themselves psychologically involved. The reasons for this have been well described by certain special investigations.[41] Most workers remain alienated from their jobs, which seem to them merely a tedious, and sometimes even a degrading and exhausting, means of securing periodically a pay packet of a certain size. But receiving wages, although economically vitally important, neither implies nor leads to any real participation by the worker in the work for which he is paid. Peter Drucker quotes a remark by a skilled hand, a 'craftsman' of the old school, who had just decided to throw up a well-paid post in the motor industry. 'Why were you unhappy at Detroit?' he was asked. 'The whole place is like an unemployment exchange,' he replied. 'Even though they are in jobs, the guys behave and act as if they were out of work.'[42] That is a far-reaching remark. He had grasped the fact that, when work is done under conditions which are degrading and empty of all content, it becomes for the man doing it as if he had no work at all.

Industrial jobs, which have lost their content through being split up by the organization required by Scientific Management, necessarily lead to the worker *losing interest* in his work. This decrease in intrinsic content as well as in variety has been recognized by the orthodox, and an attempt has been made to readapt the accepted principles by interesting the semi-skilled worker in satisfactions outside his job and by providing physical and social surroundings to act as a kind of compensation: special lighting, colourful walls and machines, a canteen, easier relations with his fellow workers and immediate superiors and so on. Each of these measures is good in itself, but as a whole they tend to enshrine the abandonment of any attempt to restore a real value to atomized labour. This change in *emphasis, now put on what is not work*, must itself be considered as one aspect of alienation. The current practice among personnel officers, notes Douglas McGregor, is to look upon work 'as a kind of punishment to which people must submit in order to be able to find satisfaction elsewhere'.[43]

We must not minimize the importance of the compensation which some men, and still more women, find in the concessions made to them *in connection with* their work properly so-called: the right to smoke, to talk to their neighbours when the working speed is not too great, to have real relations with the executive staff, whom the new type of Scientific Management is training to be more understanding, more concerned for each individual worker, more conscious of the distant ideal of the 'human engineer'. But let us remember the remark Joe made in the course of the interview previously analysed: for the worker, in the final resort, it is 'what he spends most of the time doing that counts'.

From the observations and reports we have recorded in this book it is clear that for many semi-skilled workers engaged upon very fragmentary and repetitive jobs work is something disagreeable, lacking in meaning and interest and often in dignity, something that is in fact unnatural. Their comments show that they consider overspecialization bad, because it *deprives them of the valuable need to train* for a job and confines them to a purely muscular skill which becomes more and more a matter of habit; this skill can of course be perfected through constant repetition but leaves them with no difficulties to overcome and no objective save an increase in speed. Undoubtedly the part played by speed is not psychologically negligible, and we have already referred to the interest certain industrial psychologists take in it, even going so far as to make a new ideal out of the concept of speed as a skill. However, as English experiments in job enlargement show,[44] the satisfaction that comes from increasing one's speed cannot compare with that achieved by mastering a more complicated task. In short, the overspecialized worker is very often the victim of a sort of 'bad conscience', a subjective aspect of alienation, the influence of which should not be underestimated.

This attitude, let us note, is not peculiar to the manual worker, or to the office employee engaged in simplified work, like the multi-copier. I have noticed it in other occupations and types of employment involved in this tremendous movement. I have seen it in industrial designers who, in certain big research offices, specialize on a single type of machine; in planning departments, where the division of labour has affected the heirs of Taylor's Thinking Department in their turn; and, again, among surgeons forced to give in to a movement that has swept over their profession as over so many others, compelling them, for example, to specialize in a particular bone operation, which they repeat more and more often (as required by the very dialectic of specialization) until they perform it perfectly, but also, so one of them confessed to me, with increasing boredom.

A most interesting piece of research could be undertaken into people's reactions to certain very advanced forms of specialization. It seems to be accepted as a necessity by those in widely differing walks of life but is considered by many of them, so it appeared to me during the course of my interviews, as abandoning any attempt at a general view of reality, as mastering or dealing with any problem as a whole. Specialization then seems to them the tragic price we pay for technical progress, and in consequence they work with a bad conscience and find no real satisfaction in what they are doing. Erich Fromm goes so far as to say that war and what he calls 'robotism'[45] are two of the greatest dangers facing mankind to-day. I also have felt that many highly specialized people of very different levels of skill and technical knowledge are more or less consciously aware, when at work, of being attacked by a disorder which is troublesome and, at times, even profoundly alarming.

This uneasiness is all the more marked because very often, in spite of its high degree of specialization, their work is not concentrated on one activity, institution or business in which they are involved and to which they can give the best of themselves. They too are carried away by this vast flood of distracting forces, which overwhelm so many dwellers in our big cities and are now so widespread that they constitute a social phenomenon well deserving of a special and searching investigation. Many specialists, so one might think, ought to be free from this owing to the narrow limits of their specialism. But even these do not escape. Their work leads to alienation not only because of its excessive specialism but also because of the distracting conditions under which it is done.

First of all, like a growing number of their contemporaries, they are engulfed in the new environment of our technical age, characterized as it is precisely by the increasing number and pressure of the attractions and stimuli it offers, as much during hours of work as during hours of leisure. Besides, as a result of this very complexity, a well-known specialist is in constant demand. Whether engineer, doctor or surgeon, a skilled technician of authority in a definite sphere, whatever it may be, does not know where best to give his time. Organizations, both public and private, societies, institutions, individuals, all require him. The lure of money plays its part, all the more in that his needs grow with the growing complexity of the life in which he is involved. His environment also 'sticks' to him and may often spoil his work, leading the specialist to misuse his technical knowledge and to apply the same methods in supposedly similar circumstances without ever taking the time needed to study the situation or problem properly so as to get a real grasp of it. This *failure* to concentrate, marked by a lack of interest (it may even be boredom), frequently accompanies the dispersal of the specialist's energies. In other cases, this dispersal may be the result of a need for diversity. Allowing himself to be swept away by stimuli from all sides, and making no defence against them so as to retain his balance, the specialist comes to the point where he no longer considers it possible to act in any other fashion, in a more concentrated and deeper way which would bear more fruit, although perhaps it would not be so amusing. When once caught in this whirlpool he loses his 'bad conscience' of course; but he is not less, but rather *doubly*, alienated.

VI. GROWING AWARENESS, HOPES

Man's chances of finding means of self-realization and self-fulfilment in our technical age would be very small if there were not signs to-day of other possible solutions which therefore give us leave to hope. It is true that specialization, as it is developing at present, threatens both our sensitivity and our intelligence, and tends to increase the type of dry-as-dust *technical expert*, to deprive the individual of the sense of being personally involved and of accomplishing something, and to encourage instead a process of 'robot-making', some aspects of which I have just described. But here and there we find increasing signs that many are aware of what is happening and are showing a vigorous and healthy reaction.

On every hand we see people who are dissatisfied with what life has to give them and who try to regain possession of themselves to pursue real activities, and to find opportunities for participation, self-cultivation and self-enrichment. With this in view they utilize whatever means may come to hand according to their circumstances; they go to concerts or listen to good music on the wireless; they support enthusiastically the classical plays put on by the pioneers of the *Théatre National Populaire*, and try to make a choice between the better and the poorer TV programmes, although most of them have no standards to go by owing to lack of education. They make models of monuments or machines, paint or redecorate their rooms, build boats, work in the garden and take to any kind of activity into which they can throw themselves. Adult education is increasing. The business world itself has begun to realize that technical competence is not everything, and that specialism can be dangerous when not accompanied by a deeper culture, opening up new horizons.[46] But this brings us to the future of the humanities in education, about which point I must say a few words.

People with the most diverse backgrounds are now beginning to realize that the world to-day with its technical civilization needs more than at any previous epoch a real education, enabling it to profit from our cultural heritage, from the masterpieces of the past, which show us the nature and greatness of man when confronted by the uncertainties, hopes and fears of his human condition and destiny.

I have stated elsewhere[47] my conviction that, if the classical humanities are to be really fruitful and capable of answering man's pathetic questionings in the face of the unrestrained development of modern technology, they must be thought out afresh and remodelled both in spirit and in method, as must also be the training of those who teach them. It is only by their bold re-integration into a new humanism, such as our age requires, that they can be saved. But if the classical tradition can be rejuvenated and made available to all, instead of remaining encased in an out-of-date framework of Latin and Greek as the preserve of a happy few, it can be of incomparable assistance in man's struggle (which will continue during the rest of this century) to find a new balance and to control his environment. In 1950 I wrote:

> Whereas in the future the grammar school and *university* education of doctors, lawyers, politicians, magistrates, teachers and administrators, will have to be enriched with concrete social and economic matter, with a sense of history and of man's efforts, and even with technology, conversely future technicians, whatever their function and the level of their job, will need the firm support of the humanities upon entering into life.[48]

Nothing is more significant in this respect than certain new ventures taking place in the United States, where of course the dangers are greatest, since the tremendous pressure of technology is being exercised in a young society without traditions and lacking the protection of a long-established way of life.

The famous Massachusetts Institute of Technology (M.I.T.), that astonishing institution in which specialized research workers, engineers and architects are trained in the United States, now contains a School of Humanities and Social Studies, in which the courses given form an integral and compulsory part of the education of the Institute's 3,000 undergraduates. The aim of the School is 'to impress upon the student how important human relationships are in any society, and to develop in him the first-rate human and social values which must accompany technical competence if an individual is to make his maximum contribution as a citizen'.[49]

As J. E. Burchard, the dean of the School, forcefully declares, there is no question of putting back the clock and attacking specialization. Society to-day needs more specialists and better ones. But if the specialist has not had a 'liberal' education so that he is able to see his specialist knowledge as part of a whole set in space and time, he runs the risk of either limiting his interests to his narrow specialism, or else of naïvely going beyond his own field and making deplorable 'extrapolations', by which his authority is greatly diminished.[50]

At M.I.T. they are convinced that humanistic and social studies, just as much as technical and professional training, require to be approached with a mature mind. So they have refused to confine them to the elementary level and have spread them over the four years of the Institute's course. There is no attempt to give students 'universal' knowledge. During the first two years they all share in a common course, the core-curriculum, which consists of (a) the study of the foundations of Western civilization, with the accent on four societies of different periods, their history, philosophy and literature being made the centre of interest; (b) a choice between two series of courses and seminars, the one concerned with 'The United States: Ideas and Men', the other with 'Modern Western Ideas and Values'. The emphasis is laid on texts, i.e. contact with great writers, and on problems rather than solutions, so that students go out into life with a 'stronger feeling that a college education is something *they have* — to use continuously — not something they *have had*'.[51]

During the last two years of study, 'juniors' and 'seniors' select three subjects out of one of a number of fields, together with a fourth from another field to which they feel attracted and which they will study as a new interest. It is noteworthy that a student may also take two 'humanistic' subjects instead of two 'technical' ones without his training as a specialist being in any way compromised thereby.

Here in abridged form is a list of the nine fields from which technicians and research workers can choose their 'liberal' courses: History, Literature, Modern Languages, Music, Economics, Political Science, International Relations, Labour Relations, and Psychology. Each field offers a wide choice of subjects. Students are also free to use the School's libraries as well as its gramophone records to which they can listen in special audition rooms which are reserved by the hour like tennis courts and seem always to be full. There are also lectures and discussions, exhibitions of modern art and of ethnography, cinema clubs, and music, dramatic and choral groups.

One had only to talk to the teaching staff to be convinced that so far from being of second-class calibre, they were often of the very highest quality. The directors of M.I.T. are anxious that their School of Humanities should be able to rival the best centres of literary and artistic education in the States. 'In fact,' says Dean Burchard, 'the humanities and social sciences at M.I.T. have progressed to a point where they are given status entirely equivalent to that of the professional fields of science, engineering and architecture.'[52]

This experiment, intended to 'break through the opaque curtain which has needlessly separated technologists and humanists',[53] has obviously been conceived by clear-sighted people, its methods being carefully thought out. What will be the effect in the long run of such an education upon the young engineer specialists at M.I.T., once they are caught up in the technical whirl of the United States? How far will it enable them to resist its power and help them to full self-realization as men and as citizens? It is too early yet to give any answer to these questions.

Among other innovations of the same kind, let us next take that of the Bell Telephone Company, one of the largest firms in the United States. In 1953 it collaborated with the University of Pennsylvania in establishing at Philadelphia an Institute of Humanistic Studies intended for its 'executives', i.e. its middle and higher grade staff. For ten months, from September 1953 to June 1954, and for the same period in 1954–5, young staff members of the Bell Company were released from their jobs to go and live in Philadelphia, where they underwent a special training, the aims of which, as outlined for 1955–6, are summarized here:

A. — To widen the perspectives of potential future executives and enable them to understand and interpret the social, political and economic changes, both national and world-wide, which will influence the problems of corporate management to an increasingly greater decree in the future.

B. — To indicate the importance, impact and use of history, science, philosophy and arts in the world to-day, particularly as they influence large groups of people such as employees, customers and stockholders.

C. — To motivate participants to accept the concept of intellectual activity as a never-ending process to be continued throughout life. (We noted earlier the same concern among the directors of M.I.T. in relation to their students.)

D. — To compensate by a humanistic education for the one-sided attention given by young people, once they are in business, to the acquisition of further technical knowledge and competence, as the result of the climate of intense individual competition where they work.

E. — To offset a tendency to overconformity which is bound to occur in a business which is highly specialized and which promotes almost entirely from within the organization.

The methods used are flexible and intelligent, giving much more time to seminars and discussions than to formal lectures. The full curriculum consists of 550 hours of courses, i.e. about 16 hours a week, divided among 11 subjects: Practical Logic; Economic History and the History of Economic Thought; History and Aesthetics of Music; Art throughout the World (68 hours in all, spread over a period of 24 weeks); Literature: (*a*) How to learn to Read; (*b*) Comparative Literature; (*c*) Study of James Joyce's *Ulysses* (18 hours, spread over six weeks); the Social Sciences, i.e. Sociology, Anthropology, Psychology (42 hours, spread over 11 weeks); Ethics, i.e. the history of moral ideas and human values; History and Meaning of Science; Modern Architecture and Town Planning; Political Science and International Relations; American Civilization.

According to the intention of its founders the Institute of Humanistic Studies should be much more than a group of lectures, seminars and reading. It is spoken of as 'an experiment in total education',[54] in which the relations between the students themselves and between students and staff are as important as the utilization of the rich cultural resources of Philadelphia, with its museums, concerts, and scientific societies, filled out by visits to

New York and Washington, in all of which the students' wives are invited to take part.

Many other American experiments show the same concern. Of these let us mention two, both originating in Chicago. The first is the 'Committee on Social Thought' of Chicago University, which was established by the historian John U. Nef. He wished to transcend departmentalism and specialization and return to a humanistic education, based upon wholes and the relationships between subjects. The second is the 'Hundred Great Books' movement, which, although highly dubious owing to its naïveté, was encouraged by Robert Hutchins while he was Chancellor of Chicago University. It is a network of simple unpretentious clubs, where business men, generally belonging to the higher ranks of industry and finance, can meet privately and get mental food and refreshment by reading and discussing the 'hundred greatest books' in the world.

THE LONGING FOR CULTURE

This longing for culture is found in many countries at the most varied levels, and is a phenomenon of which we must take account if we are to judge rightly as to the effects of our technical civilization. For instance, it is owing to the progress of the book industry, and to a network of communications and distributors, that *Pocket Books* have been printed by the million in the United States and sold at 25 cents each. Many of these, it is true, are seasoned with 'sex' and 'crime', and many are badly compiled digests. But the majority are world classics, as David Riesman tells us, when reporting on a small industrial township of 75,000 inhabitants in the Ohio valley, where more than 750,000 of these *Pocket Books* were sold during 1951, in restaurants, drug stores and newspaper kiosks (*not* in book-shops).[55] This longing for culture is also to be found in the Soviet Union, in a completely different ethical and socio-economic background. Striking proofs of this have been reported by recent visitors to Russia, whose observations are similar to those I made during my pre-war and post-war visits, when huge State editions of the classics were already being flung on a constantly buoyant market, only to be exhausted in a few days.

The demand for popular education in France, which has been studied by J. Dumazedier, is paralleled in many other countries, although its expression is different. Spontaneous 'leisure'-time associations are springing up on every side and are as characteristic a feature of our modern age as the call for a new type of humanities. Here mass media play a part, which is often already a positive one. Their ambivalent character goes unrecognized by many critics of technical civilization. They see their dangers clearly enough but overlook the benefits and cultural value, even to-day, of such things as the wireless and television. We gather, for instance, from British investigations into the social effects of television, that it stimulates the curiosity of quite a number of viewers and leads to a wish to take part in the kind of activities watched.[56] Thus a 'journey' on TV, a concert, a talk, a ballet performance or a visit to an art centre, all arouse new interests. Books are read, real visits made to museums and libraries, and even, when finances permit, a journey undertaken for which the televised show has been a valuable preparation.

There are certain encouraging signs of the present situation which show that the battle is still undecided, that the destiny of mankind in our technical age *may* yet be glorious; for instance the reform movement which is freeing the teaching of the humanities from the antiquated framework in which so many of its clumsy defenders try to keep it, the ferment in popular education, and the contribution of the 'mass media of communication', which is bound to increase if an enlightened policy on the part of our rulers (the only possible hope in this sphere) will make these mass media into a means of individual self-realization and development instead of using them to support conformity and corruption. To these promising movements should be added those described in this book, i.e. the recombination and integration of jobs, running counter to the excessive subdivision of labour, the healthy reaction against the errors of Scientific Management, and the revaluation of certain sectors of working life, where the 'atomization of work' is losing ground through the introduction of new responsible, supervisory activities.

POSSIBILITIES OF PROGRESS

Let us stop here to consider in the light of the recent development of specialisms what possibilities of progress there are, and along what lines specialization is tending to evolve.

Along one line of development we can see it everywhere lessening and eliminating the drudgery connected with man's labour. Owing to the advance of automatism, the physical and mental operations that the worker is required to perform are decreasing in number and becoming easier all the time, thus approaching the 'press-button' ideal. This is well expressed in a slogan invented by the Ford Company and illustrated on two pages of the magazine *Life*. In front of a charming house, elegant in its simplicity, stands a shining 'Lincoln' decked out with phrases of wise advice intended for present and future owners: 'Your house has glass walls. Your kitchen is a technical marvel. Your clothes and furniture are the height of functional beauty. Work easily, play hard.'

This inversion of a current maxim* for publicity purposes displays quite a deep insight into certain facts of modern life. Since all labour is becoming increasingly easy and for many people working life is losing content and interest, we must look for new content and our interests and efforts must be fixed elsewhere, our life being centred about 'play'.

Following another line of development, however, we find weight being given both to work and to play. Transcending the traditional, ascetic, dichotomy between work and play, we see the commencement of an integration, giving us each 'more work in work and more play in play'.[57] David Riesman, the inventor of this brilliant formula, believes that most of his fellow countrymen do not know how to amuse themselves precisely because their work has been debased and has become monotonous and without meaning for them. Such being the case, this suggested form of mutual interaction, of happy interplay between what we prefer to call work activities and free time ones, will not in practice bring about a real revival in the life of the majority of the citizens of the United States — at least not for a long time yet.

Let us now remind ourselves of the points where, in the present state of economic and technical development, we found constructive solutions to the problems here discussed. Two separate steps are required. First, there must be a revaluation of work, which, to be complete, must be carried out simultaneously on three different planes, intellectual, social and moral. Secondly, there must be opportunities of self-realization and self-development for the individual in non-work activities.

* 'Work hard, play easily.'

In an earlier book I have examined the conditions of this revaluation. To these the present study adds a few new facts, the importance of which has since then become clear to me, i.e. the increase in transfer and job rotation, and the movement for the recombination and enlargement of jobs, the effect of which upon the valuation of labour I have already discussed. Moreover, the type of multispecialist worker is on the increase. He is not of course a trained professional controlling a whole group of operations like the artisan craftsman of old, a mechanic, a boilermaker or a tool-setter. But the multispecialist benefits from the *integration* ($\sum$ dt) of a whole *series* of partial operations which he knows how to perform. And this integration, when backed by technical know-ledge, can create a new and original type of skilled worker, one who can find satisfaction and take a pride in his work. Finally, the increase in supervisors and operators responsible for multipurpose auto-matic machines also constitutes in itself a fact with sociological implications. I have mentioned other phenomena of the same kind in administration and commerce.

But we must not give way to tempting illusions. These new movements, whatever their importance and however excellent their effects, are far from affording a universal solution to our problem. As I have said, and must now repeat at the end of this book, there are still to-day millions of jobs which cannot be revalued in such ways, and this will continue to be the case for a long while yet. The work that millions of men and women do every day for a living neither enriches their lives nor acts as a balancing factor. Such people can only look for true satisfaction and the means of self-realization in leisure-time activities, more particularly in the 'free time' which is progressively increased as the working week is shortened. It is the time spent away from work, as Marx (and Hegel before him) saw, that should constitute the 'true realm of freedom' for mankind.[58]

To a certain number of workers and employees this 'free time' also gives the possibility of self-expression through the collective struggle of political and trade union organizations. Let us recall an admirable sentence written by a man who knows the worker's condition personally, Georges Navel: 'There is a worker's illness which can only be cured by taking part in politics.' But it is essential that all parties and trade unions should give their militant supporters the chance of civic action, and a sense of achievement and of self-realization — together, of course, with consideration for others. This can only be done if their structure is truly democratic and if they show more than their present small concern for education and further training, encouraging free discussion at all levels including the lowest and allowing a margin for individual initiative and responsibility.

A GRAVE PROBLEM

But here arises a serious problem, which was noticed for the first time by Freud and which will become increasingly pressing as automatism develops between now and the end of the century.

As we have seen, work, when its scope is sufficient and the personality can to some extent be involved in it, has a fundamental part to play in the balance of the individual, in fitting him into his social environment, in fact, in his physical and mental health. This is the role it has always played in history in the most varied social and cultural surroundings; although, of course, as ethnographers rightly remind us, it has meant very different things for those performing it.[59] From this standpoint, may not the reduction in the part played by it in human life, the progressive suppression of manual work by automatism, have exceedingly harmful results? Can work be replaced in a psychological sense by 'non-work' and particularly 'free-time' activities? Can they assume the role it used to play in regard to the personality? Can the transference of the centre of personal activity and self-realization to leisure hours guarantee equal benefits, confer comparable psychological advantages? What indeed will happen when men in growing numbers find themselves gradually deprived of 'work' in the traditional sense of the term? Will the active employment of leisure-time be a balancing factor in the whole of an individual's life and aid in the formation and development of his character?

To some people these problems may seem very vague and remote. But we are not the only people they disturb. Eric Fromm, whose disquiet, although it comes from a completely different background is very like my own, writes as follows:

> Is man, during the next few hundred years, to continue spending most of his energy on meaningless work, waiting for the time when work will hardly require any expenditure of energy? What

will become of him in the meantime? Will he not become more and more alienated, and this just as much in his leisure hours as in his working time? Is the hope for effortless work not a daydream based on the fantasy of laziness and push-button power, and a rather unhealthy fantasy at that? Is not work such a fundamental part of man's existence that it cannot and should never be reduced to almost complete insignificance? Is not the mode of work in itself an essential element in forming a person's character? Does completely automatized work not lead to a completely automatized life?[60]

That grounds exist at the present day for these anxieties is truer than it may seem at first sight. Powerful movements are tending to weaken the part played by work in people's lives. Job simplification is increasing the sector of atomized labour, while automatism, on the other hand, is already reducing it at certain points. But the effects of both taken together converge, and lead to a decrease in the number of manual jobs in which the personality can really be involved and by which it can be benefited. Is there any way of judging whether the new forms of escape from work will fit a man into the human community as well as work did, will offer him as many possibilities of self-realization, of a balanced life, of self-development? These problems, though they have been stressed by thinkers such as Fromm, have in fact not been studied at all yet nor been made the subject of any systematic investigation. They constitute a field of observation that should attract social psychologists and sociologists and might lead to researches of the greatest value during the next few decades, helping to enlighten the policy of all administrators, reformers and statesmen anxious to think out and plan the institutions of the new age.

The possibilities we have just described might finally be illustrated by two remarks. First of all, the elimination or transformation of atomized jobs should be carried out as quickly as possible in all the ways we have suggested. Such tasks possess none of the balancing virtues of real work. Their disappearance entails no danger. The happiness and dignity of those enslaved to them to-day will not suffer at all.

Secondly, the dangers to which we have referred are far from being universal. Even if all fragmentary manual jobs were to disappear, many functions would still remain, in agriculture, industry, commerce and the whole of the 'tertiary' services, in which the personality could be involved in many different ways;

the contemporary development of technology seems indeed to be increasing their number, as we have seen. It is vitally important that those responsible for our societies — statesmen, heads of departments, technicians — should, wherever such direction is possible, seek by carefully planned and co-ordinated measures to enlarge the sector containing these humanly valuable and beneficial activities. It is important, too, that the mass of the workers, enlightened by those in whom they have placed their trust, by their political and trade union leaders, should make this their aim, and from now on count it as one of the chief objectives of their struggle.

TECHNOLOGY SERVES NOTICE ON MAN. WHERE SHALL HE FIND A NEW HOME?

Thus the study of specialization leads to the heart of our problems to-day. This should not be astonishing, as it gives us a central observation point from which to see clearly and take the measure of both the immense hopes and the great dangers connected with technical progress.

One of the most alarming of these dangers seems to me to be *the failure of human beings to participate* in an environment which they can now control from outside by means of increasingly efficient, autonomous and widespread techniques. Needs and desires, capacities and aspirations, which are an essential part of man, remain unused and run to waste. He is present, and listens more or less absent-mindedly, without giving anything of himself. He is acted upon passively, and shows no power of concentration, being influenced more and more by a 'press-button' attitude. And this is as true during work as during leisure. Technical progress has served notice on man everywhere. We have mentioned some of the effects of this development upon his mental attitudes and equilibrium.

From this point of view traditional capitalism exerts a permanently harmful influence upon the wage-earner in his employment, maintaining an unbridgeable psychological gulf between him and the managerial staff, constantly frustrating his deep desire to participate and preventing him from utilizing all his moral and professional capacities in his work. This is one of the fundamental vices of the capitalist régime, one that makes it essential that it should be transcended through the action of the working masses, so that, while full use is being made of technical progress, the spiritual needs of man may be properly satisfied.

State socialism, whatever help it can give the individual through the provision of educational facilities and opportunities for advancement, does not seem to satisfy his complex desires for participation. Its over-centralization and the excessive growth in bureaucracy discourage these desires, as do the screen formed by a layer of managers imbued with purely technical ideals, and a hoard of committees and jurisdictions whose decisions are in fact imposed upon him. Businesses and administrative units combine into larger groups, where there is much too small a margin of freedom left to the individual, too little time in which he is listened to and can express himself. If he is to be more fully involved and interested in his work, showing his capabilities and feeling that his initiative and sense of responsibility are of use, industrial and administrative units must be limited in size and be given the largest possible measure of autonomy within the general framework of a planned economy. Teamwork must be increased at all levels, team members being free to distribute specialized jobs within the group as they wish and attention being paid to their suggestions, while a full use is made of the technical training and talents of each person.

Communitarian socialism, based on flexible and decentralized institutions, seems a better method than State socialism of satisfying the individual's psychological requirements, since it harmonizes them with modern techniques of group organization and production. In this sense, in spite of their very modest limits, the experiences of the French 'work communities'* seem to deserve close attention. They are one of those interesting experiments taking place in the immense laboratory in which the foundations of the world of to-morrow are being tested. Notwithstanding their difficulties, on which recent objective investigations have thrown light,[61] one must recognize that their vitality depends upon the unique forms of individual integration and participation they have evolved. These difficulties are, moreover, inseparable from the social context in which the Communities are working, since it is both economically and morally foreign to them, when not

* 'Communautés de travail'.

definitely hostile. Their experience, nevertheless, shows certain practical ways in which a new value can be given to specialized work within a small productive group, of which the worker can feel himself a member with full rights, since he is constantly informed of how things are going and is associated with the running of the whole.

But communitarian socialism could only give a new value to labour on a widespread scale if it possessed a varied network of schools and universities, giving everyone, whatever his economic function, the elements of a humanist culture and, on that foundation, the necessary technical knowledge to enable him to take an interest in his job and see it in relation to a whole. Furthermore, in the ideal state of which we are allowing ourselves to dream, now that our book is at an end, decentralization would not prevent its rulers from exercising an enlightened, though only limited and provisional, control over the direction and use of the mass media of education at present in existence or later to be evolved. We do not forget that man's leisure is essentially freedom and choice, and will correspond to individual character and tastes, in fact, to a complex of drives lodged in the very heart of his personality, which society should respect so far as it can. Leisure, if used by the State to impose its doctrines, beliefs, or ideology on the individual, to force him in a particular direction and 'mass-produce' him according to its momentary interests, is not the kind of leisure one would wish mature human beings to enjoy.

On the other hand, when one looks at the way in which many men and women of our age really occupy their leisure, for instance in watching mediocre films, shows, and variety entertainments, or in reading stories and magazines with huge circulations specially 'adapted' to the masses (so their producers say) and therefore 'attractive' to them, one cannot help thinking that some collective action is required, at any rate so long as society is as it is to-day. Only some such action can prevent people, when they leave work (work, as we have seen, often morally unprofitable, or even harmful), from being debased rather than enriched by their leisure. For it alone will give them the maximum of cultural value and effectiveness. Confronted by the corrupting anarchy which is too often the sad reality of to-day, there now seems a need for an intermediate zone of planned intervention, centralized at State level, though of course devoid of all totalitarian tendencies. Even within the framework of a reformed society, it will for a long while be important to provide all citizens working on specialized jobs with the coin of humanist values as an inspiration during both working and leisure hours. Alain, paraphrasing Berthelot, used to say: 'Our power is greater than our knowledge.'[62] This power, developing day by day at increasing speed and in a more and more frightening manner, now lies in the hands of an ever-growing number of people: it *must* be united with wisdom. However the problems of technical progress are viewed, conclusions of this kind are inescapable.

That is also a reason why we cannot share the enthusiasm and illusions of the prophets of 'automation'. As one of the phases of automatism, no doubt to be followed by many more, it can indeed pour out floods of consumer goods, creating abundance and freeing men from many physically and morally degrading tasks. Its possibilities are immense. Of course! But, as I have insisted, this programme demands such extensive economic and social reforms that it will be equivalent to a revolution. Moreover, we must be extraordinarily naïve or blind, if we imagine that the suppression of all manual labour, should just social institutions and wisdom be lacking, will not have as its final result a further alienation of man's spirit.

Then let us not repeat incessantly this new version of the 'technicians' utopias'. If man is to rise to his full stature in the new civilization to which the present upheavals are giving birth, if he is to reach the height of his calling, and the whole of his personality is to be involved and developed by his work, something other, and much more, than the most miraculous applications of the physico-chemical sciences is required. The results of technical progress will only be beneficial if they are accompanied by progress in the social sciences, whose findings must be wisely applied to the problems of individual and State. Plato in his *Republic*, in order to secure good government, demanded that philosophers should become kings, and kings philosophers. From the foregoing pages it becomes clear that the guides of the world of tomorrow should be, if not psychologists or sociologists, at least surrounded by advisers who are prepared to remind them constantly, amid the ups and downs of man's great struggle with technology, of the conditions that are essential for a balanced and happy life.

Statistical Appendix[*]

THE PROPORTION OF UNSKILLED, SEMI-SKILLED
AND SKILLED WORKERS IN THE WORKING POPULATION

IN THE course of this book I have discussed in their concrete and individual aspects the simplified jobs of mechanized industry, and have described their principal psychological effects upon the worker and his behaviour, both during and outside working hours. I have also indicated ways in which under certain conditions work and non-work activities may involve the personality and lead to its development.

But my study would be incomplete, even within the limits to which I have restricted it, if it did not enable the reader to measure at least approximately the place occupied by 'atomized work' among all the activities by which the working populations of industrial lands earn their livelihood. This statistical information is all the more useful because of the success of cybernetics and more particularly of the flood of noisy propaganda let loose by the advocates of 'automation', which has encouraged the public to believe that the problems this book discusses are out of date, or about to become so. The worker, they say, released from all heavy and tedious tasks through the mechanization of manual work and of all forms of communication, a mechanization which has been going on since the beginning of the century, is being increasingly freed from repetitive and fragmentary jobs. Already we can see the dawn of an era in which new technical qualifications will take the place of all the old forms of muscular and manual skill.

I shall be careful not to adopt any dogmatic position here as regards future trends or the pace at which occupational skills will develop. It is very probable that sooner or later technical progress will diminish very considerably the multitude of repetitive and fragmentary tasks I have been describing, and eventually it may even succeed in suppressing them. In this modest appendix I do not claim to throw any light upon the way in which occupational qualifications are changing in the main branches of industry according to age, sex, and social and ethnic origin. For that a very wide statistical analysis would be needed such as has

* I have to thank Mlle. Jacqueline Gauthier, Research Assistant at the *Centre national de la Recherche scientifique*, for her valuable help in preparing this appendix.

never yet been directly made, so far as I know. There seems no doubt that the reason for this is that no good *qualitative statistics*, confirmed by *systematic studies* of *sample jobs* made in the workshop, exist at present, and lacking these it is in fact impossible to treat the subject in all its ramifications with any pretence at scientific exactitude.

My intention here is only to indicate the actual importance of un-skilled labour in certain industrially advanced countries, although I shall not hesitate in passing to point to a few interesting trends. It may be noted that as a result of the progress of mechanization most of the workers classified as 'specialized', or 'semi-skilled' workers, or whatever they may be called in different countries, are performing repetitive tasks with cycles of very short duration that need no thorough and systematic training and may involve the personality only slightly, if at all.

The statistics we summarize must be regarded with a cautious and critical eye. First of all they must be considered in relation to the whole industrial structure of the countries concerned and to the technical progress achieved by different industries, and especially to the age of their machines. Then, as we shall see, the criteria according to which these statistics have been drawn up are not always comparable. Finally, in several of the countries mentioned, and particularly in France, they must be treated with great reserve from the point of view that interests us, for the following reasons in particular:

(1) Many workers counted as skilled have been accorded too high a classification, being included in categories above their real occupational value. This is particularly true during periods when, after a freezing of wages, the unions attempt to get round it by obtaining increased pay for the categories they consider ill-treated. In consequence 'specialized labourers' are often classed as 'O.S.1'. Moreover, many 'O.S.3' are promoted to 'O.P.1', for instance in the manufacturing workshops of big motorcar firms, although, if one watches carefully the operations they perform, one can see that these do not contain anything like the complexity, the time taken by the unit of work, the variety and versatility, skill and initiative, which 'skilled' jobs are generally said to demand.

(2) Conversely, we often notice in certain branches of production, for example in chemical industries, oil refineries and electrical power stations, workers who are classed as 'semi-skilled' but whose jobs in fact require attention, responsibility, and supervisory functions, such as should lead to their being given a higher classification.

More generally, where the statistics are derived from occupational categories based upon the wage scale, we notice a downgrading during times when the labour market is slack. Thus on 1 January, 1947, a period when labour was in great demand, the Minister of Labour's inquiry reported 9·5 per cent of the workers as 'highly skilled' (*Revue française de Travail*, June–July 1947, p. 633), whereas on 1 July, 1948, the percentage had gone down to 7·2 (ibid., January–February 1949, p. 79).

The relations existing between the employers' associations and the trade unions and the wages policy pursued during certain phases of capitalism often lead to reclassifications that do not correspond to real qualitative differences and so distort the occupational scale.

(3) The figures given below concern unskilled or semi-skilled workers in industry, transport, and occasionally in activities called 'commercial and liberal'. But if we wish to make an estimate, be it only an approximate one, of the total number of occupations characterized to-day by highly subdivided and downgraded jobs, we must not forget that rationalization and mechanization have also penetrated into office work of all kinds, and have already profoundly altered it in big administrative units, in insurance companies, banks, and industrial and commercial firms. Many of the posts occupied by typists, multicopiers, accountants, etc., present striking similarities with those in factories concerned with repetitive and fragmentary operations. It would be wrong to omit this large section of the working population in the general sketch we are making here. Its size can be judged from the fact that those considered in France as office-workers numbered 846,100 persons on 1 July, 1952, that is 18·6 per cent of the total number employed in the same branches of activity on that date. We must add that these figures are far from covering the whole of the working population of our country, since they leave out of account businesses with fewer than ten employees, and have been drawn up to exclude important sections of the community in undertakings containing a large number of mechanized white-collar jobs, such as water, gas, electricity, and solid fuel companies, the S.N.C.F., R.A.T.P., and P.T.T.*

In default of general investigations, and even of partial sample inquiries, we have been unable to discover from the statistics at present available the proportion of office-workers employed on fragmentary and mechanized jobs. But the tremendous increase in the production of different kinds of office machines is an indication of the rapid growth in the number of these employees.

The reservations I have just made should be borne in mind as well as others I shall have occasion to formulate later on. Nevertheless, I should not have inflicted this appendix upon the reader if, in the final resort, it did not contain a number of convergent indications which will enable him to get a better view of the actual importance of the problems to which I have drawn his attention.

I shall arrange the statistics and my comments on them in three groups. The first, and most important, concerns France, and here I

* i.e. *Société Nationale des Chemins de Fer; Régie autonome des Transports parisiens; Postes, Télégraphe, Téléphone.*

shall go into greater detail, since this book is addressed in the first place to French readers. In the second, certain information will be given in a very concise form about a few industrially advanced countries, i.e. Great Britain, Western Germany, Italy and Belgium. Finally, so that comparisons may be made with the classification of occupations in the technically most advanced nation, I shall add certain data relative to the United States.

I

The statistical data available in France concerning the proportion of semi-skilled workers in industry come from very different organizations and vary much in scope. So it is vitally important to be clear as to their provenance and the methods employed in their collection and use.

The general statistics come from:

(1) *L'Institut national de la Statistique et des Études économiques* (I.N.S.E.E.), which since the war has had charge of the general census of the population and of its evaluation. The figures and commentaries I cite are derived from the censuses of 1946 and 1954 and all are taken from the publications of the I.N.S.E.E.

(2) The Ministry of Labour and Social Security; its inquiries concern industry and are addressed to employers. Their results are published in the *Revue française du Travail*.

Partial statistical data can also be obtained from:

(a) Associations of Employers. They deal with a particular branch of industry and are only concerned with firms that are members of the association.

(b) Research workers of the *Centre d'Études sociologiques* who collect information on this subject in the course of their investigations. Certain of these have already been published.

The variety of these sources leads one at first to expect very little coherence in the mass of figures given. We shall in fact see later all the reasons that lead us to show the greatest caution in interpreting, and particularly in comparing, these statistics. Nevertheless, the official organizations, that is to say the I.N.S.E.E. and the Ministry of Labour, have made an effort since the war to remedy the lack of co-ordination in the methods used and in the presentation of the results.* A statistical division has been set up at the Ministry of Labour and its co-operation

* A. Aboughanem, head of the Statistical Division of the Ministry of Labour and Social Security, 'L'organisation et le développement des statistiques sociales en France', *Revue française du Travail*, July–August–September 1951.

A large part of my information about the researches of the Ministry of Labour has been taken from this article.

Those concerned with the sample enquiries of 1952 come from a communication made on 17 November, 1954, to my seminar at the *École pratique des Hautes Études* by M. Raymond Lévy-Bruhl, M. Aboughanem's successor.

with the I.N.S.E.E. has been assured by the exchange of qualified staff.

The I.N.S.E.E. also tries to reclassify all the information it receives from employers and private sources. Inquiries concerning the distribution of workers in certain branches of industry (electrical engineering for instance) have been conducted jointly by the I.N.S.E.E. and the employers' associations.

In spite of these beginnings of co-ordination many difficulties remain, due either to the subject of our investigation or to the inquiries themselves.

To make a reliable estimate of the total number of a definite category of the population, the term defining it must be unambiguous in the minds of those answering the questionnaire. Now, though the term *semi-skilled worker* possesses a quite definite sense in metallurgy, this is not the case in the other branches of industry, in chemical products for example. Besides, many employers and personnel managers are very hesitant when asked to give figures, or to indicate the proportion of semi-skilled and skilled workers, since these distinctions are not sufficiently clear in their firm.* On what then do they base their replies to a questionnaire from the Labour Ministry when it asks them for the same information? Exclusively on the wage scale. Now this, as we have already seen, is far from corresponding strictly to the scale of skill. Those concerned, the semi-skilled workers themselves, may say they are turners or drillers, for instance, but they cannot always declare whether they are O.S.2 or P.1. Finally, in the provinces as well as in certain firms in the neighbourhood of Paris the term *manoeuvre spécialisé* represents what others mean by *ouvrier spécialisé. This fact must therefore always be taken into account when interpreting the following tables, and the two categories should in most cases be combined.*

There is an explanation for these difficulties. The term *ouvrier spécialisé* is of comparatively recent creation, and was imposed in a quite artificial manner. Between 1936 and 1938, during discussions on wages and on the extension of collective agreements, it was considered necessary to establish a classification and stricter definitions of the hierarchy of labour. After the war the Parodi law imposed these fixed categories upon all branches of industry, starting with metallurgy. Some industries hastened to abandon them as soon as they were free to do so. Thus the textile trade now refers to occupations (*métiers*) and not to occupational categories. Other sectors, like the Mines, the S.N.C.F., l'Électricité de France, le Gaz de France, each have their own scale. Thinking that a forced comparison would be illusory, the statisticians of the Labour Ministry have excluded these different nationalized industries in presenting the results of their inquiries.

* We may cite: (1) a large textile business, where all the information we wanted, except these figures, was given to us; (2) a large undertaking concerned with chemical products where the figures were given to us with many reservations.

Secondly, if the statistical data are to do what we hoped and allow us without arbitrary assumptions to distinguish trends, we must have a series of figures as well as comparable proportions, referring to different dates and spread over a sufficiently long period. But no trustworthy pre-war census of semi-skilled workers exists, for various reasons: (1) the designation *ouvrier spécialisé* was not at that time widely used; the census of 1936, in particular, only distinguished workers and employees, grouping under the one common heading of 'workers' skilled and unskilled workers, day labourers, watchmen, and transport and delivery staff; (2) the inquiries of the Labour Ministry, begun in 1930, were mainly concerned with certain characteristics of employment, their principal object being to find answers to the urgent questions resulting from the economic crisis; moreover, the technical training of the labour inspectors charged with the inquiry was inadequate.

In general, scarcely any attention was paid to this problem either by official organizations or by business firms, and very few of the latter have preserved in their archives any details of the occupational distribution of those days or are able to bring them out now for the benefit — and to the joyful surprise — of the curious researcher.

We are therefore limited to the post-war period. Here there are figures and percentages. But the difficulty lies partly in their interpretation and partly in deciding how legitimate it is to make comparisons between the results of the different inquiries.

The co-operation established between the I.N.S.E.E. and the Statistical Division of the Labour Ministry has great advantages in this respect:

(1) It has allowed the preparation of a more reliable and complete sample of the different strata of the working population. 'In principle, the inquiry covers *all* concerns employing 50 persons, 25–30 per cent of the concerns employing 20–50 persons, 10–15 per cent of the concerns employing 10–20 persons. In practice no concern employing less than 5 people was questioned. The information received from concerns employing less than 10 persons can only be used with great caution and must in many cases be eliminated because of its too scattered nature or because of misleading divergencies.'* In the final result the Labour Ministry received about 30,000 replies from the 45,000 concerns questioned. Its inquiries therefore give an accurate picture of the different economic sectors, but the sample is spoiled to a certain extent by the fact that 90–95 per cent of the firms with more than 50 employees replied, but only 40 per cent of those with less than 20.

The sample inquiry of 1952 tried to find a remedy for these defects, in the first place by enlarging the sample of firms with less than 50 employees, and secondly by making the inquiry compulsory. Sanctions had been allowed by the law of 1951 but had not been applied earlier.

* A. Aboughanem, art. cit.

At the same time, the general results of preceding inquiries (to which a few comments were added) were given on the questionnaire. Thanks to this there were more replies. 50,000 firms answered, that is 80 per cent.

(2) It also established a nomenclature co-ordinating the presentation of the results. The first list was concerned with collective activities and grouped the different industries under 26 headings.* This is now used by both organizations in dealing with all their inquiries. The second concerned trades and individual activities, and one of its purposes was to distinguish between skilled and unskilled workers.†

Since 1945 the Ministry of Labour has undertaken several sample investigations among firms in order to gather information about the distribution of different occupational categories. They took place on the following dates:‡

1 January, 1946

1 January, 1947

1 July, 1948

1 July, 1952.

Before making any comments on the results which are presented in the following tables, let us see to what extent the four inquiries are comparable and the figures reliable. Unfortunately they are far from satisfactory; there are many reasons for this:

(1) With a view to improving the nomenclature applied to collective activities it was altered from 1948 on. A simple examination of the list of headings§ shows that the heading 'Oil' appears in 1948 and 1952, while it does not appear at all in 1946 and 1947; the book industry, too, is replaced by the 'polygraphic' (printing) industry. Rubber is separated from the chemical industry in 1946 and 1947 but included in it in 1948 and 1952. The metallurgical industries have undergone the greatest alteration. In 1946 and 1947 the headings concerned with them are entitled 'Metallurgy' and 'Metal Work', in 1948 and 1952 'Metal Production' and 'Engineering and Electrical Industry'. The commentator of the *Revue française du Travail* gives a warning to those wishing to use these results: 'Whereas in 1946 and 1947 the classification of activities was based upon the nomenclature adopted in 1936 for dealing with the general census of the population, a new nomenclature, now official owing to the decree of 16 January, 1947, had to be used in the present study (1948). Thus it is difficult to make detailed comparisons, since the

* Table I gives an idea of these headings.

† Cf. P. Naville's *Essai sur la qualification du Travail*, for a detailed critical analysis of these lists.

‡ The results have been published by the *Revue française du Travail* in the following numbers in chronological order: No. 2, 1946; Nos. 15–16, 1947; Nos. 1–2, 1949; No. 3, 1954.

§ Cf. Table I.

content of each group, in spite of a similarity of title, is generally different in each of the two lists. On the other hand, new sectors have been included and a comparison of general averages may be falsified by this.'*

I am therefore only showing detailed comparative tables for the results of the samplings of 1948 and 1952 (cf. Table I).

(2) A second source of difficulty arises if we try, merely as a pointer, to compare the percentages of the different occupational categories in relation to the total of the manufacturing industries and to the total of all the activities considered. The occupational categories are not strictly the same. We are thus forced to regroup certain headings and to restore the scale of categories to the three categories of 1946, i.e. unskilled, semi-skilled (specialized), and skilled.

(3) At first sight the proportions of the different occupational categories seem to have differed greatly in 1946 from those in subsequent years. Were they abnormal? I cannot definitely say so. But it is as well to remember a third source of inaccuracy. The occupational distribution of these samplings is based upon a classification of workers according to their place in the scale of wages. Hence there is a distortion in times of labour shortage and the proportions are then larger at the top of the scale (as in 1946–7, for example), while they increase at the bottom of the scale during periods of unemployment.

(4) Finally, the very conditions under which the data of Table I have been drawn up lead one to interpret them as indicating an order of size, and not as actual figures. 'The proportions of each category have been calculated in relation to the whole of the personnel employed in each group of activity and each region. These percentages have then been weighted, the coefficients being made proportional to the importance of the effectives in each group of activity and in each region, in order to obtain the total results.'†

In spite of all these reservations, do these figures nevertheless indicate certain general trends?

Table I will enable us to realize what results can be obtained from these inquiries. If I put together *ouvriers spécialisés* and *manoeuvres spécialisés*, the totals arrived at are striking, although certain firms are excluded. In the non-agricultural working population of 7 million in 1948, manual workers numbered nearly 5 million, and the semi-skilled workers constituted almost half the total of workers — to be exact, 2,438,500 out of 4,727,500.

We shall see that the proportions of the three main occupational categories tend to oscillate around a third of the total workers (Table II). It is undoubtedly better not to worry too much about the results of 1946, since it is hardly possible to estimate the effect of certain exceptional

* *Revue française du Travail*, January–February 1949, p. 71.
† *Revue française du Travail*, June–July 1947, p. 625.

factors existing at that time. The general variations from 1948 to 1952 are quite small in respect of the manufacturing industries. In Table III, containing the figures dealing with all activities, the difference between the proportions of *ouvriers spécialisés* in 1948 and 1952 is a little more noticeable; but ought one to interpret this as due to an increase in the number of *ouvriers spécialisés* in activities other than the manufacturing industries?

However, the Ministry of Labour's inquiries do not deal with the whole of the working population. We have seen that businesses employing less than 10 persons could not be taken into account. But these are very important. Table IV in fact shows that more than a third of the non-agricultural working population (34·06 per cent) works in undertakings of this size. It is probable also that the proportions of semi-skilled and skilled workers are not the same in small and big firms, if we are to judge by Table V. These proportions have been calculated regularly by the I.N.S.E.E. from the time of the 1946 census. There are certainly many reasons that lead us to mistrust indications obtained in this way. The proportions of semi-skilled workers rise to double when we pass from businesses employing less than 10 persons to those employing more than 50. We may also notice that there is a difference of almost 10 per cent in the percentage of skilled workers (49·5–40·2 per cent), and of more than 10 per cent for the semi-skilled (17·6–28·9 per cent) between firms employing less than 10 persons and those employing from 11 to 20. So we may take it that in a third of the non-agricultural working population there are 10 per cent more skilled workers than in the other two-thirds, and that it is this third that the samplings of the Ministry of Labour leave out of account.

Nevertheless, there are certain ways of finding out the size of occupational categories within the whole labour force. First of all we can use the censuses of 1936, 1946 and 1954. As we have already mentioned, the census of 1936 does not distinguish the semi-skilled workers. The individual questionnaires of 1946 have no definite question about the worker's occupational category, but a sheet is included asking for information from all managers of firms. The result of this part of the census is poor, either because of the carelessness of those who conducted it, or of the unwillingness of managers to give the information, so that replies were obtained from only 72 per cent.

The 1954 census is still more open to dispute. The data given in Tables III and VI are not those of the whole census, but are partly derived from a sampling of one-twentieth taken from it by the I.N.S.E.E.* The final results will not be disclosed for a long time, six or seven years after the census itself, and they will then be out of date.

* *Bulletin hebdomadaire de Statistique* (28 May, 1955): *Annuaire statistique de l'I.N.S.E.E.* (1955).

What this preliminary sampling suggests, it must be admitted, is disconcerting, not because of the proportion of semi-skilled workers, which is only a little below the figures we are used to, but because of the large proportion of the skilled and the small proportion of the unskilled (48·7 per cent and 17·7 per cent). Since it dealt with all undertakings, including those employing less than 10 persons, we ought of course to expect an increase in the percentage of the skilled as against the figures given by the Labour Ministry. No doubt we should also deduct from this 48·7 per cent about 3 per cent representing foremen; but even so this vast increase is odd. We should doubtless remember too that the census was taken by means of individual questionnaires, and that a considerable number of workers, whether skilled or semi-skilled, may have described themselves as 'millers' or 'turners' without furnishing any further details or proof. They may therefore have been wrongly classed as skilled. But we must admit that these explanations do not appear entirely satisfactory. So we shall avoid using these figures, not knowing how reliable they are.

Some more plausible, though incomplete, information comes to us from another source, the analysis made by the I.N.S.E.E. and contained in Bulletin 1024 of the employers' declarations to the Finance Ministry. These declarations come from every firm, but a number do not mention the qualifications of their workers. Table VII shows the totals obtained.

In this Table the number of skilled workers is slightly higher and the number of semi-skilled workers slightly lower *than in the Tables of the Ministry of Labour*; but we still cannot place full reliance on its figures, since more than half the workers are classed under the heading 'qualification not given'.

Taking all this into account, we are then probably right in supposing that *semi-skilled workers constitute as a whole one-third of all manual wage-earners*. They are to be found everywhere. At the same time we must not forget that the jobs done by *manoeuvres spécialisés* are often very similar to those performed by the semi-skilled worker. Putting the two categories together, we find that they include more than half the labour force and have slightly increased in proportion between 1948 and 1952 (51·6 per cent and 52·2 per cent), although the number of *manoeuvres spécialisés* taken alone has decreased in almost all branches of industry.

Some samples taken from particular firms and industries furnish similar proportions. Here are a few instances:

(1) In electrical engineering in the Paris region (137,000 workers distributed among 28 branches of production and 255 firms):*

---

* These results come from a periodical inquiry made by the I.N.S.E.E. in conjunction with the *Syndicat général de la Construction électrique*. They are published in the *Annuaire de l'I.N.S.E.E.* for 1953 and 1954.

	March 1953	February 1954	March 1955
Labourers	6·47	6·38	6·12
Semi-skilled workers	57·6	56·78	57·85
Skilled workers	35·93	36·84	36·03

(2) In an electrical engineering firm in the neighbourhood of Paris in 1955 (1,230 employees—760 manual workers):

Labourers - - - - - - -	3%
Semi-skilled workers - - - - -	55%
Skilled workers - - - - - -	42%

(3) In engineering industries in France* in 1952:

	Labour Force	Percentages
Factory apprentices	72,000	8
Semi-skilled workers	444,000	49
Skilled workers	396,000	43
	912,000	100

These figures refer not only to the labour force in engineering firms, but also to those employed in engineering work in other undertakings, such as textiles, food, chemical products, etc. It is probable that the proportion of skilled workers is therefore unduly increased at the expense of that of the semi-skilled workers.

(4) In a firm in the neighbourhood of Paris, in 1955, (2,000 to 3,000 workers):

	Manufacturing		Factory Total	
Labourers	2%		2%	
Manoeuvres spécialisés	25%⎫		22%⎫	
	⎬ 63%		⎬ 55%	
Ouvriers spécialisés	38%⎭		33%⎭	
Skilled workers	35%		43%	
	100%		100%	

This last example shows clearly a well-known phenomenon, a greater proportion of semi-skilled workers in the manufacturing part than in the whole of the undertaking. We find the same phenomenon in Table VIII, which is concerned with another industry and a much greater number of workers since it is from the Renault factories.

Samples of this kind, when they deal with particular firms, have of course a more limited scope than inquiries concerning a country's total

* We owe these figures to the kindness of the *Fédération des Industries mécaniques et transformatrices des Métaux.*

labour force. Nevertheless they have two advantages. They increase our confidence in the more general inquiries when the results of both are similar, and they also suggest possible explanations.

Thus Table IX, which outlines the whole development of occupational categories in the Renault factories from 1925 to 1954, shows first a larger proportion of semi-skilled workers in this vast modern enterprise than in any other firm or branch of industry. Secondly we can see a slight decrease in this proportion since 1952. Table VIII shows us which sectors have a growing need of semi-skilled workers (foundry) and of skilled men (manufacturing). When we know precisely with what jobs we are concerned as well as their technical framework, the hypotheses we may make, although of course only hypotheses, acquire a much more solid foundation.

II

The statistical data obtainable in France concerning the distribution of occupational categories are then far from satisfactory. But at any rate they possess a few elements which may, we hope, lead to more ample information being provided in the course of the next few years. The information available in other European countries from which we have tried to gather statistics is still less adequate.

GREAT BRITAIN

In England the Statistical Department of the Ministry of Labour and National Service has sent us information about the year 1940, obtained from employers' declarations, which were only made compulsory for the period of the war. Table X, which presents a summary of this information, gives us very little that we want, since the women workers are divided into only two groups, one containing the unskilled, and the other the semi-skilled and skilled, lumped together. Now, the distinction between the last two groups is fundamental for us, particularly since women are more often semi-skilled than skilled workers.

Are they called such in English statistical literature? The rare percentages we have discovered for Great Britain all actually confirm the importance of the category of skilled workers — an unusual importance in comparison with what we know about other countries. Let us look at Table XI from this standpoint. It has been drawn up according to the census of 1951 and covers the whole working population, except those employed in fishing, agriculture and the armed forces. The skilled workers are two and a half times more numerous than the semi-skilled and, if we add to them the foremen, represent 35·71 per cent of the whole, while the semi-skilled and unskilled scarcely reach 24 per cent.

One might wonder whether the abnormal size of the category of skilled workers was not partly due to the fact that in earlier evaluations commerce, insurance and the banks are grouped with industry. But this explanation will scarcely hold water, as Table XII shows us still higher percentages for metals and textiles, i.e. 81·5 per cent and 70 per cent being skilled. We may also notice that the textile industry does not recognize the presence in its factories of any unskilled worker or labourer.

These surprising figures, which may even be regarded as mistaken when compared with the corresponding ones in France or the United States, can only be explained by fundamental differences in the definition and titles given to different occupational categories, partly perhaps also by the traditional policy of the British trade unions, which attempt to maintain the status, and so far as possible the wages, of skilled trades for occupations that have been downgraded by mechanization.

WESTERN GERMANY

The German statistics are abundant. We have therefore been able to calculate the proportions of workers in the three groups for the whole of the non-agricultural population (Table XIII), and for two branches of industry, metallurgy (Table XIV) and textiles (Table XV).

The documents give us chiefly an order of size, and here again we must be cautious in attempting to make comparisons with other nations. In fact:

(1) The collective agreements of the different German provinces (*Länder*), and of the different branches of industry, take account of a wide range of occupational categories, starting with the three common ones we are here using and ending with a continuous scale not unlike American job evaluation.

(2) The way in which jobs are distributed among occupational categories varies sometimes very noticeably from one factory to another.

(3) The list of 'recognized occupations' in certain industries is peculiar to Germany, as for instance in the iron industry.

(4) A large number of young skilled workers in Germany are employed in jobs that are specifically semi-skilled, for instance in the case of turners, who may be working on automatic lathes or on mass-production jobs supervised by machine operators. It is not possible to discover how many of these workers are entered as skilled and how many as semi-skilled.

With these reservations let us note the large number of semi-skilled and unskilled workers, the total (Table XIII) forming 57·55 per cent of the labour force as given in the census of 30 October, 1955. Taking metallurgy and textiles alone, we find this proportion rising to 72·4 per cent and 76·1 per cent (Tables XIV and XV). That is to say, out of every ten workers in these industries at least seven are semi-skilled workers or labourers.

ITALY

Our principal sources of information for Italy have been:

(*a*) A sample taken on 1 April, 1947, in 838 concerns, employing 242,623 workers (*Compendio statistico italiano*, 1947–8, Ser. II, Vol. II, p. 60); (*b*) a study by Agostino de Vita, 'Salari e Costo del Lavoro nell' Industria' (*Congiuntura Economica*, 20 October, 1948); and above all (*c*) the third general Census of Industry and Commerce, taken on 5 November, 1951.

But the Italian names for occupational categories are very different from ours, and include among 'skilled workers' levels of skill which often would be called 'semi-skilled' in France.

Thus in the textile trade we find (Census of 5 November, 1951) 32,082 'highly skilled' women workers (in Italy they are called *operai specializzati*, a denomination that is liable to cause confusion in any comparisons with France), 295,393 skilled and 55,673 'common' women workers (*operai comuni monovali specializzati*), corresponding to our *ouvriers spécialisés* and *manoeuvres spécialisés*.

Here is another example of the results of a nomenclature peculiar to Italy. In the engineering and metal industry (cf. *Index*, the monthly review of the 'Centro per la Statistica Aziendale', 12 May, 1949), 35·2 per cent of the workers are classed as 'semi-skilled' and 'skilled', and 26·9 per cent as 'common' workers or labourers.

Because of this distortion, the census of 5 November, 1951, out of a total of 3,014,867 manual workers, classes only 1,205,429 as 'common' workers or labourers. It is clear that this figure would be considerably higher if the Italian statistics had adopted the usual French criteria for the 'semi-skilled worker'.

BELGIUM

We have been unable to obtain any Belgian data concerning the tripartite classification of labour. Here is a summary of the Belgian situation as it appears from the information kindly given us by the *Institut de Sociologie* of the University of Liège.

In practice there exists in Belgium no official or non-official definition of a skilled or semi-skilled worker. In businesses we often meet with more than a score of occupational distinctions, based upon the performance of definite jobs rather than upon a comparable level of skill in the performance of different tasks.

When industrial employers or scientific observers want to group under one general tripartite classification the multitude of occupational distinctions met with in practice, they use as their chief criterion either the wage level, or the level of vocational training, or the capacity shown in adapting or readapting to a change of job.

III

The American statistics concerning the distribution of occupational categories, as in other matters, are much more exact and varied than those we have for European countries, among which France is not the least well served, as we have seen. Censuses, having been taken every ten years since 1900, allow us to go back to that date and contain sufficiently precise headings to permit of distinguishing different occupational categories, so that by making a few adjustments, we can describe their development since that time. Various writers have used these sources in order to draw up tables of manpower, but, owing to differences of definition, these are far from always strictly coinciding. We shall compare some of them.

Anyone who takes an interest in the development of the American population as a whole or of one of its sectors of activity, must always keep one vital fact in mind, the great and constant growth in numbers that they show. In this matter, absolute and relative figures, total number of workers and general percentages, each have a particular meaning. This is shown very clearly by Table XVI, in which we can see the non-agricultural working population almost doubling. If we consider percentages alone manual workers have hardly increased. In 1910 they were 47·9 per cent of the working population, and in 1950 49·9 per cent. Between these dates, however, the number of manual workers increased by about 11·5 million.

If we look at Table XVIII, which is taken from a group of official sources, we shall note: (1) the increase in the number of skilled workers and foremen, which grew by about 50 per cent between 1910 and 1930, and by about 33 per cent between 1930 and 1950; (2) the fall in the number of labourers, i.e. unskilled workers. Between 1910 and 1930 this number was still slightly increasing in absolute figures, although its increase was much less than that of the total population. From 1930 to 1950 the proportion of unskilled workers diminished by about 40 per cent; (3) the large growth in the number of semi-skilled workers. Between 1910 and 1950 their number more than doubled, as did the industrial population as a whole during the same period. There is no doubt that this growth included the absorption of a section of the unskilled workers, who have thereby benefited from a certain amount of upgrading. Nevertheless, one should not overestimate the importance of

this, and the results of the inquiry made by Mr Julius Hirsch in the
Ford factories in 1926 should be borne in mind:*

Percentage of workers	43	36	6	14	1
Length of Training in the Factory	Not more than one day	1 to 8 days	1 to 2 weeks	1 month to a year	Up to 6 years

We can see the relationship of this development to that of the other
occupational categories by referring to the percentages given in Tables
XIX and XX and the numbers given in Tables XXI and XXII.

Tables XVII and XIX, the data of which come from the excellent
book by Jaffe and Stewart, unfortunately do not allow us to distinguish
between the development of the semi-skilled and the unskilled from
1940 to 1950. But they are completed in this respect by Table XX,
which shows the considerable increase in the sector of the semi-skilled,
and the equally considerable reduction in that of the unskilled worker.
The proportion of manual workers remains comparatively stable (Table
XIX) and even decreases slightly between 1940 and 1950, in line with
the ceiling reached in the United States by the 'secondary' sector of
occupations, as is shown elsewhere by the analyses of Colin Clark and of
Jean Fourastié. Moreover, by comparing Tables XIX, XXI and XXII,
we shall see that the proportion of skilled workers does not greatly
increase (it even diminished in relation to 1920). So it is the growth in
the number of the semi-skilled that compensates for the decrease in the
number of the unskilled.

As regards the striking differences that exist between Tables XIX and
XX the following remarks about the latter table should be made:

(*a*) It excludes female labour and therefore tends to show a considerably smaller proportion of semi-skilled and unskilled workers.
In fact, according to Jaffe and Stewart, in April 1950, 1·1 per cent of the
women included among the working population were skilled, and 42 per
cent formed a part of the semi-skilled or unskilled labour force, while for
men these proportions were respectively 18·6 per cent and 28·6 per cent.

(*b*) It includes artisans, which increases the volume of skilled labour.

On the other hand, according to the figures for 1930, 1940 and 1950
included in Tables XIX, XX, XXI, a development seems to be taking
place of which we cannot as yet say whether it will be continued or
accelerated. The number of skilled workers, which decreased between
1930 and 1940, is slightly rising again and is contributing (with the
increase in the number of the semi-skilled) to compensate for the
diminution in the proportion of unskilled labour. During my own
personal inquiries I have noted that this triple tendency is also to be
found in some highly mechanized and rationalized European firms.

* Cf. *The Social Aspects of Rationalization*, Bureau international du Travail,
Geneva, 1931, p. 344.

It will be interesting during the next few years to see how this trend has been affected by the introduction of 'automation'. Tables VIII and IX show that a similar phenomenon has appeared in France in certain departments of the Renault works.

These comments are not intended in any way to dispute the tendency to an increase of the semi-skilled sector. In spite of the different ways in which Tables XIX and XX were drawn up, they both show that, from 1940 on, the proportion of semi-skilled workers is greater than that of either the skilled or the unskilled. *Semi-skilled workers now constitute the largest group among the manual workers of American industry.* Tables XXI and XXII underline this fact and show the rate of increase in each category. Our calculations (Table XXI), made on the basis of Jaffe and Stewart's data, do not lead to exactly the same figures as those of F. Pollock (Table XXII). But the general results of both are the same:

(1) There has been a relatively considerable increase in the number of the semi-skilled, particularly since 1930.

(2) There has been a relative decrease in the number of the unskilled. The differences noted for this category are probably due to differences of definition, as in the case of Tables XIX and XX.

(3) There has been a relatively slight increase, and recently a more decided growth, in the number of skilled workers.

Tables

TABLE I.—*Distribution per 1000 workers in 1948 and 1952 according to classified skill and occupational group (Ministry of Labour).*

Occupational Group	1948				1952			
	Skilled Workers	Semi-skilled Workers	Semi-skilled Labourers	Ordinary Labourers	Skilled Workers	Semi-skilled Workers	Semi-skilled Labourers	Ordinary Labourers
Oil	405	315	247	33	498	252	189	61
Mining	284	362	283	71	284	328	246	142
Metal Production	280	444	201	75	319	457	182	42
Engineering and Electrical Industries	406	418	113	63	414	439	90	57
Glass Industry	294	298	295	113	312	309	223	156
Pottery and Building Materials	199	353	307	141	188	337	262	213
Building and Public Works	497	242	162	99	503	228	154	115
Chemical and Rubber Industry	236	336	330	98	289	372	246	93
Agricultural and Food Industry	182	235	332	251	162	226	304	308
Textile Industry	252	463	159	126	266	456	143	135
Garment Industry	445	325	122	108	283	413	111	193
Leather and Skins	320	345	241	94	309	338	207	146
Timber and Furniture	346	293	224	137	241	296	224	239
Paper and Cardboard	214	327	326	133	244	323	294	139
Printing	556	269	83	92	597	237	62	104
Various Industries	214	452	180	154	232	454	145	169
Manufacturing Industries, including Building	355	359	181	105	352	369	157	122
Manufacturing Industries, excluding Building	—	—	—	—	324	395	158	123
Transport Other than the S.N.C.F. and R.A.T.P.	361	252	190	197	341	382	142	135
Total of all Groups	343	333	183	141	345	361	161	133

516　　　　522

TABLE II.—*Proportion of labourers, specialized workers and skilled workers per 1000 workers (Ministry of Labour).*

	Total of Manufacturing Industries*			
	1946	1947	1948	1952
Skilled Workers	289	350	355	352
Specialized Workers	452	347	359	369
Labourers	259	303	286	279

* For the list of manufacturing industries see Table I.

TABLE III.—*The combined results of the samplings of the Ministry of Labour and of the 1946 and 1954 censuses.*

Occupational Category	Census 1946	Sample 1946*	Sample 1947*	Sample 1948*	Sample 1952*	Census 1954 Sample of 1/20
Skilled Workers	335	264	327	343	345	487†
Specialized Workers	363	436	334	333	361	301
Labourers	267	300	339	324	294	177
Apprentices	35	—	—	—	—	35
	1,000	1,000	1,000	1,000	1,000	1,000

* All Activities.
† Including Foremen.

TABLE IV.—*Percentages of those working in concerns employing less than ten persons (Sampling of the Ministry of Labour, 1952).*

Occupational Group	Proportion of those working in concerns employing less than 10 persons (per cent)
Timber and Furniture	48·17
Garment Industry	47·81
Agricultural and Food Industry	42·27
Building and Public Works	41
Various Industries	41
Transport, excluding S.N.C.F. and R.A.T.P.	36·4
Leather and Skins	27·26
Pottery and Building Materials	26·07
Mining	23·33
Printing	21·55
Engineering and Electrical Industries	18·91
Paper and Cardboard	16·48
Chemical Industry, Rubber	12·54
Glass	11·62
Textiles	9·82
Oil	0
All Activities	34·06

TABLE V.—*Differences in distribution of occupational skills according to size of concern (Census of 1946).*

Occupational Category	Total of Concerns	Number of Persons Employed							More than 500
		0–9	10	11–20	21–50	51–100	101–200	201–500	
Skilled Workers	363	495	427	402	358	331	321	306	327
Semi-skilled Workers	330	176	256	289	328	352	370	375	406
Labourers	250	167	239	250	273	284	278	291	234
Apprentices	57	162	78	59	41	33	31	28	33
	1000	1000	1000	1000	1000	1000	1000	1000	1000

TABLE VI.—*Census taken in 1954, sampling of 1/20.*

Occupational Category	Total	Per cent
Foremen and Skilled Workers	2,999,680	487
Specialized Workers	1,855,700	301
Worker Apprentices	212,860	35
Labourers	1,093,040	177
	6,161,280	1,000

TABLE VII.—*Numbers and percentages in the different occupational categories according to the analysis of Bulletin 1024 (I.N.S.E.E.).*

1951. *Analysis of Bulletin 1024*

Occupational Category	In Thousands	Percentage
Labourers	746·6	33·6
Semi-skilled Workers	649·6	29·2
Skilled Workers	827·9	37·2
Total	2,223·1	100

'Workers' without further qualification; 2,540·1

TABLE VIII.—*Development of occupational skills in the Renault works by type of department (in percentages).* Source; A. Touraine, *L'Évolution du Travail ouvrier aux Usines Renault*, éd. du C.N.R.S., 1955, p. 94. The figures in italics indicate how greatly the proportion of specialized workers varies according to the departments of the same firm.

	Departments			
	Manufacturing	Assembly	Foundry	Tooling and Maintenance
	Labourers:			
1948	7·6	9·0	11·3	5·6
1952	7·7	13·2	8·2	6·1
1954	8·0	13·5	6·9	6·2
	Specialized Workers:			
1948	74.9	58·2	64·3	*26.9*
1952	74.2	62.5	68.0	*23.7*
1954	*71.9*	61·9	70·8	*19·3*

	Manufacturing	Assembly	Foundry	Tooling and Maintenance
	Skilled Workers:			
1948	17·5	32·8	24·4	67·5
1952	18·1	24·3	23·8	70·2
1954	20·1	24·6	22·3	74·5

TABLE IX.—*Corrected percentages of skilled workers and of specialized workers and labourers in 1925, 1939, 1948, 1952 and 1954 in the Renault works.* Source; A. Touraine, *op. cit.*, p. 84.

	Skilled Workers	Specialized Workers and Labourers
1925	46·3	53·7
1939	31·8	68·2
1948	30·5	69·5
1952	29·9	70·1
1954	32·4	67·6

GREAT BRITAIN

TABLE X.—*Distribution of different types of workers in the metallurgical and engineering industries in June 1940.* According to information furnished by the Statistics Department of the British Ministry of Labour.

Occupational Category	Men	Women
Skilled* and Semi-skilled Workers	81	75
Paid as if Skilled	50	—
Others	31	—
Unskilled	19	25
Total	100	100

* Including apprentices.

TABLE XI.—*Distribution of occupational skills in Great Britain in 1951 according to a sampling of 1 per cent taken from the census of 1951.*

	Total Number of Workers in Thousands	Percentage
Industry, Commerce, Banks, Transport, etc. (All except Fisheries, Agriculture and the Armed Forces.)	20,580·2	
Foremen and Inspectors	564·25	2·74
Skilled Workers	6,785·9	32·97
Semi-skilled Workers	2,731·9	13·28
Unskilled Workers	2,163·8	10·51
Others (Executive Staff, Clerks, etc.)	8,334·1	40·49
	20,580·2	99·99

TABLE XII.—*Distribution of occupational skills in two industries in Great Britain according to a sampling of 1 per cent taken from the census of 1951.*

Occupational Category	Metals (in 1000's)	Textiles (in 1000's)	Metals (%)	Textiles (%)
Foremen	134·4	29·3	4·5	4·55
Skilled Workers	2,248·8	451·6	81·5	70·00
Semi-skilled Workers	306·3	164·0	13·0	25·45
Unskilled Workers	3·4	—	1·0	—
Total	2,750·3	644·9	100·0	100·00

GERMANY

TABLE XIII.—*Distribution of occupational skills in Western Germany according to the census of 30 September, 1955.* Source; *Die nichtlandwirtschaftlichen Arbeitsstätten in der Bundesrepublik Deutschland, Vol. 45, t. I.*

	Numbers			Percentage		
	Skilled	Semi-skilled	Unskilled	Skilled	Semi-skilled	Unskilled
Men	2,815,798	1,583,131	1,285,284	38·25	21·45	17·50
Women	305,442	695,612	668,758	4·20	9·50	9·10
Total	3,121,240	2,278,743	1,954,042	42·45	30·95	26·60
	=7,354,025			=100		

TABLE XIV.—*Distribution of occupational skills in metallurgy in Western Germany according to the census of 30 September, 1955.*

(Source as indicated in the previous table.)

Occupational Category	Total	Percentage
Skilled	78,133	27·6
Semi-skilled	134,903	47·6
Unskilled	70,160	24·8
Total	283,196	100·0

TABLE XV.—*Distribution of occupational skills in textiles in Western Germany according to the census of 30 September, 1955.*

(The same source as in Table XIII.)

Occupational Category	Total	Percentage
Skilled	126,003	23·9
Semi-skilled	299,974	56·7
Unskilled	102,710	19·4
Total	528,687	100·0

THE UNITED STATES

TABLE XVI.—*Development of the population of the United States from 1910 to 1950.* From A. J. Jaffe and C. D. Stewart, 'Manpower Resources and Utilization', *Principles of Working Force Analysis*, New York, 1951, p. 190.

	Numbers in Thousands			Percentages		
	1910	1930	1950	1910	1930	1950
Working Population	37,271	48,595	58,668	100	100	100
Non-agricultural Working Population	25,731	38,396	51,648	69·0	79·0	88·0
Manual Workers	17,848	23,861	29,268	47·9	49·1	49·9

TABLE XVII.—*Numbers in the different occupational categories from 1910 to 1950 in the United States.* From A. J. Jaffe and C. D. Stewart, *op. cit.*, p. 501.

Occupational Category	1910	1920	1930	1940	1950
Skilled Workers and Foremen	4,364*	5,571	6,283	6,105	7,500
Semi-skilled Workers	5,489	6,632	7,973	10,918⎫	21,768†
Unskilled Workers	7,995	8,263	9,605	9,749⎭	

* In millions.

† The book by Jaffe and Stewart was published in 1951 and does not contain figures differentiating between these two categories for 1950.

TABLE XVIII.—*Numbers in the different occupational categories from 1910 to 1950 in the United States.* Table drawn up by F. Pollock (*Sociologica*, Vol. I, Frankfurt a/M, 1955, p. 113), from the official American sources indicated, ibid., pp. 109–10.

Occupational Category	1910	1930	1950
Skilled Workers and Foremen	4·4*	6·3	8·2
Semi-skilled Workers	5·5	8·0	11·7
Unskilled Non-agricultural Workers	5·5	6·3	3·8

* In millions.

TABLE XIX.—*Proportional development of different occupational categories in relation to the whole working population of the United States.* From Jaffe and Stewart, op. cit., p. 190.

Occupational Category	1910	1920	1930	1940	1950
Skilled Workers and Foremen	11·7	13·5	12·9	11·7	12·8
Semi-skilled Workers	14·7	16·1	16·4	21·0⎫	37·1
Unskilled Workers	21·5	20·0	19·8	18·8⎭	
Total of Manual Workers	47·9	49·6	49·1	51·5	49·9

TABLE XX.—*Proportional development of different occupational categories in relation to the whole working population of the United States from 1910 to 1950* (Men only). Source; 'A Study of Census Data on the Craftsman Population of the United States, 1870–1950', *The Skilled Labor Force*, Technical Bulletin no. T. 140, Washington, April 1954.

Occupational Category	1910	1920	1930	1940	1950
Skilled Workers	14·5	16·7	16·4	14·8	18·6
Semi-skilled Workers	11·2	13·3	14·4	18·1	20·1
Unskilled Workers	18·2	17·7	16·1	11·4	8·5

TABLE XXI.—*Development of the occupational index from 1910 to 1950 in the United States in relation to the whole of the non-agricultural working population and all manual workers.* Calculated from the figures provided by Jaffe and Stewart, op. cit., p. 190.

Occupational Category	1910	1930	1940	1950
Non-agricultural Workers	100	149	166	200
Manual Workers	100	133	150	164
Skilled Workers	100	145	143	174
Semi-skilled Workers	100	145	199	—*
Unskilled Workers	100	120	121	—*

* The absence of certain data makes it impossible to determine these figures.

TABLE XXII.—*Indices showing the development of different occupational categories in the United States in relation to 1910.* From F. Pollock, op. cit.

Occupational Category	1900	1910	1930	1950
Manual Workers, Agricultural Workers not included	63	100	134	154
Skilled Workers	98	100	143	186
Semi-skilled Workers	—	100	145	213
Unskilled Workers	98	100	115	69
Total Working Population	76	100	131	170

Notes

INTRODUCTION

1. Cf. Camille Arambourg, *La Genèse de l'Humanité*, Presses universitaires de France, new ed., 1955: André Varagnac, *De la Préhistoire au Monde moderne*, Plon, 1954: Henri Breuil, *Quatre Cents Siècles d'Art pariétal*, Centre d'Études et de Documentation préhistorique de Montignac, Dordogne, 1952.

2. Cf. Raymond Lantier, 'Sociologie protohistorique', Deuxième Semaine internationale de Synthèse sur *Les Origines de la Société*, La Renaissance du Livre, Paris, 1931, p. 65.

3. Cf. Pierre Waltz, *Le Monde égéen avant les Grecs*, 2nd ed., A. Colin, Paris, 1947, Pt. II, Ch. III.

4. Xenophon, *Cyropaedia* (trans. Walter Miller, Loeb Classical Library), Bk. VIII, Ch. II. This text is quoted in part by Marx, *Das Kapital* (trans. from the 3rd German ed. by S. Moore and E. Aveling), William Glaisher Ltd, London, 1918, Vol. I, pp. 361–2.

5. Herodotus, *Euterpe*, p. 84.

6. Cf. G. Renard and G. Weulersse, *Le Travail dans l'Europe moderne*, Paris, 1920: E. Coornaert, *Les Corporations en France avant 1789*, Gallimard, Paris, 1941.

7. Cf. the author's *La Crise du Progrès*, Gallimard, Paris, 1936, pp. 30, 31.

8. Henry Ford, *My Life and Work*, 1922 and *Moving Forward*, 1930.

9. Cf. the author's *Problèmes du Machinisme en U.R.S.S. et dans les pays capitalistes*, Éditions sociales internationales, Paris, 1934, pp. 53–4.

10. Cf. A. Arakelian, Professor at Moscow University, *Upravlenie Sotsialistisheskoi Promyshlennost'iu*, Moscow, 1947, Rabotshizdat; English trans., *Industrial Management in the U.S.S.R.*, Public Affairs Press, Washington, 1950, p. 131 *et seq.*

CHAPTER I

1. Cf. *Où va le travail humain?*, new ed., Paris, 1954, Pt. III, Ch. I, pp. 207–24; Pt. IV, pp. 319–20, 343–4.

2. Harvard University Press, 1952. In these notes this book will be indicated by the letters WG.

3. *Où va le travail humain?*, pp. 326–33.

4. D. Cox, in collaboration with K. M. Dyce Sharp and D. H. Irvine, *Women's Attitudes to Repetitive Work*, National Institute of Industrial Psychology, Report 9, London, 1953, p. 17 *et seq.*

5. *Où va le travail humain?*, pp. 343–8.

6. *Problèmes humains du Machinisme industriel*, new ed., Paris, 1955, pp. 208–14.

7. WG, p. 148.

8. WG, p. 149.

9. *Satisfactions in the White-Collar Job*, Survey Research Center, University of Michigan, Ann Arbor, 1953.

10. For instance, in the centres organized in England by O'Connor and Tizard, in Holland by J. de Smet, and in France by P. Sivadon. See Chapter VIII, p. 134.

CHAPTER II

1. Morris S. Viteles, *Motivation and Morale in Industry*, W. W. Norton, New York, 1953. On the experimental studies see Pts. III and IV of this work.

2. Cf. *Problèmes humains du Machinisme industriel*, p. 167.

3. Cf. above, Chapter I, p. 10.

4. Cf. *Où va le travail humain?*, p. 137.

5. WG, p. 150.

6. WG, pp. 150–1.

7. We take this example from an inquiry conducted, under the direction of J.-D. Reynaud and A. Touraine, during 1954–5 by the *Institut des Sciences sociales du Travail* (University of Paris) in a large Lorraine steelworks. The investigators were J. Dofny and B. Mottez. Cf. on the development of the same industry Maurice Verry, *Les Laminoirs ardennais*, Paris, 1955, p. 87 *et seq.*

8. Documents made available by the *Centre d'Études pratiques des Techniques de Production.*

9. WG, p. 148.

10. *Où va le travail humain?*, pp. 141–2.

11. WG, p. 121.

12. WG, pp. 56–7.

13. WG, p. 111.

14. Experimental studies have been made of the need for workers' participation in the organizing of their work; these show their resistance to changes of method and job where this participation is lacking, and indicate ways of overcoming this resistance to change. Among these studies I should particularly like to mention the excellent series of investigations carried out under the auspices of Kurt Lewin in a clothing factory, the Harwood Manufacturing Company, by a group of psychologists, including, apart from Lewin, A. J. Marrow, A. Bavelas, J. R. P. French and L. Coch. Cf. K. Lewin, 'Group Decision and Social Change', in the collection published by T. N. Newcomb and E. L. Hartley, *Readings in Social Psychology*, Henry Holt, New York, 1949, pp. 330–44; L. Coch and J. R. P. French, 'Overcoming Resistance to Change', *Human Relations*, 1948, Vol. I, pp. 512–32; and the report of these experiments given with comments by M. S. Viteles in the book mentioned above, p. 164–9.

15. The works of H. M. Vernon and S. Wyatt, assisted by J. A. Fraser,

J. N. Langdon, A. D. Ogden and F. G. L. Stock, cf. the Industrial Fatigue Research Board (from 1930 the Industrial Health Research Board), Reports 26 (1924), 32 (1925), 52 (1928), 56 (1929), 77 (1937), London, Her Majesty's Stationery Office.

16. Apart from the English works mentioned in the preceding note, cf. L. G. Reynolds and J. Shister, *A Study of Job Satisfaction and Labor Mobility*, Harpers, New York, 1949; E. Roper, 'The Fortune Survey', *Fortune*, May 1947, pp. 5–12; 'Factory's Fourth Annual Report of Worker Opinion', *Factory*, 1947, Vol. 105, pp. 86–90; E. Krause, 'Leistungsbereitschaft durch Arbeitswechsel', *Industrielle Psychotechnik*, 1933, Vol. X, pp. 97–106.

17. S. A. Raube, 'The Problem of Boredom', *Management Record*, December 1948, pp. 565–75.

18. Ibid.

19. George C. Homans, *The Human Group*, Harcourt, Brace, New York, 1950, p. 102.

20. I am following here the analysis made by P. F. Drucker in the series of articles which he published under the title 'The Way to Industrial Peace', *Harpers Magazine*, November, December 1946, January 1947. Cf. the number of November 1946, p. 390 *et seq.*

21. The English psychologists have noted that when, in teamwork, jobs are highly subdivided and rigidly determined, they have to be fixed nearer to the minimum output of the least efficient worker than to the maximum of the most efficient. Cf. S. Wyatt and J. A. Fraser, Industrial Fatigue Research Board, London, 1925, p. 13 *et seq.*; H. J. Rothe, 'Output rates among butter wrappers: work curves and their stability', *Journal of Applied Psychology*, June 1946, Vol. XXX, pp. 199–211.

22. Cf. *Où va le travail humain?*, pp. 239–41.

23. P. F. Drucker, *Harpers Magazine*, November 1946, pp. 389–90.

24. Ibid., p. 390.

25. 'A working philosophy of personnel management', Industrial Relations Association of Chicago, 11 June, 1951.

26. Ibid.

27. 'Organizational structure and employee morale', *American Sociological Review*, April 1950, Vol. XV, Pt. 2, p. 177.

28. F. W. Taylor, *Shop Management*.

29. Stanford University Press, 1948, p. 85.

30. This is the great problem of the separation between planning and execution. Most followers of Taylor fail to recognize its seriousness and obstinately deny the responsibility for it incurred by their system, to which they remain uncritically attached.

Certain points to be mentioned later must be briefly discussed here.

In various books I have dealt with Taylor and his system at some length, attempting to show its relation to his times and comparing it with investigations carried out during the last half-century by the physiology of of labour, psychotechnics and industrial sociology. As the result of this examination I concluded that 'if we leave out of account considerable benefits due strictly to applied engineering and metallurgy, it would be a mistake to call a science what is only a perfected system of ways of increasing the immediate output of machines and tools and of the labour force' (*Problèmes humains du Machinisme industriel*, p. 57).

Now, as we have just seen, the conclusions of the classical investigations of Atzler, O. Lipmann, C. S. Myers, J. M. Lahy and their teams are supported by the views of American specialists and prominent industrialists. Is it then sensible to persist in considering Taylor a sacred figure, as my excellent colleague, L. Danty-Lafrance, did in the course of his farewell address at the *Conservatoire national des Arts et Métiers*, which is reproduced in the *Bulletin du Comité national de l'Organisation française* (C.N.O.F., June 1954, 'Éloge de F. W. Taylor')? Clearly we must begin by making a distinction between Taylor the man, who was certainly a very sincere and excellent person, possessing the best of intentions, and the reality of his system, the actual role it has played in the history of industry and management. In spite of all his expressed confessions of faith, which are easy enough to find, his influence has not in fact been on the side of the 'primacy of the human personality', as Danty-Lafrance maintains, but has actually been dangerously antagonistic to it.

Visibly irritated by the criticisms levelled at his master, Danty-Lafrance goes so far as to denounce those who 'sadistically spread and amplify a remark attributed to Taylor, and that without even being able to show proof that he ever made it'. He means Taylor's retort to Shartle, the worker who often asked him questions and to whom he is once said to have replied: 'You aren't asked to think, there are other people here who are paid to do that.' Since, I believe, I was the introducer of this remark to France (*La Crise du Progrès*, 1936), I am very willing to accept responsibility for it and give my sources. The remark, and Shartle's fine reaction to it, are reported by Copley in his classical biography of Taylor (New York, 1923, Vol. I, pp. 188–9), the work of an enthusiastic disciple of Taylor; Copley should then be considered the first of the 'sadists'! But never mind. It is always dangerous to make a man, whatever his merits, your infallible guide, the pioneer who 'has seen and predicted everything', instead of looking at him in terms of his own age, in the historical circumstances which explain his action and knowledge and their limitations, as well as his aims and methods. Danty-Lafrance, quoting a passage from Simone Weil's *La Condition ouvrière*, thinks it amusing to call her 'a worthy visionary' (p. 29). But have not the beliefs of certain of Taylor's followers not only an orthodox, but also a mystical, tinge?

31. Industrial Relations Association of Chicago, 11 June, 1951.

32. *American Sociological Review*, April 1950, Vol. XV, Pt. 2, p. 174.

33. Ibid., pp. 176–7. J. C. Worthy has also repeated his arguments in an excellent general account of his ideas contained in the *Harvard Business Review*, January 1950, which is reproduced in a collection published by S. D. Hoslett, *Human Factors in Management*, new ed., Harpers, New York, 1951, p. 315 *et seq.*

34. For the methods employed and the details of these investigations cf. J. C. Worthy, 'Discovering and evaluating employee attitudes', *Personnel Series*, American Management Association, New York, 1947, No. 113.

35. S. D. Hoslett, *Human Factors in Management*, p. 318.
36. 'Planned executive development: the experience of Sears, Roebuck and Co.', *Personnel Series*, American Management Association, New York, 1951, No. 137, p. 7.
37. S. D. Hoslett, *Human Factors in Management*, p. 311.
38. *The Human Group*, pp. 90–4.
39. Ibid., p. 103.
40. Ibid., p. 84.

CHAPTER III

1. Taken from P. F. Drucker's account, *Harpers Magazine*, November 1946, p. 390.
2. Cf. the recommendations of E. Atzler, *Körper und Arbeit, Handbuch der Arbeitswissenschaft*, Leipzig, 1927, p. 486 *et seq.*, and the author's *Problèmes humains du Machinisme industriel*, pp. 65–7.
3. P. F. Drucker, *Harpers Magazine*, November 1946, pp. 391–2.
4. P. F. Drucker, *Harpers Magazine*, December 1946, pp. 517–18.
5. Graham W. Parker, *Simplification du Travail*, éd. Hommes et Techniques, Paris, 1949; Jean Bénielli, *La Simplification du Travail*, two pamphlets, éd. Travail et Maîtrise, Paris, 1954.
6. Cf. L. Couffignal, *Les Machines à penser*, Éd. de Minuit, Paris, 1950, p. 32 *et seq.*
7. C. R. Walker, 'The Problem of the Repetitive Job', *Harvard Business Review*, May 1950, p. 55.
8. Ibid., p. 56.
9. Ibid., p. 56.
10. *Wall Street Journal*, 11 March, 1954, art cit. on p. 44.
11. C. R. Walker, *Harvard Business Review*, May 1950, p. 56.
12. The matter to be found in the course of these pages is largely derived from two articles by J. D. Elliott: 'Increasing Office Productivity Through Job Enlargement', *Office Management Series*, no. 134, American Management Association, New York, December 1953; 'Job Enlargement Increases Productivity', lectures delivered at the University of California from 28 January to 1 February, 1955, roneotyped and communicated by the Detroit Edison Company (these two articles are indicated in the following notes by A and B respectively). We have also consulted the Annual Report of the Company for 31 December, 1955.
13. A, pp. 3–4.
14. A, p. 5.
15. A, p. 5.
16. A, p. 7.
17. B, p. 12.
18. In his lecture delivered at the University of California, J. D. Elliott (B, pp. 14–15) makes an interesting comparison between work simplification and job enlargement. The first aims at simplifying work (and not at subdividing jobs, though some of its supporters unfortunately do so in practice in obedience to the tradition of Scientific Management).

The second attempts to enlarge the jobs of individuals, but not the whole work cycle. It leads to a *unification* of many overspecialized activities, and this fits in with work simplification. The latter, on the other hand — but on this point Elliott gives no examples, although he is very definite as to the facts — leads to a unification of separated activities and so to job enlargement.

Elliott concludes that, if one keeps to these principles, there cannot be any contradiction between the two movements. However, I should have liked to have his opinion about work simplification as it has been spreading in the United States and in Europe during recent years under the influence of Allan H. Mogensen and his collaborators.

19. In France particularly by Bernard Juilhet and Jacques Lobstein.

20. A, p. 8.

CHAPTER IV

1. WG, p. 58.

2. B. Zeigarnik, 'Ueber das Behalten von erledigten und unerledigten Handlungen', *Psychologische Forschungen*, 1927, Vol. 9, pp. 1–85.

3. M. Ovsiankina, 'Die Wiederaufnahme unterbrochener Handlungen', *Psychologische Forschungen*, 1928, Vol. 11, pp. 302–79.

4. G. W. Allport, *Personality*, Henry Holt, New York, 1937, p. 198.

5. M. Ovsiankina, *Psychologische Forschungen*, 1928, Vol. 11.

6. H. Wunderlich, 'Die Einwirkung einförmiger Zwangsläufiger Arbeit auf die Persönlichkeits-Struktur', *Zeitschr. für angewandte Psychologie*, Vol. XXV, pp. 321–73.

7. Press Conference of 24 March, 1953. Cf. *The Times* editorial of the next day, entitled 'Human Problems in Industry', and an article describing the work programme of the two committees and giving a list of their members.

8. D. W. Harding, 'A Note on the Subdivision of Assembly Work', *Journal of the National Institute of Industrial Psychology*, January 1931, pp. 261–4.

9. David Cox and K. M. Dyce Sharp, 'Research on the Unit of Work', *Occupational Psychology*, April 1951, pp. 90–108.

10. D. Cox, in collaboration with K. M. Dyce Sharp and D. H. Irvine, *Women's Attitudes to Repetitive Work*, National Institute of Industrial Psychology, Report 9, London, 1953. These investigations are being continued at the moment and other publications are in preparation. Cf. the communications of D. Cox and C. B. Frisby at the Rome Conference on Human Relations in Industry (29 January to 4 February, 1956) 'Interchangeability of jobs'; 'The division of labour'.

11. D. Cox and K. M. D. Sharp, *Occupational Psychology*, April 1951, pp. 95–6.

12. WG, pp. 47, 146–7.

13. D. Cox and K. M. D. Sharp, *Occupational Psychology*, April 1951, p. 97.

14. Cf. L. Walther, *Psychologie du Travail*, Éd. du Mont-Blanc,

Geneva, 1947, and 'L'Horlogerie en face de la psychologie du travail', *Mélanges Albert Michotte*, Louvain and Paris, 1947.

15. As Cox and Sharp have noted, *Occupational Psychology*, April 1951, p. 99.

16. Cf. *Où va le travail humain?*, pp. 324–5.

17. It is interesting to consider here the bitter complaints made by American workers, who stress that the jobs at which they are kept require no apprenticeship, and who show signs of professional pride as soon as these jobs become a little harder to perform correctly and rapidly. (Cf. WG, pp. 56–7.)

18. D. Cox, National Institute of Industrial Psychology, Report 9, 1953, p. 16.

19. D. Cox and K. M. D. Sharp, *Occupational Psychology*, April 1951, p. 99.

20. D. W. Harding, *Journal of the National Institute of Industrial Psychology*, January 1931.

21. Industrial Fatigue Research Board and Industrial Health Research Board, Reports 26 (1924), 32 (1925), 52 (1928), 56 (1929), 77 (1937), London, Her Majesty's Stationery Office.

22. L. S. Hearnshaw 'Le but et le domaine de la psychologie industrielle' (communication made to the Eleventh International Congress of Psychotechnics, Paris, 1953), *Le Travail humain*, 1954, Vol. XVII, Nos. 1–2. C. B. Frisby in his inaugural address (ibid., p. 1), takes the same position. Cf. also L. S. Hearnshaw, 'Attitudes to Work', *Occupational Psychology*, July 1954, p. 132.

23. D. Cox, National Institute of Industrial Pscyhology, Report 9, 1953, p. 26.

CHAPTER V

1. Taylor has often been given this title in the United States and elsewhere. Cf. the classic biography by Copley, *Frederick Winslow Taylor, Father of Scientific Management*, 2 vols., Harpers, New York, 1923.

2. Émile Durkheim, *The Division of Labour in Society* (trans. George Simpson), Free Press, Glencoe, Illinois, U.S.A., 1947, p. 40. This translation will be referred to in the following notes by the letters DL.

3. DL, p. 372.

4. DL. We take this formula from the analytical table of contents drawn up by Durkheim.

5. This preface is entitled by Durkheim 'Some Remarks on Professional Groups'.

6. DL, p. 421.

7. *Cours de Philosophie positive*, Vol. IV, p. 429. For Comte, the independent organ which brings about unity in spite of the diversity of specialized functions can only be the State or the government.

8. DL, p. 365.

9. DL, p. 365.

10. DL, p. 367.

11. DL, p. 370.

12. DL, p. 371.

13. DL, p. 372.

14. DL, p. 373.

15. Cf. particularly the works of I. N. Spielrein, A. I. Kolodnaya, S. Gellerstein and W. Kogan; the report of the Soviet communications to the Seventh International Conference of Psychotechnics (Moscow, 1931) and the manual of I. M. Bourdiansky (in Russian), *Principles of the Rationalization of Production*, 3rd ed., Gos-Sotsekizdat, Moscow, 1934.

16. DL, p. 390.

17. DL, p. 392.

18. Karl Marx, *Das Kapital* (Eng. trans.), Vol. II, Ch. XV, Sect. 3, p. 408.

19. Cf. the author's *Problèmes humains du Machinisme industriel*, pp. 82–3; C. S. Myers, *Industrial Psychology*, London, 1929, p. 73.

20. DL, p. 29.

21. DL, pp. 365–7.

22. G. C. Homans, *The Human Group*, p. 101.

23. Cf. Hans Rupp, *Report of the Fourth International Conference of Psychotechnics*, Alcan, Paris, 1929, p. 235 *et seq.*

24. *Problèmes humains du Machinisme industriel*, p. 316.

25. Georges Navel, *Travaux*, Stock, Paris, 1945, p. 217.

26. As C. Bouglé observes in his 'Théories sur la division du travail', *Qu'est-ce que la Sociologie?*, Alcan, Paris, 1921, pp. 140–1.

27. Ibid., p. 142.

28. Ibid., p. 139.

CHAPTER VI

1. Cf. above, Chapter I, p. 9 *et seq.*

2. *Médecine et Monde moderne*, Éd. de Minuit, Paris, 1953.

3. Ibid., p. 79.

4. We are utilizing here the descriptions given by J. Larcebeau in his interesting study 'La hiérarchie professionnelle; promotion professionnelle, formation, perfectionnement', *Bulletin de l'Institut national d'Orientation professionnelle*, January–February 1955, p. 6 *et seq.*

5. A clear distinction must be made between work activities and leisure time activities which are undertaken quite apart from work. This active use of leisure is growing and polyvalence is an essential aspect of it. (Cf. farther on, Chapter VII, p. 105 *et seq.*)

6. F. W. Taylor, *Principles of Scientific Management*, pp. 125–6.

7. F. W. Taylor, *Shop Management*.

8. *Principles of Scientific Management*, pp. 66–7.

9. F. B. Gilbreth, *Motion Study*, New York, 1911.

10. P. Naville, *Essai sur la Qualification du Travail*, Marcel Rivière, Paris, 1956, p. 43.

11. Cf. their communications to the Seventh International Conference of Psychotechnics (Moscow, 1931), and the two collections: *The Workers and Mass Production* (in Russian), Gos-Sotsekizdat, Moscow, 1929, 1931;

with prefaces by Bourdiansky and Spielrein who elaborate in a very significant way the thesis we have summarized here.

12. Cf. *Problèmes humains du Machinisme industriel*, 'Expériences depuis 1945', pp. 338–49.

13. Georges Duveau, *La Pensée ouvrière sur l'Éducation pendant la Seconde République et le Second Empire*, Domat, Paris, 1947, p. 201. Of the theorists it is particularly Proudhon who developed ideas (new in his time) concerning 'polytechnical education during apprenticeship' in its connection with the division of labour. Cf. in particular *De la Justice dans la Révolution et dans l'Église*, 6th Study, Ch. VI.

14. *Das Kapital* (Eng. trans.), Vol. I, Ch. XIV, Sect. 2, p. 330.

15. This is how Marx's argument runs on this point in *Das Kapital* (op. cit., p. 489). Large-scale industry has a 'revolutionary basis'. Constantly renewing the processes of production, it 'sweeps away the manufacturing division of labour, under which each man is bound hand and foot for life to a single detail operation'. In other words it makes of him in actual fact a 'semi-skilled worker', able to change his speciality, this being performed each time by fragmentary and intense labour, devoid of gaps or 'pores'.

But large-scale industry in its capitalist form cannot reap the fruits of its revolutionary character and overcome the evils of the manufacturing division of labour. It reproduces them 'in a still more monstrous shape; in the factory proper, by converting the workman into a living appendage of the machine; and everywhere outside the factory, partly by the sporadic use of machinery and machine workers, and partly by re-establishing the division of labour on a fresh basis, through the general introduction of the labour of women and children and of cheap unskilled labour' (pp. 489–490). On the 'closer filling up of the gaps or pores of the working day', see p. 408.

16. *Das Kapital* (Eng. trans.), Vol. I, Ch. XIV, Sect. 2, p. 332.

17. *Das Kapital* (Eng. trans.), Vol. II, Ch. XV, Sect. 9, p. 489.

18. Ibid., p. 494.

19. *Anti-Dühring* (trans. Emile Burns, ed. C. P. Dutt, Martin Lawrence), 1935, Pt. III, 'Production'; Ch. III, 'Socialism'; p. 332.

20. *Les Problèmes économiques du Socialisme en U.R.S.S.*, special number of the review *Études soviétiques*, November 1952, p. 43.

21. Éd. de la Librairie de l'Humanité, Paris, 1922, p. 36.

22. *Das Kapital*, Hamburg, 1894, Vol. III, 2nd part, Ch. 48, p. 355. (Eng. trans. by Ernest Untermann, Charles H. Kerr & Co., Chicago, 1926, Vol. III, p. 954.)

23. *Problèmes du Machinisme en U.R.S.S. et dans les pays capitalistes*, pp. 19–36; *De la Sainte Russie à l'U.R.S.S.*, Gallimard, Paris, 1938, pp. 48–62. Among recent accounts of polytechnicalization and its development in the U.S.S.R. it is useful to consult the overdetailed but well documented book by Luigi Volpicelli, *Storia della Scuola Sovietica*, 3rd ed., Brescia, 1953, 'La Scuola', Editrice (an abridged French trans., *L'Évolution de la Pédagogie soviétique*, Delachaux et Niestlé, Neuchâtel-Paris, 1954).

24. N. Dombre, *France-Observateur*, 29 July, 1954.

25. *Problèmes du Machinisme en U.R.S.S. et dans les pays capitalistes*, pp. 19–20, 25–6.

26. *De la Sainte Russie à l'U.R.S.S.*, pp. 56–62.

27. L. Volpicelli, *L'Évolution de la Pédagogie soviétique* (French trans.), p. 228.

28. N. Dombre, art. cit., p. 16.

29. For the Z.O.T. circles (initials of the Russian words 'For the Control of Technique') cf. *De la Sainte Russie à l'U.R.S.S.*, pp. 96–7; for the Children's Technical Centres (D.T.S.), cf. *Problèmes du Machinisme en U.R.S.S. et dans les pays capitalistes*, p. 24, note.

30. L. Volpicelli, *L'Évolution de la Pédagogie soviétique* (French trans.), p. 229.

31. *Où va le Travail humain?*, pp. 152–3.

32. Cf. Alain Touraine, *L'Évolution du Travail ouvrier aux Usines Renault*, Centre national de la Recherche scientifique, Paris, 1955, pp. 171–2.

33. John Diebold, *Automation, the Advent of the Automatic Factory*, D. van Nostrand, New York, 1952.

34. *Problèmes humains du Machinisme industriel*, p. 179.

35. J. Diebold, op. cit., p. 164.

36. Eugene Staley, *Technology and Human Values*, quoted by Diebold, *op cit.*, pp. 164–5.

CHAPTER VII

1. Ferdynand Zweig, *The British Worker*, Penguin Books, London, 1952, p. 97. I have italicized certain words in this quotation.

2. Cf. the investigations mentioned and documents brought together by J. Dumazedier in Vol. XIV of the *Encyclopédie française*, Paris, 1955, Sect. G: 'Les Loisirs dans la vie quotidienne'.

3. Cf. *Où va le Travail humain?*, pp. 348–56, and, as concerns the U.S.S.R., *De la Sainte Russie à l'U.R.S.S.*, p. 53 *et seq.*, p. 96 *et seq.* We may note the success in France of the 'Salon du Modéliste', which every year exhibits at the Palais Berlitz the most varied types of small models. Cf. the report of the Ninth Salon in *Le Figaro*, 9–10 October, 1954.

4. Jacques Ellul has strongly criticized the commercialization and standardization of leisure in *La Technique et l'Enjeu du siècle*, A. Colin, Paris, 1954, pp. 340–4, 346, 361–3, 368, 379–80.

5. To the facts mentioned in *Où va le Travail humain?* (pp. 148–9) which come chiefly from American life, let me add here the widespread diffusion in Great Britain of gambling on football matches, the 'football pools': John Cohen has made some interesting comments on them in his article, 'The Ideas of Work and Play', *British Journal of Sociology*, December, 1953, p. 318.

6. Daniel Bell, 'Notes on Work', *Encounter*, June 1954, p. 12.

7. Ibid., p. 13.

8. Erich Fromm, *The Sane Society*, Rinehart, New York, 1955, p. 207.

In *Le Monde* of 20 March, 1956, Henri Pierre published a 'Lettre des Etats-Unis', full of examples of these 'Do it Yourself' activities. Innumerable amateur craftsmen of every social class spend more than six thousand million dollars a year on pots of paint, cement, plywood, planes, saws, drills and other tools, sold in ingeniously devised holders. 'At the basis of these innumerable crafts,' he writes, 'lies the revolt of the individual who seeks to escape from the mechanization of life.' But economic reasons also play a large part, the expense and difficulty of getting hold of skilled manual workers, plumbers, mechanics, electricians, etc. An amateur craftsman has thus summarized the situation: 'An accountant getting 1.25 dollars an hour cannot afford the luxury of employing a carpenter at 3.50 dollars an hour.'

9. Daniel Bell, *Encounter*, June 1954, p. 13.

10. Cf. *Recreation in Industry*, Publications of the Industrial Welfare Society, 2nd ed., London, 1949.

11. F. Zweig, *The British Worker*, p. 97.

12. Ibid., p. 155.

13. Henri Colas, 'Le Problème de la Culture dans le milieu des employés', an unpublished memorandum (archives of the Institut national d'Étude du Travail et d'Orientation professionnelle, Paris). Cf. also some interesting material in Michel Crozier's *Petits Fonctionnaires au Travail* (report of a sociological inquiry made in a big Parisian administrative organisation), 'L'activité de loisir et les attitudes culturelles', Centre national de la Recherche scientifique, Paris, 1955, pp. 112–19.

14. P. Louchet and J. Frisch, an investigation published by the Éditions du Centre national de la Recherche scientifique, Paris, 1961.

15. P. Fougeyrollas, *Population*, January–March 1951, pp. 83–103.

16. Amicale du Personnel, 'Exposition de l'Art des travailleurs', Ougrée-Marihaye, 1949.

17. I. Meyerson, 'Comportement, travail, expérience, oeuvre', *L'Année psychologique*, 1951 (Hommage à Henri Piéron), p. 78.

18. L. S. Hearnshaw, 'Le but et le domaine de la psychologie industrielle', *Le Travail humain*, 1954, nos. 1–2, p. 8, and 'Attitudes to Work', *Occupational Psychology*, July 1954, p. 132.

19. On domestic work in working-class homes cf. P. Chombart de Lauwe, *La Vie quotidienne des familles ouvrières*, Centre national de la Recherche scientifique, Paris, 1956, p. 46, and P. Fougeyrollas, *Population*, January–March 1951, pp. 96–7.

20. This is also the term proposed by Pierre Naville, *De l'aliénation à la jouissance*, Éd. de Minuit, Paris, 1956.

21. J. Dumazedier, 'Les loisirs dans la vie quotidienne', *Encyclopédie française*, Vol. XIV, pp. 14, 54–5 *et seq.*

22. Cf. later on my analysis of an interview obtained by R. H. Guest, Chapter VIII, p. 138.

23. On contrasting attitudes to time see the remarks of Jean Daric, *Villes et Campagnes*, A. Colin, Paris, 1953, pp. 416–18; Lucien Bernot and

René Blancard, *Nouville, un village français*, Institut d'Ethnologie, Paris, 1953, Ch. XII, 'Le temps et l'espace', pp. 321–32, 355–8; P. Durand, Communication on Work in Negro Africa at the Twelfth International Congress of Psychotechnics, London, 1955, and the bibliography contained in *Le Travail en Afrique noire*, collection made under the direction of P. Naville, Éd. du Seuil, Paris, 1953.

24. M. S. Viteles, *Motivation and Morale in Industry*, W. W. Norton, New York, 1953; C. W. Mills, *White Collar: the American Middle Classes*, Oxford University Press, New York, 1951, p. 229. From a study of job satisfaction based on a national sample, it appears that 85 per cent of the members of the liberal professions and of executives, 64 per cent of the white-collar class, and 41 per cent of the factory workers, gave positive answers: in another inquiry 74 per cent of the managers, 56 per cent of the skilled, 48 per cent of the semi-skilled workers, and 42 per cent of commercial employees, expressed satisfaction in their work.

25. Eric Fromm, *The Sane Society*, pp. 296–7.

26. 'In this democracy,' declares the well-known journalist Dorothy Thompson, 'to be as happy as one can has become a public duty' ('The United States seen by the Americans', *Économie et Humanisme*, September–October 1954, No. 87, p. 5).

27. Erich Fromm, *The Sane Society*, p. 297.

28. Cf. *Où va le Travail humain?*, pp. 343–8, and R. H. Guest, 'Men and Machines: An Assembly-Line Worker Looks at his Job', American Management Association, New York, 1955, p. 7 (an article published previously in the review *Personnel*, May 1955).

29. Cf. Martha Wolfenstein, 'The Emergence of Fun Morality', *Journal of Social Issues*, 1951, No. 7, pp. 15–25.

30. Erich Fromm, *The Sane Society*, pp. 205–6.

31. *Problèmes humains du Machinisme industriel*, p. 179.

32. *Automation* (A Report to the U.A.W.-C.I.O. Economic and Collective Bargaining Conference), Detroit, 12–13 November, 1954, pp. 16–18.

33. Cf. Norbert Wiener, *The Human Use of Human Beings, Cybernetics and Society*, new ed., Doubleday, New York, 1954.

34. C. R. Walker, 'The Problem of the Repetitive Job', *art. cit.*, pp. 57–8.

35. Ibid., p. 57.

36. Cf. Chapter II.

37. P. F. Drucker, *The Practice of Management*, Heinemann, London, 1955.

38. Ibid., p. 21.

39. Ibid., pp. 21–2.

40. Ibid., p. 289.

41. Ibid., p. 295.

42. Ibid., p. 266.

43. Ibid., p. 265.

44. Ibid., p. 267.

45. Cf. *Automation* (Conference of the U.A.W.-C.I.O., Detroit, 12–13 November, 1954) report quoted; declarations of Walther Reuther to the 'Congressional Joint Committee on the Economic Report', 10 February,

1955; *Automation*, C.I.O. Committee on Economic Policy, Washington, 1955, no. 270.

46. P. F. Drucker, *The Practice of Management*, p. 21.

47. Ibid., p. 267.

48. *La Crise de Progrès*, Ch. III.

49. *Cours de Philosophie positive*, Vol. IV, pp. 430–1.

CHAPTER VIII

1. Let me mention among the many good books on technical progress previous to the industrial use of the steam engine: A. P. Usher, *History of Mechanical Inventions*, new ed., Harvard University Press, 1954; F. Russo, *Histoire des Sciences et des Techniques* (bibliography), Paris, 1954, P. Hermann; B. Gille, *Les Origines de la grande Industrie métallurgique en France*, Domat, Paris, 1947; also his 'Les problèmes techniques au XVIIe siècle', *Techniques et Civilisations*, 1954, pp. 177–206; T. S. Ashton, *The Industrial Revolution*, Oxford University Press, 1948; F. George Kay, *Pioneers of British Industry*, London, 1952; Maurice Daumas, *Les Instruments scientifiques aux XVII et XVIIIe siècles*, P.U.F., Paris, 1953.

2. F. Gallais, *Chimie minérale*, Masson, Paris, 1950, p. 181. My attention was drawn to the possibility of applying the Van't Hoff-Le Chatelier law to our industrial civilization, considered as a system in equilibrium, by P. Maurer, the author of some interesting studies of automatism which I have quoted in a former book (*Problèmes humains du Machinisme industriel*, p. 170 *et seq*).

3. H. Bergson, *L'Évolution créatrice*, 26th ed., Alcan, Paris, 1924, p. 393.

4. Ibid., p. 281.

In connection with this aspect of Bergsonism it is interesting to note that palaeontologists agree to-day on the great importance of the concept of *equilibrium* considered from a biological point of view. 'Nature,' writes C. Arambourg (*La Genèse de l'Humanité*, pp. 126–27), 'at every moment of its history constitutes a harmonious whole, all parts of which coexist in a state of mutual equilibrium. When this equilibrium ceases, for whatever reason, there results inevitably, after a shorter or longer period of great difficulty, a general readjustment, usually fatal to the cause of the disturbance.'

During the course of his recent history man has completely upset the biological equilibrium of this planet: certain large animal species have been almost totally wiped out, there has been an artificial distribution of other species and of plants, the population of mankind has multiplied, and the play of natural selection has been disturbed by the survival and reproduction of many defective and diseased human beings, etc.

From another angle, one which is of particular importance to us here, the palaeontologists have introduced the idea of equilibrium in relation to the specialization of organs, overspecialization at first encouraging the development and spread of species, but leading finally to its complete extinction (ibid., p. 127). As regards man, we can consider him as tending to overdevelop the brain.

Specialization from this standpoint concerns the means and capabilities of the species and is thus part of biological evolution.

The observations made by palaeontologists from these two different angles thus suggest that we should consider the crisis of specialization against the background of the fundamental laws of biology. In their light we can say that our study points to certain dangers *for the species* which derive from the overspecialization of the individual.

5. L. S. Hearnshaw, C. B. Frisby, I. Meyerson. Cf. p. 108.

6. S. Freud, *Das Unbehagen in der Kultur*, Vienna, 1929 (Eng. trans. Joan Rivière, *Civilization and its Discontents*, Hogarth Press, 1930, p. 34, note).

7. K. Marx, *Das Kapital*, Pt. II, Ch. VII, Sect. I.

8. Institut scientifique de Recherches économiques et sociales, *Enquête sur le chômage*, Vol. I, *Le Chômage en France*, Recueil Sirey, Paris, 1938.

9. Milton L. Blum, *Industrial Psychology and its Social Foundations*, Harpers, New York, 1949, pp. 351–2. Cf. also G. Adams, *Workers on Relief*, Yale University Press, New Haven, 1939; E. W. Bakke, *Citizens without Work*, Yale University Press, 1939; P. Eisenberg and P. F. Lazarsfeld, 'The Psychological Effects of Unemployment', *Psychological Bulletin*, 1938, Vol. XXXV, pp. 358–90; M. Jahoda, 'Incentives to work, a study of unemployed adults in a special situation', *Occupational Psychology*, 1942, Vol. XVI, pp. 20–30; G. Watson, 'Morale during Unemployment', *Civilian Morale* (ed. G. Watson), Houghton Mifflin, Boston, 1942.

10. Kimball Young, *Personality and Problems of Adjustment*, Appleton Century, New York, 1940, particularly pp. 618–20.

11. Pauline V. Young, *Interviewing in Social Work*, McGraw Hill, New York, 1935, p. 162, quoted by D. C. Miller and W. H. Form, *Industrial Sociology*, Harpers, New York, 1951.

12. Report of the Industrial Hygiene Group on 'La reprise du travail', presented by Dr Claude Veil, *Journées de la Santé mentale*, Paris, 27–28 November, 1955. Cf. *L'Hygiène mentale*, 1956, No. I, pp. 61–82.

13. Cf. J. Daric, *Vieillissement de la population et Prolongation de la vie active*, Institut national d'Études démographiques, cahier 7, 1948. In his conclusions concerning the participation of the whole population in all work activities Daric notes (p. 111) that there has been a constant decrease from 1906 to 1936 in the rate of activity of the older ages (from 50 to 59) as a result of earlier retirement. By the same author: 'Vieillissement de la population, besoins et niveau de vie des personnes âgées', *Population*, January–March 1952. Cf. also J. Bourgeois-Pichat, 'Perspectives sur la population active européenne', *Population*, July–September, 1953.

14. A. Sauvy, 'Vue générale et mise au point sur l'économie et la population française', *Population*, April–June 1955, pp. 210–11.

15. Miller and Form (*Industrial Sociology*, p. 770) expect the number of retired workers to increase at an accelerated rate during the next thirty years.

16. Cf. *Social Adjustment in Old Age*, Social Science Research Council, New York, 1946; *Criteria for Retirement* (a Report of a National Conference on Retirement of Older Workers), Putnam's, New York, 1953;

E. A. Friedmann and R. J. Havighurst, *The Meaning of Work and Retirement*, University of Chicago Press, 1954.

17. T. Caplow, communication to the Industrial Sociology Group (Centre d'Études sociologiques), 4 March, 1955: "L'adaptation à la retraite chez les travailleurs de l'industrie: résultats et interprétation d'une enquête américaine'.

18. E. J. Briggs, 'How Adults in Missouri use their leisure time', *School and Society*, 1938, pp. 805–8.

19. Cf. references, p. 197, n. 13.

20. I.N.E.D., cahier no. 7, 1948, pp. 77–8.

21. Ibid., p. 79.

22. We have used here the tables drawn up by Erich Fromm (*The Sane Society*, pp. 8–9) with the help of the following publications of the World Health Organization: (1) *Annual Epidemiological and Vital Statistics*, 1939–46, Pt. I, 'Vital Statistics and Causes of Death', Geneva, 1951; (2) the same publication, Geneva, 1952, Report 5; (3) Committee of Experts on Mental Health, report on the first session of the Sub-committee on Alcoholism, Geneva, 1951. As regards the figures given in this last document, it must be noted that the statistics on alcoholism in France are calculated for the year 1945, a year which marked the end of a period of restrictions, and therefore, alas, show an exceptionally low rate of alcoholism.

Cf. also H. Goldhamer and A. Marshall, *Psychosis and Civilization*, Free Press, Glencoe, 1953, and the excellent analysis of P. Chombart de Lauwe, 'La maladie mentale comme phénomène social', *Monographie no. 7* de l'Institut national d'Hygiène, Paris, 1955.

23. E. Fromm, *The Sane Society*, p. 10.

24. M. Halbwachs, *Les Causes du Suicide*, Alcan, Paris, 1930, pp. 109, 112.

25. P. Sivadon, 'Psychopathologie du travail', *L'Évolution psychiatrique*, 1952, Vol. III, p. 470; 'L'adaptation des psychopathes au travail', *Revue de Psychologie appliquée*, July 1952; 'L'adaptation au travail en fonction des niveaux de maturation de la personalité', *Le Travail humain*, July–December 1954, pp. 173–9; 'Étude sur le travail rythmé', (in collaboration with C. L. Balier), *Le Travail humain*, July–December 1955, pp. 224–9. Cf. also the theses for a doctorate in medicine of his pupils, Koechlin (Paris, 1951) and Claude Balier (Paris, 1954).

26. Russell Fraser, *The Incidence of Neurosis among Factory Workers*, Industrial Health Research Board, London, 1947.

27. Karen Horney, *The Neurotic Personality of our Time*, Norton, New York, 1937, p. 290.

28. This figure was given us at the Banstead Hospital.

29. Centres with similar ideals have been created or reorganized at Bonneval (Dr Henri Ey) and at Villejuif (Dr L. Le Guillant).

30. English occupational therapists have been particularly interested in the adaptation of mental defectives to work. (Cf. J. Tizard and N. O'Connor, 'The occupational adaptation of high grade mental defectives', *Lancet*, September 1952).

31. *Où va le travail humain?*, pp. 40–75.

32. R. H. Guest, 'An Assembly-line Worker looks at his Job', *Personnel*, May 1955. We are quoting from the reprint of this article in pamphlet form by the American Management Association (New York, 1955).

33. Ibid., p. 6.

34. Ibid., p. 6.

35. Ibid., p. 6.

36. Ibid., p. 7.

37. Ibid., p. 7.

38. Cf. the classical study of Hans Rupp, 'Psychologie der Fliessarbeit', Fourth International Conference of Psychotechnics, Paris, 1927.

39. A. R. Heron, *Why Men Work*, Stanford University Press, 1948, pp. 121–2.

40. We may recall here the 'solidary self-governing teams' commended by E. Rimailho and H. Dubreuil.

41. *La Participation des travailleurs à la Gestion des entreprises privées*, investigations undertaken under the direction of Marcel David, Dalloz, Paris, 1954.

42. P. F. Drucker, *Concept of the Corporation*, John Day, New York, 1946, p. 179.

43. D. McGregor, 'Line Management's Responsibility for Human Relations', American Management Association Manufacturing Series No. 213, New York, 1953.

44. Cf. above, Chapter IV.

45. Cf. E. Fromm, *The Sane Society*, p. 360.

46. Cf. Chapter VIII, p. 148 *et seq.*, the programme carried out by the Bell Telephone Company for training its middle and higher grade staff.

47. 'Humanisme du travail et humanités'; cf. *Où va le Travail humain?*, Pt. III, Ch. IV.

48. Ibid., p. 306.

49. *Massachusetts Institute of Technology Bulletin*, Catalogue Issue for 1954–5 Session, p. 47.

50. *Liberal Education at M.I.T.*, Cambridge, U.S.A., September 1952, Intro., p. 3.

51. Ibid., 'The underclass core curriculum', p. 13.

52. Ibid., Intro., p. 7.

54. 'A New Educational Opportunity', M.I.T., October 1955. In 1955–1956 M.I.T. offered four new four-year programmes combining the 'liberal arts' with pure or applied science. The students choosing them devote 40 per cent of their time to the humanities and social sciences. The courses end with a diploma of Bachelor of Science (B.Sc.) with a mention of either Humanities and Science or Humanities and Engineering.

54. 'Institute of Humanistic Studies for Executives (July 1955)', a roneotyped document communicated by the University of Pennsylvania.

55. David Riesman, 'Some observations on changes in leisure attitudes', *The Antioch Review*, winter issue, 1952–3, p. 432.

56. *Television and the Family*, Report by the Coventry University

Tutorial Class in Psychology, compiled by Max Gordon, 1953; cf. also J. Dumazedier, *Télévision et Éducation populaire. Les Télé-Clubs en France*, Unesco, Paris, 1955.

57. D. Riesman, 'The themes of work and play in the structure of Freud's thought', an article reproduced in his collection of essays *Individualism Reconsidered*, Free Press, Chicago, 1954; cf. p. 333.

58. Cf. K. Marx, *Das Kapital* (trans. Ernest Untermann), Chicago, 1926, Charles H. Kerr & Co., Vol. III, p. 954, and the passage in the *History of Economic Doctrines*, Pt. VII, where Marx writes in regard to free time: 'Free time, the time of which one can dispose either to enjoy the products of industry or to develop oneself freely, that is real wealth'.

As regards the origin of these views in Hegel see particularly the text of his *Philosophy of Right* (§§ 195, 198), as quoted and commented on by Éric Weil, *Hegel et l'État*, Vrin, Paris, 1950, p. 90 *et seq.*

59. Cf. Paul Mercier, 'Travail et service public dans l'ancien Dahomey', and Henri Labouret, 'Sur la main-d'oeuvre autochtone' in *Le Travail en Afrique noire*, Éd. du Seuil, Paris, 1952. Cf. also R. W. Firth, *The Primitive Economics of the New Zealand Maori*, Routledge, London, 1929, and Margaret Mead (ed.), *Cultural Patterns and Technical Change*, Unesco, Paris, 1953.

60. Erich Fromm, *The Sane Society*, pp. 288–9.

61. Henri Desroche and Albert Meister, *Une Communauté de Travail de la banlieue parisienne*, Éd. de l'Entente communautaire, Paris, 1955.

62. Berthelot wrote in *La Chimie organique fondée sur la Synthèse* (1860): 'It is essential to note that our powers are greater than our knowledge'.

Index of Names